Ancient Egypt

Discovering its Splendors

Ancient Egypt

Discovering its Splendors

NATIONAL
GEOGRAPHIC
SOCIETY

Ancient Egypt
Discovering its Splendors

Published by
The National Geographic Society

Melvin M. Payne
Chairman of the Board

Robert E. Doyle
President

Owen R. Anderson
Secretary

Melville Bell Grosvenor
Editor Emeritus

Gilbert M. Grosvenor
Editor

A volume in the
Story of Man Library
Prepared by
National Geographic
Book Service
Jules B. Billard, *Director*

Chapters by

Karl W. Butzer
Virginia Lee Davis
I. E. S. Edwards
Barbara Mertz
William H. Peck
Edna R. Russmann
William Kelly Simpson
Anthony J. Spalinger

Staff for this Book

Jules B. Billard
Editor

Charles O. Hyman
Art Director

Anne Dirkes Kobor
Illustrations Editor

Mary H. Dickinson
Chief Researcher

Thomas B. Allen
Ross S. Bennett
Seymour L. Fishbein
Mary Swain Hoover
Edward Lanouette
David F. Robinson
Verla Lee Smith
Editor-Writers

Carol Bittig Lutyk
Shirley L. Scott
Elizabeth C. Wagner
Editorial Research

Robert C. Firestone
Production Manager

Karen F. Edwards
Assistant Production Manager

Molly Kohler
Illustrations Research

Victor R. Boswell, Jr.,
and Farrell Grehan
Photography

John T. Dunn
William W. Smith
Engraving and Printing

Suzanne P. Kane
Lise Swinson
Assistants

George I. Burneston, III
Index

Contributions by
Thomas J. Abercrombie
Constance Brown Boltz
Effie M. Cottman
Margaret Deane Gray
John D. Garst, Jr.
Michael A. Hampshire
David M. Seager
George E. Stuart
Lloyd K. Townsend, Jr.
Anne E. Withers

326 illustrations,
306 in full color

First edition 425,000 copies
Library of Congress CIP Data Page 256

Pages 2-3: Shadowed by a winter
sunset, the pyramids of Chephren
(right) and Mycerinus at Giza
evoke the enduring fascination
of ancient Egypt—land of sun
and sky and mighty splendor.
Page 7: Desert hills edge the west
bank of the Nile near Aswan, where
the river's First Cataract marked
ancient Egypt's southern frontier.

Contents

Foreword

Day after day through chill winter months the line of people snaked around the block from the building's entrance. For four, six, and as much as ten hours, men, women, and children waited as the queue inched into the National Gallery of Art in Washington, D. C. Enterprising sidewalk vendors did land-office businesses selling coffee, hot chocolate, and sandwiches—even knitted wool caps—to the patient throngs. What was the attraction that drew so many? The treasures of Tutankhamun, from the Egyptian Museum in Cairo, which we at the National Gallery had the privilege of starting on a seven-city tour of the United States.

From November to March nearly 7,000 persons a day wound into the rooms where 55 priceless pieces from the boy-king's tomb were shown. Visitors were drawn from miles away—altogether a number larger than the entire population of the District of Columbia. The crowds taxed the National Gallery's facilities in surprising ways—for example, we had to put a man to work cleaning air filters full time just to keep up with the dust that came in with the people.

The same enthusiastic acceptance greeted the Tutankhamun exhibit in the other cities where it was shown. The public's response became a powerful tribute to the sheer visual quality of the pieces, and to the fascination of their breathtaking age, the drama of their discovery, and the ancient Egyptian's obsession with life's ability to transcend death.

These thoughts and scenes came back as I leafed through page proofs of this book. And I was carried back to the sun-drenched days of my own first trip to Egypt, taken when I was a student at the Louvre in Paris and studying with the great Egyptologist Christiane Desroches-Noblecourt. The impact of the monuments in their settings was as great as any artistic experience I have ever had: the forms straining toward the sun, as pyramids or obelisks; or flattened lizard-like against the stone in relief; and in Cairo's Egyptian Museum, the taut elegance, purity, and restraint of objects made a thousand years before Tutankhamun.

Egypt has offered our civilization so much more than the treasures of Tutankhamun, dazzling as they are. The book for which I write these words makes that point in an eloquent way. Created under the guiding hand of a friend of many years, William Kelly Simpson, the eminent Yale Egyptologist and curator of Egyptian art at the Boston Museum of Fine Arts, it tells the story of a great civilization in very human terms.

Outstanding scholars have contributed the text to the volume. They trace the origins of the people who launched a nation at a time when the rest of the world was hardly more than a collection of city-states. They tell how those enduring wonders of time, the pyramids, may have been built—and why. They recount how religion interwove itself in the daily activities of pharaoh and noble and peasant, shaping their expectations in the life they lived and the afterworld to come. They unfold the painstaking drudgery—and the rewards—of archeological finds, the detective work of deciphering the hieroglyphs that have helped reveal more about ancient Egypt than we know about any other civilization of that long-ago time.

The quality of the color photography is the envy of all of us who have ever held a camera. The ancient Egyptians were intensely visual; even their writing was visually based, and the imagery of their poetry bears this out. I believe they would have loved this book. I know of no other book on the Egypt of the pharaohs that presents its treasures and its grandeur with this visual quality, and with such impressive scale.

To the fortunate reader I can only wish the injunction carved on the white lotus goblet in the Tutankhamun exhibition: "May your *ka* [spirit] live and may you spend millions of years, you who love Thebes, sitting with your face to the north wind, your two eyes beholding happiness."

The Constant Lure

William H. Peck

*Concerning Egypt itself I shall
extend my remarks to a great length,
because there is no country that
possesses so many wonders.*
                    Herodotus

*I had seen a hundred things, while a
thousand others had escaped me; and
had, for the first time, found access
to the archives of the arts and sciences.*
                    Vivant Denon

Two travelers separated in time by 2,250 years—one from the fifth century B.C., the other from the 19th century A.D.—sound a common chord. Egypt is a land of so many wonderful things the mind can hardly encompass them. The sheer quantity of remains from the past exists because the country's dry climate preserves. Man has been the worst destroyer.

What has made Egypt, its culture, and its monuments a source of fascination throughout the ages? The country resembles no other in the world. The physical situation of the land—cut off, protected, and isolated from its neighbors by mountains, desert, and sea—made it an ideal nurturing place for a unique civilization. The regularity of the Nile River floods provided a way of life that seems to have been almost changeless. Egypt has always been a land of mystery to the non-Egyptian, its monuments a source of more inspired fantasy than those of any other country. Nowhere else is there such a long, continuous tradition revealed by preserved structures, which, by their nature, seem somehow on a more than human scale.

"Egyptian king . . . receive my salutation"

Facing the life-giving Nile, a massive statue of Amunhotep III embodies the majesty of Egypt's pharaohs. Standing in western Thebes, it is one of a pair that guarded the king's mortuary temple, destroyed ages ago. Greek travelers named the northern colossus Memnon in honor of a Trojan war hero; generations of tourists engraved it with greetings and commemorative verses.

The systematic study of Egypt's past had to wait until the late 18th century when foreign scientists began to arrive. But travelers in every age tried to make sense of the mysterious country. The first students of Egypt were the Egyptians themselves. We know this because we can still read a number of graffiti scratched on monuments in pharaonic times. A tourist who visited Djoser's Step Pyramid at Saqqara a thousand years after the pharaoh's reign wrote: "The scribe, Ahmose, son of Iptah, came to see the temple of Djoser. He found it as though heaven were within it, Re rising in it." Another visitor recorded that he was on a holiday in Memphis and wanted to amuse himself. Then he added a pious prayer, which he hoped would benefit him in the afterlife.

The Egyptians knew their country to be one of great antiquity. They pondered a tradition that stretched back thousands of years. In the Song of the Harper, carved on a tomb wall, the ancient author wonders about the disappearance of the tombs of famous men:

*Their walls are dismantled,
And their cult places exist no more,
As if they had never been.*

In the seventh century B.C. the Greeks had established regular contact with Egypt. They became fascinated with the temples and tombs that still remained along the banks of the Nile. By the sixth century Greek mercenaries serving under Pharaoh Psamtik II had left graffiti at Abu Simbel, more than 600 miles from the sea. In the western Delta, the town of Naucratis was founded as a Greek trading enclave on Egyptian soil.

Persia ruled Egypt in the fifth century B.C., when the Greek historian Herodotus visited the Nile Valley. His delightful account of the trip combines hearsay, myth, and personal observation. Describing Egyptian customs, he tells us they were opposite to those practiced by the rest of the known world: "The women attend the markets and trade, while the men sit at home at the loom. . . . In other countries the priests have long hair,

"Soldiers, forty centuries look down upon you"

Napoleon, one of countless invaders of Egypt, pointed to the Giza pyramids as he uttered these words. Although his soldiers would know defeat, success crowned the efforts of scholars who joined the expedition. Here they measure the Sphinx, a human-headed lion that served as a guardian spirit. Medieval Moslems chiseled away the statue's nose. The French were eager sightseers—even Napoleon's aging officers, egged on by the young general's taunts, scaled the Great Pyramid and shared a little brandy at the summit.

in Egypt their heads are shaven. . . . other men pass their lives separate from animals, the Egyptians have animals always living with them. . . . When they write or calculate, instead of going, like the Greeks, from left to right, they move their hand from right to left."

Herodotus visited the pyramids and apparently became the gullible victim of a tour guide. He tells us with confidence that an inscription on the Great Pyramid, read to him by an interpreter, reveals the amount of onions and garlic consumed by the workmen who built it. And he repeats an old story—that when the pharaoh needed money to continue building, he put his daughter to work as a prostitute. The pyramid's casing stones, carried off long ago by the Arabs, probably never bore any inscriptions except graffiti.

Manetho, a high priest in the temple at Heliopolis in the third century B.C., prepared a history of Egypt that still influences historians. The document no longer exists intact, but pieces of it have been assembled from extracts found in other ancient writings. Manetho divided Egyptian history into 30 dynasties—groups of hereditary rulers—a scheme we still use, though details are missing. We wonder, for example, why one dynasty replaced another. When the French scholar Champollion deciphered the Egyptian language in the early 19th century, Manetho's lists could be compared to inscriptions on monuments, and his history turned out to be far more reliable than anyone had supposed.

To bring order to 3,000 years of history, Egyptologists divide Manetho's numbered dynasties into several phases. They designate the three great periods of Egyptian history the Old Kingdom, the Middle Kingdom, and the New Kingdom, with each followed by an Intermediate Period of political unrest. They also modified Manetho's list by adding a 31st dynasty.

Each of the three kingdoms can be characterized by certain accomplishments. Old Kingdom pharaohs raised the pyramids at the edge of the western desert. Middle Kingdom pharaohs consolidated power by controlling the nobles. The New Kingdom ushered in

"A fit prison-house for fallen angels"

Napoleon's savants explore by torchlight the cavernous Grand Gallery deep in the heart of the Great Pyramid. The sloping aisle, walled in polished limestone, stretches 153 feet and rises 28 feet to a stepped roof. The Frenchman on the ladder (opposite) disappears into a hole that leads to a compartment directly above the burial chamber—where Cheops's sarcophagus stands empty. The first visitors—robbers—came in pharaonic times; the curious have been drawn to the monument's eerie interior for centuries. Huge bats and a terrible stench greeted medieval visitors—an Arab doctor fainted from fright in a dark passage. To Victorian novelist Harriet Martineau the pyramid was a gloomy prison, but she hitched up her long skirts and climbed to the King's Chamber.

the nation's zenith as a military power. Culture and the arts flourished. At the end of the New Kingdom, about 1100 B.C., Egypt began to decline. It saw a brief renaissance with the Saite Dynasty, but felt the battering of wave after wave of invaders—culminating in the conquest by Alexander the Great in 332 B.C. Three centuries of domination by Macedonian and Ptolemaic kings ended with the country's fall to Rome in 30 B.C.

With the Roman occupation, Egypt became a thoroughly administered Roman province. Travelers could come and go in safety, using the excellent post roads maintained for the imperial mail service. Emperors and senators arrived to inspect the principal tourist attractions and to study the quaint customs of the Egyptians, who continued to live, work, and worship in the age-old way. The emperor Hadrian not only traveled in Egypt but also founded a city on the Nile. When he returned home, he ordered part of his villa at Tivoli designed Egyptian-style.

In Roman times, travelers stopped at the Giza pyramids and the Sphinx, then traveled upriver to Memphis to see the sacred bull at the Apis sanctuary. The Faiyum oasis had more attractions—the Labyrinth, a maze-like temple complex named by the Greeks for the legendary structure in Crete, and nearby, the pool of the sacred crocodile.

Thebes, capital of Egypt at the height of its power, was a ruined city even in those days, but the tourists admired the damaged temples and hiked the rocky trail to the Valley of the Kings, burial place of New Kingdom pharaohs. Most tombs had already been plundered when the Romans crawled inside and scratched their names on the walls by torchlight.

Roman emperors, who considered Egypt their personal preserve, collected antiquities on a grand scale. They carted off hundreds of statues and other objects to decorate their capital. But it was the tall obelisk, topped by a small pyramid and chiseled with mysterious hieroglyphs, that the Romans most fancied. Obelisks were dedicated to the sun god and inscribed

with names of pharaohs; the foreigners, however, knew nothing of this. Pliny the Elder believed the inscriptions interpreted "the operations of Nature according to the philosophy of the Egyptians." Today more obelisks stand in Rome than in Egypt. Others are scattered about the world from New York to Istanbul.

During the Middle Ages, the association of Jewish and Christian history with Egypt gave Europeans a new motive for visiting. They made the journey not as traders or tourists, but as pious pilgrims. Old Testament stories about Joseph in Egypt, the bondage of the Israelites, the Exodus, and the New Testament account of the Holy Family's flight from Herod made Egypt a place of consuming interest.

Travel grew difficult and dangerous after the Arab conquest about A.D. 640, when Egypt became part of the Moslem world. A long silence settled over the country during this period. The Arabs, who felt disdain for a culture so alien to their own, searched the temples and pyramids for treasure and used them as quarries for building stone. Not until a thousand years after the last hieroglyphs were written could Europeans travel in safety again. By that time no one understood the ancient writings. Scholars had not forgotten the Nile Valley—the works of ancient authors were still available. But they could shed no light on current conditions, and the country remained terra incognita.

Most of the adventurers who braved the sea voyage or the overland route along the eastern Mediterranean were German, French, and English. Some wrote accounts of their travels. In 1547 Pierre Belon entered the Great Pyramid at Giza and saw the royal sarcophagus. So did André Thevet, chaplain to Catherine de Medici, in 1549. Thevet entered the so-called "mummy pits" at Saqqara, looking for the bodies of dead Egyptians. The shriveled corpses excited a great deal of interest, for by the 16th century, "mummy" had become a popular drug found in apothecary shops all over Europe. Tombs were ransacked to supply the constant demand for mummies. The Egyptians themselves broke up

mummy cases for firewood and sold the powdered bodies of their ancestors as medicine. "Mummy is become merchandise," wrote physician-author Sir Thomas Browne in 1658, ". . . and Pharaoh is sold for balsams." At a time when the going price in Scotland was eight shillings a pound, one canny trader exported 600 pounds in one shipment—and made a killing.

The word mummy comes from the Arabic *mumiyah*, meaning bitumen. Early Near Eastern peoples used bitumen to heal wounds. Sometimes the shiny black resins found in embalmed bodies, and even the mummy itself, were used as substitutes. If the real thing were unobtainable, the cadavers of slaves or prisoners were treated with bitumen and sold instead.

In the 11th century, the Persian physician Avicenna prescribed mummy for almost every ill—paralysis, epilepsy, nausea, ulcers, concussions, and palpitations of the heart. As late as the 1800's Arabs were still mixing mummy powder with butter as a remedy for bruises. Even today, genuine Egyptian mummy, it is rumored, can be purchased in certain New York drugstores—for forty dollars an ounce.

The curio dealers of Cairo could supply the 17th-century visitor with a complete mummy or a variety of other objects, such as amulets, scarabs, and papyri. What the Egyptians couldn't find in the desert sands they made themselves. In 1635 Archbishop Laud presented to the Bodleian Library at Oxford University one of the oldest known Egyptian fakes—a small mummiform statue, not in the least ancient. The art of faking, it seems, is as old as the tourist industry that creates a market for copies.

By the 18th century, the trickle of visitors threatened to become a torrent. Some travelers searched for antiquities to take back to collectors or museums, others were curious antiquarians who wandered from temple to temple, copying inscriptions, admiring reliefs.

If we could transport ourselves back to the Egypt of 1737, we would see a *dahabeah*—a lateen-rigged sailing vessel—moving slowly up the Nile. Aboard would be an Anglican clergyman, Richard Pococke. He had already visited Lower (northern) Egypt and was on his way to Aswan in Upper (southern) Egypt. Pococke adopted the name Yusef, let his beard grow, and wore native costume—all prudent precautions for a foreigner on the Nile. "I provided everything as for a long voyage," he wrote, "coffee, rice, tobacco, soap, red shoes of the Arabs, and several other things for presents, and took care to have sufficient arms for our defence."

At Saqqara, he had stayed in the house of a local sheikh. The Arab villagers were suspicious of foreigners and considered them fair game. Returning unexpectedly from the tombs one day, Pococke was surprised by an eight-year-old girl rushing from his room. In the ceiling was a large hole. The child's mother had let her down on a rope to rifle his baggage.

In spite of danger and inconvenience, the clergyman saw more of the country than most of his predecessors. His account of the land, the people, and the antiquities stands as one of the most reliable. Methodically, he drew plans of royal tombs, sketched monuments, and accurately described others. He observed that the Sphinx had been cut from solid rock, not constructed; and he guessed, correctly, that the receptacles found in tombs—later called canopic jars—contained the viscera of mummies. Pococke was one of the first writers to denounce the destruction he saw all around him.

He and other early travelers left us magnificent drawings and descriptions of monuments, as well as fascinating insights into village life. But ancient Egypt still wore its veil of mystery. No one understood its past or how to read its forgotten language.

In May 1798, Napoleon Bonaparte embarked from the French port of Toulon with an expeditionary force of 38,000 men for the conquest of Egypt. He hoped to expand the territory of France while limiting the power

of England in the East. The result of his military adventure would be the opening up of Egypt's wonders to the West. The French expedition can rightly be called the beginning of modern Egyptology.

With the army and the navy, the general brought a corps of scholars—more than a hundred men schooled in every discipline. He offered them the opportunity to study Egypt and record their observations for the rest of the world. With enthusiasm, the specialists set to work: Artists sketched the antiquities, engineers studied irrigation methods, mapmakers set down the topography of Egypt. Often the work was carried out in the face of hardship and danger.

Vivant Denon, a skillful young artist, risked death or capture to follow an army detachment as it marched south. Sketching furiously, engrossed in his task, Denon was often left alone among picturesque ruins, unaware that the soldiers had moved on. Then, in January 1799, Denon with his military escort rounded a bend of the Nile and saw the temples of Luxor and Karnak. We are told that the troops halted and burst into applause at the sight. "Without an order being given, the men formed their ranks and presented arms, to the accompaniment of the drums and the bands," wrote an army lieutenant.

Besides his select group of intellectuals, dubbed by the military "the donkeys," Napoleon brought with him the first printing press seen in Egypt. Works could now be published quickly and cheaply in Arabic, French, and Greek. He also founded the French Institute in Cairo, a research facility that still exists. In due course, the 24-volume *Description de l'Égypte* appeared. An encyclopedic record of the nation's antiquities, natural history, and contemporary customs, it thrust Egypt into the center of the world stage. Beautifully illustrated folios provided source material for European artists, who painted charmingly realistic scenes of

Egyptian life without ever leaving home. The *Description* contains valuable information on the crumbling monuments, including some that no longer exist.

Crucial to a real understanding of ancient Egypt were the mysterious inscriptions. French soldiers digging fortifications near the town of Rosetta found the key—a bilingual inscription in Greek, which could be read, and Egyptian, which could not. The story of the Rosetta Stone and its decipherment unfolds in a later chapter of this book.

With the coming of the French, Egypt was no longer protected by its remoteness or the difficulties of travel. The 19th century was to be the great period of European exploration and plunder. Most foreign agents were obsessed with acquisition, either for their own national museums or for anyone willing to pay. A competition began for the largest, the most unusual, and the best examples of Egyptian artifacts.

Mohammed Ali, pasha of Egypt after the departure of the French, wished to bring his country into the modern world, and he saw the advantage of using European expertise. If some of these same Europeans showed an interest in hauling off antiquities, he made no objection. Surely there was plenty for everyone; what difference could it possibly make if these foreigners took away a few statues and sarcophagi? Under Mohammed Ali, men such as Giovanni Belzoni, Henry Salt, and Bernardino Drovetti scoured the country for anything ancient and movable. Their enterprise enriched the collections of the British Museum, the Louvre, and the Egyptian Museum in Turin.

Of all those who shared in this wholesale sack of Egypt, Belzoni stands out as the most flamboyant. Italian by birth, English by adoption, he once worked as a sideshow strong man in London. At Sadler's Wells Theatre, where he carried a pyramid of men on his shoulders, he was advertised on the playbill as the "Patagonian Sampson." It was not his great strength

that took him to Egypt, but rather his inventive mind and rich imagination.

Belzoni arrived in Cairo in 1815 and offered to build the pasha a pumping machine that would efficiently move water for irrigation. Nothing came of his ambitions to improve Egyptian agriculture, but he quickly saw the possibilities in collecting antiquities. For the next four years he succeeded brilliantly, overcoming every obstacle. Agents of Drovetti, his rival, threatened to cut his throat if he continued collecting; armed Arabs attacked him; workmen refused to work, but he cajoled, badgered, and bribed them into doing the job.

In 1817 Belzoni journeyed up the Nile to Abu Simbel to uncover the temple that lay behind the gigantic statues of Ramses II. Digging alongside his workmen, he cleared away centuries of drifted sand. Light penetrated the pillared hall inside, revealing "one of the most magnificent of temples, enriched with beautiful intaglios, painting, colossal figures." The monument became so well known that it was saved by international effort in the 1960's when water rising behind the Aswan High Dam threatened to engulf it.

In the Valley of the Kings, Belzoni opened several tombs. Faced with a blocked passage, he fashioned a battering ram and smashed through, obliterating seal impressions and objects behind the door. In other tombs elsewhere the destruction went on: "I sought a resting-place, found one, and contrived to sit; but when my weight bore on the body of an Egyptian, it crushed it like a band-box. . . . I sunk altogether among the broken mummies, with a crash of bones, rags, and wooden cases, which raised such a dust as kept me motionless for a quarter of an hour. . . . every step I took I crushed a mummy in some part or other."

In 1817 Belzoni found the tomb of Seti I, who died about 1300 B.C. Down in the burial chamber stood the sarcophagus, carved from a single block of translucent alabaster and decorated with tiny inlaid figures. Here was a treasure; nothing like it had been seen before. But the tomb had been plundered—gone were the

Theirs was a legacy of giant strides

A trio of great archeologists helped bring ancient Egypt back to life. Gaston Maspero reclines on the rocks at the site where a colleague recovered some 40 royal mummies once buried in the Valley of the Kings. The Egyptian guide holding the rope, Mohammed Abd er-Rasul, received a £500 reward for revealing the resting place of the kings and queens. The meticulous excavator Flinders Petrie is shown in his later years examining pottery finds. Petrie often criticized the sloppy fieldwork of Auguste Mariette, pictured below with Fifth-Dynasty statues from Saqqara. Mariette made spectacular discoveries but kept incomplete records. His excavations at Saqqara, where he found mummified bulls in 60-ton granite sarcophagi, made him famous. **Overleaf:** Swarming over the hillside north of Queen Hatshepsut's funerary temple, diggers and basketboys—the unsung heroes of Egyptology—labor to clear a ravine outside the temple wall. Honeycombed with the tombs of nobles and priests, the area was explored by Herbert Winlock, who in 1929 found there the tomb of 18th-Dynasty Queen Merytamun, the coffin stripped by thieves.

mummy and almost everything else that was movable.

The mummy's fate is part of the long story of tomb robbery in Egypt. As early as the Fourth Dynasty in the reign of Cheops, builder of the Great Pyramid, there is evidence of pillage. Curses inscribed on early tombs threaten with vengeance those who inflict damage, and promise blessings to those who care for the tomb. With the fall of the Old Kingdom an epidemic of looting began. The starving people traded the tomb treasures for bread.

The Middle Kingdom brought better days, and the tombs flourished as before. Only with the lean years of Dynasty 20 did robbery become prevalent again, this time with the connivance of government officials. A surviving papyrus tells the story: The mayor of East Thebes charged the mayor of West Thebes, who policed the cemeteries, with neglecting his duties and helping the thieves. A commission sent to investigate found nine royal tombs intact, only one violated. But there was room for suspicion—the commission probably avoided the violated burials! Accusations continued to fly, and tombs continued to be plundered. As a last resort, the priests collected all the surviving royal mummies and hid them in a safer place, where they remained undisturbed for 3,000 years.

In 1871 a goatherd and part-time tomb robber, Ahmed Abd er-Rasul, found the cache of mummies while searching for a lost kid near the temple of Hatshepsut at Deir el Bahri. Ahmed came from the village of Qurna, whose inhabitants had been robbing tombs in the hillside west of Thebes for centuries. Often they lived in the tombs among the "hands, feet, or sculls" strewn around the dark caves. Belzoni had made friends with them and bought their antiquities; Napoleon's men had been greeted with volleys of stones.

When Ahmed found the royal mummies, he was cautious. He entered the tomb only a few times in ten years and took into his confidence only family members. Gradually, papyri, scarabs, and canopic jars began to appear on the market. By this time, the Egyptian

government had set up an organization to protect antiquities. The Director-General, Gaston Maspero, suspected that a royal tomb had been found. Some clever detective work led him and Egyptologist Emil Brugsch to the guilty family; two of the brothers were arrested, thrown on the ground, and beaten with palm rods on the soles of their feet. They refused to confess. Later, Ahmed's eldest brother Mohammed, fearing for his own safety, led authorities to the treasure.

Brugsch entered the grave deep inside the cliffs of the Theban necropolis. By flickering candlelight he beheld the mortal remains of such illustrious pharaohs as Ramses II, Thutmose III, and Seti I—Belzoni's missing mummy. "I still wonder if I am not dreaming when I see and touch what were the bodies of so many famous personages," Maspero was to write later. The buried kings were removed and sent north by boat. Along the Nile, crowds gathered for the funeral procession—the women wailing, the men shooting off shotguns. They mourned as much for the defeat of their friends, the tomb robbers, as they did for the dead pharaohs.

With the work of scholars like Maspero, Egyptology made rapid progress. Besides supervising the mummy project, Maspero went "fishing for statues" in the Temple of Amun-Re at Karnak. Rising groundwater had drowned a rich mine of objects buried by priests in antiquity. Using oil cans for pails, workmen bailed, then groped in the mud with bare hands. "Seven hundred stone monuments have already come out of the water," Maspero wrote, "Pharaohs enthroned, queens standing upright, priests of Amun . . . indeed, a whole population returns to the upper air."

Maspero followed in the footsteps of another French archeologist, Auguste Mariette. The latter had been appointed the first conservator of ancient monuments, a position he used to protect antiquities from vandals and thieves. Careless tourists enraged him, especially one American visitor who toured Upper Egypt in 1870

"I was struck dumb with amazement"

Howard Carter peered through a chink in Tutankhamun's tomb. "At first I could see nothing," he said. Then details within emerged: "strange animals, statues, and gold—everywhere the glint of gold." Lord Carnarvon asked, "Can you see anything?" Carter replied, "Yes, wonderful things." And this was only the beginning—four rooms were heaped up with treasure. The mummy lay encased in solid gold, one of three nested coffins (left). When the news broke, visitors and journalists swarmed around the tomb, impeding work. Carter had erected a steel door, and armed guards escorted workmen, shown here bearing part of a couch and a bust of the king that seems to walk by itself. It took Carter and a staff of experts ten years to clear the tomb.

"with a pot of tar in one hand and a brush in the other, leaving on all the temples the indelible and truly disgraceful record of his passage." To Mariette goes the credit for establishing an Egyptian national museum that would protect antiquities and keep them in Egypt.

Many other scholars brought special talents to the growing discipline. A pioneering English archeologist, William Matthew Flinders Petrie, was shocked by the wastefulness of early excavators who concentrated on showy objects and ignored such run-of-the-mill items as potsherds and mud walls. Petrie believed these "trifles" to be important. By applying step-by-step methodology, he transformed a treasure hunt into a science. "Most people think of excavating as a pleasing sort of holiday amusement," he wrote, "but it takes about as much care and management as any other business."

Petrie's spartan life-style became legendary. While other diggers ate elegant food on plush houseboats, he was content to live in a tomb or a mud hut and eat out of tin cans. "He has a cot bed in the tomb of Nefermaat," a visitor wrote, "a few . . . books . . . and two tents, one a kitchen with a petroleum stove." He was his own photographer, copyist, and chemist. Though his students abhorred the rigorous life in camp, they revered Petrie as a great archeologist.

In the 20th century, German, French, and English archeologists were joined by the Americans. Excavations enriched the museums of New York and Boston, until today their collections are among the finest in the world. James Henry Breasted of the University of Chicago led an intensive campaign to copy monument inscriptions before they were lost to decay or vandalism.

The scientists of this period were occupied with more than just a re-examination of known sites. In 1907 a dedicated archeologist began an association with an English nobleman that would have stunning consequences for Egyptology. In that year, the Fifth Earl of Carnarvon, having decided to do some excavating, hired Howard Carter to direct the project. Carter had worked with Petrie and other scholars. A gifted artist,

he had copied temple carvings at Deir el Bahri. The Egyptian government had appointed him an inspector of monuments.

Theodore Davis, a rich American, relinquished his rights to dig in the Valley of the Kings in 1914. Almost everyone believed the valley to be exhausted, but Carter disagreed. With Lord Carnarvon's financial backing, he took up the concession. Their efforts were interrupted by World War I, and even Carnarvon had become discouraged. Carter pleaded for one more season to pursue the goal that had become his obsession— the tomb of Tutankhamun. He knew that Davis had found some Tutankhamun artifacts. The tomb itself had never been discovered because it was concealed by the rubble quarried out of a larger tomb just above it. Even the ancient robbers had been fooled; except for an abortive break-in, probably soon after Tutankhamun's funeral, the tomb remained intact until our own time.

Like Heinrich Schliemann, who discovered the site of ancient Troy, Carter found exactly what he believed to be there. In November 1922, his workmen uncovered a staircase. As they cleared it, a doorway came into view, affixed with royal seals showing the jackal symbol of the god Anubis above nine defeated captives. "It was a thrilling moment," Carter wrote. "Literally anything might lie beyond that passage, and it needed all my self-control to keep from breaking down the doorway, and investigating then and there."

But for nearly three agonizing weeks he waited for the arrival of Lord Carnarvon from London. Then the clearing continued. Finally, on November 26, 1922, they entered the tomb, where the glitter of gold and the sight of beautiful things made the onlookers "strangely silent and subdued." Carter's reward was spectacular. "King Tut" became a household phrase. The press carried daily bulletins from the Valley of the Kings as work progressed. Today the wealth of Tutankhamun's tomb fills gallery after gallery in Cairo's Egyptian Museum. Some of these treasures appear in the portfolio that follows, and elsewhere in this book.

Spectacular finds come along once in a lifetime, but there are always perplexing riddles to tease the imagination. New scientific tools help solve them. An intriguing example is the recent identification of Queen Tiy. Eighty years ago a female mummy with wavy brown hair and no identifying marks turned up in the tomb of Amunhotep II. She was called simply "Elder Lady." In 1975 scientists X-rayed the mummy's head and discovered that the facial contours resembled those of Queen Thuya, mother of Tiy. With the maternal link suggested, electrons were used to "fingerprint" the minerals in Elder Lady's hair and in a known lock of Queen Tiy's hair—found in Tutankhamun's tomb. The results positively identified the mummy as Queen Tiy, wife of Amunhotep III and possibly the grandmother of Tutankhamun.

New discoveries are coming out of Egypt. I was fortunate to participate in the ongoing excavation of the Mut Temple complex at Karnak, a part of the Brooklyn Museum Theban Expedition in Egypt. Two Englishwomen dug there in the 1890's, but archeologists have all but ignored the site. The Karnak temples honor the Theban gods Amun, his consort, Mut, and their son, Khonsu. An avenue lined with sphinxes, connecting Mut's temple with Amun's, may have been built by Tutankhamun. Nearly surrounded by a lake symbolizing the water from which all life came, the Mut Temple is the centerpiece of a 25-acre complex. We uncovered foundations of walls and colonnades, potsherds, and sculpture—the puzzle pieces of Egyptian history. But it may take years to understand the temple's intriguing story.

Most people believe the sands of Egypt have yielded all the secrets of the past. Nothing could be further from the truth. So much lies buried that it will take generations of digging even to begin to fill the gaps in our knowledge. The search goes on for clues to the civilization that has already given us, as Herodotus said, "such a number of works which defy description."

A boy-king's golden trove

A rarity among archeological finds, Tutankhamun's tomb held treasures today beyond price. Court goldsmiths fashioned exquisite works of art to accompany the pharaoh on his last journey, expressing the ancient Egyptian's fervent hope that life could indeed be eternal. Arms outstretched, the goddess Selket guards a chest (inset) containing the king's viscera, which were preserved separately. The scorpion on Selket's head suggests her magic power against its sting. Encased in gold, the wooden shrine (opposite) is covered with intimate scenes from the everyday life of king and queen. A pedestal inside once held a statue stolen by tomb robbers in antiquity. **Overleaf:** To see Tutankhamun's solid gold funerary mask is to look into the king's face—the features resemble those of the mummy. Very little is known about the young pharaoh who ruled Egypt some 1,350 years before Christ.

27

In the kingdom of the dead

Alive again in the shadowy spirit world, the entombed pharaoh lived as he had on earth. Tutankhamun's tomb was crammed with the ritual objects and personal possessions he would need. As high priest he might wear on his chest the leopard's head device with eyes of translucent quartz. In life the young king loved to hunt. On his mummy lay a sheathed dagger of superb craftsmanship, the handle adorned with floral designs and overlaid with tiny balls of gold. In a statuette of solid gold, the pharaoh crouches, holding royal emblems—a crook and flail. From the tomb's innermost room came 22 shrines containing images of the king or of a deity. Tutankhamun believed that this gilded cobra would help him pass safely through the underworld. On its base an inscription describes the dead ruler: "Beloved of the living god."

The People of the River

Karl W. Butzer

Hail to you, O Nile!
Sprung from earth,
Come to nourish Egypt! . . .
Food provider, bounty maker,
Who creates all that is good.

These lines from an ancient hymn to the Nile summarize the vital part the river played in the great civilization that grew along its banks. When the Nile overflowed its channel in a rhythmic annual pattern, it spread life-giving waters across the sun-parched land. Moisture soaked deep into the ground to help nourish crops. A plentiful flood brought laughter and jubilation; low waters could mean starvation.

Equally important, Nile inundations carried with them fine clays and silts, rich in minerals, washed from highlands upstream. The river dropped these loads on the fields, spreading a natural fertilizer and replenishing plow-worked land. Egypt is "the gift of the river," wrote Hecataeus of Miletus, a Greek who visited the Nile Valley about 500 B.C. He referred not so much to the livening waters as to the alluvium they carried—the soil that built a lush delta on the coast and a strip of green across the eastern Sahara.

Some 450 years after Hecataeus, Diodorus the Sicilian speculated on the source of the waters that appeared so profusely in a land where little rain fell. Egypt then had much the same climate as it has today: notoriously dry and warm. Delta regions get an average of some four inches of rain a year. Around Cairo the amount totals an inch or so. Farther inland a shower may come only once in two or three years. So little rain falls that for the last 1,600 miles of its trip to the sea the Nile counts not a single tributary. Yet until the high dam at Aswan tamed the river in 1970, it swelled with the regularity of clockwork each summer. It brought a vast volume of runoff—a rise that filled the entire channel and spread to an average depth of five feet over the fields of the floodplain. Diodorus suggested a solution to the mystery of the annual inundation. He spoke of continuous rains that fell on the mountains of Ethiopia between June and September each year. In response, the river rose, flooding its valley.

Ancient Egyptians took a less analytical view of their river than did the early Greek travelers. Egyptian attitudes toward the Nile were simultaneously more practical and more symbolic. They knew the Nile in every mood and season, and regulated their lives accordingly. To them the river was the source of life, not an object of curiosity. They saw in the Nile a wholesome cosmic order. They personified the river with the god Hapi, who represented its spirit and its inherent forces. He flowed with the waters of Nun, the primordial ocean out of which the first mound of earth emerged—in turn to give rise to Re, the sun. Here, in the realm of the gods, the Nile had its inexhaustible source. So the function of the river was divine. And Egyptians could hymn:

Hail to you, Hapi . . .
When he floods, earth rejoices!
Every belly jubilates,
Every jawbone takes on laughter,
Every tooth is bared.

The reliance placed on the Nile by the ancient Egyptians was understandable. In general the Nile is the most predictable of the world's great rivers. It taps two major climatic regions for its water: Ethiopia and the southern Sudan with its summer monsoons, and central Africa with its double (spring and autumn) rainy seasons. Spectacular lightning, crashing thunder, awesome sheets of rain mark the storms that can sweep the highlands and forests. Their runoff blends, south of the Sahara, through a number of tributary basins to provide a remarkably reliable flood pattern.

Other rivers that nourished early civilizations—the Tigris, Euphrates, or Indus, for example—are far more affected by random weather events. Heavy rains or sudden melts from mountain snowfields race down watercourses. Flood volume fluctuates wildly, both

Prehistoric people of the Nile Valley shaped clay and stone to meet both pious and practical needs. Winglike arms and beaked head of a female figure suggest a dancer or a supplicant spirit that may represent a fertility symbol. An artisan made it about 4000 B.C. A finely worked flint knife, its ivory handle carved with marching animals, dates from about 3100 B.C. The urn, from the same period, shows evidence of early use of the potter's wheel. Pottery types give us a dating system for predynastic Egyptian cultures.

from week to week and from one year to the next. Yearly flood peaks vary by as much as a month or two. In contrast, ancient Egyptians could almost set their calendar by the arrival of the annual inundation, and though the crest of the flood might include extreme highs and lows, during most centuries it was predictable within a few feet.

Today a complex irrigation system rigidly controls the Nile Valley, carefully regulating water from day to day and from place to place. Great panoramas of cultivated fields, separated by rows of palms and dotted by countless villages and towns, accompany the river from Aswan to the sea. Amid this thickly settled, man-made landscape, it seems difficult to imagine the original look of the land. Was it a hostile morass of marsh and jungle-like thickets that required draining, clearing, and taming by generations of prehistoric colonists? Or was it an inviting, fertile environment of woods, meadows, streams, and occasional lakes—a primeval Eden that enticed settlers from the earliest times? Who were the people that colonized the land? And where did they come from?

The original Nile landscape must have resembled that of other great rivers whose annual floods cover broad plains. Such rivers have well-defined channels that meander between banks—natural levees—raised as heavier sediments drop first from the overflowing stream. Their floodplains include broad basins that catch the muddy waters spilling from the channel. When floods are moderate, water brims across low spots in the banks, and only parts of the basins become inundated. In exceptionally high floods, even the banks may be submerged. As the crest passes, much of the water flows back into the river channel. But enough moisture normally remains in the soil, and as groundwater, to allow a crop to grow and ripen.

You find this pattern in parts of the Mississippi Valley and with many tropical rivers. Two such streams in Africa, the Senegal and the Logone-Chari, course through the southern Sahara. There, until recent

Birth of a nation: a story in stone

Immortalized on a palette of slate, a king named Narmer—his name appears in hieroglyphs between the horned heads—smites an enemy. His size befits his importance, a convention of Egyptian art. On one side of the slate he wears the domed crown of Upper Egypt, on the other the curled one for Lower Egypt—symbolically uniting the nation. Snake-necked leopards encircle the hollow where pigment was ground, then mixed with fat to make eye shadow. Plain at first, palettes acquired decoration and ceremonial use. This, carved about 3000 B.C., is 25 inches high.

decades, native people practiced successful agriculture without the aid of artificial drainage, irrigation, or flood control. Villages sat atop the riverbanks or other bits of high ground. Inhabitants sowed their crops on the fresh silts of the flood basins as soon as the high-water season ended. While the crops grew, cattle grazed in meadows and scrublands. When the waters rose again, the crops had been taken in and the herds moved to the dry margins. The farmers waited out the flood in their high-perched villages. No special technology was needed to colonize such regions—only the know-how to profit from a bountiful environment.

We can guess that the same way of life was followed in prehistoric times in Egypt. And the argument finds ample support in the archeological record. Cemeteries and settlement sites tell the story.

Until a half-century ago most of the prehistoric camps and graves that had been studied lay along the edge of the low desert that borders the Nile floodplain. We know from recent radiocarbon dating that the majority of such sites belong to the fifth and fourth millenniums B.C., a period in Egypt called the Predynastic Era. Early archeologists felt that the sites represented the first agricultural settlements of the Nile Valley. They also argued that these earliest settlers at first couldn't colonize the flood basins—by building villages there. That had to wait until people learned how to drain the basins and irrigate them. Presumably this came a few centuries before the joining of Upper Egypt and Lower Egypt—kingdoms named for their locations on upstream or downstream stretches of the north-flowing Nile. That union came around 3050 B.C.

Nineteenth-century archeologists opened thousands of predynastic graves at dozens of sites all along the edge of the valley. Settlements, however, were few and far between. They represented mainly tiny villages, some of them probably seasonal camps of herders or even desert-edge nomads. The number of cemeteries and graves argues that more people lived in the region than could be accounted for by the size of the desert-edge settlements. These colonists must have populated locales well within the floodplain. But the early archeologists didn't know about those sites. They were buried under a mantle of later Nile mud, or they lay hidden beneath tens of feet of rubble at the bottom of village mounds settled over the millenniums.

Then a new era of archeological research began in Egypt about 1960. The start of the Aswan High Dam brought its certainty of drowning Nile sites. Scholars swarmed over ancient Nubia, the strategic region of black rocks and scorched sand that overlaps the present-day border between Egypt and Sudan. As one of the scientists put it, they had "temples to save, thousands of inscriptions and graffiti to record, untold numbers of cemeteries [and] town mounds . . . to excavate, acres to map archeologically." They examined areas where new villages were to be built for people who would be displaced as the waters rose. They made geological studies that helped reconstruct old wanderings of the Nile. And as a result, a totally new picture of Egypt's prehistory emerged.

The Kom Ombo plain, some 30 miles north of Aswan, turned out to be an ideal area for finding out what the Nile Valley was like 10,000 to 15,000 years

ago. At that time the river meandered in several channels across the plain. Some filled with overflow waters only during flood stage. Others carried water all year. Hundreds of prehistoric sites around Kom Ombo date to this period. Almost always those sites lie on former riverbanks. But in some cases people set up camps along the ephemeral desert streams, or in Nile overflow channels after the flood receded. Similar patterns occur elsewhere. To the north, near Esna, camps stood on low dunes that surround grassy swales or ponds fed by seepage from the nearby Nile. The findings show how consistently the people chose riverside living sites. More important, with the digs came a wealth of information about how these prehistoric folk lived.

Stone tools—axes, knives, drill tips, arrowheads—turned up in abundance at the campsites. By carefully classifying the tools with the help of computers, we can put them into specific groupings—and a surprising number of groupings at that. These differ not only in how frequently certain tools turn up and what they were used for, but also both in the styles and in the techniques with which they were made.

People in some settlements made relatively large tools in painstaking ways. Others made a great number of small tools, as if by mass production. Even among these small-tool—or microlithic—groups, specialization existed. Some emphasized broad, scraping instruments. Others concentrated on narrow points, tips, and borers—obviously hafted to arrows, spears or other wooden shafts that long ago disappeared.

What all this means is that the makers of these several kinds of tool kits had differing skills and backgrounds—differing cultures. Careful study leaves little doubt that, at any given time, at least three and sometimes five or more cultural groups lived along the Nile. They were distinctive ethnic populations. Each probably consisted of several scattered bands of 50 or more people. The related bands roamed adjacent areas, although sometimes also beside other ethnic groups.

Some of these populations had tool-making traditions similar to those in northwest Africa dating from the same time. Others derived from older peoples who had lived along the Nile 25,000 or more years ago. Some groups may originally have had roots in Asia, although this is not by any means proven. Thus the prehistoric Nile Valley clearly belonged to the North African cultural sphere, not that of the Near East. It attracted Stone Age people of different life-styles, evidently because of the many opportunities it offered for subsistence. But some competition for resources can be expected in such a situation. And discovery of a contemporary cemetery with many skeletons showing broken bones or embedded arrowheads gives impressive evidence of warfare at this early date.

Bones, shells, and other finds unearthed at their campsites tell us much about the habits of these river dwellers of 10,000 or 15,000 years ago. We know that they hunted wild cattle, several kinds of antelope, and an occasional wild ass or hippo. They caught fish and gathered shellfish. One site at the northern end of the Kom Ombo plain had an enormous number of bird remains; somehow settlers must have netted or snared migratory geese and ducks.

Hand-held grinding stones tell us other stories of their skills. Some of these stones found near Kom Ombo date as far back as 14,500 years ago. Such stones have been used to grind meat and pigment for cosmetics. They also can turn wild grass seeds into flour. Near Esna, stones dating from about 10,700 to 10,000 B.C. came to light in deposits that also contained pollen, perhaps from wild barley. With them were stone blades that had a lustrous sheen on their cutting edges. The sheen resulted from silica in plants—the blades must have been used to reap stalks. Such tantalizing hints may well be the record of sophisticated gathering and processing of plant foods. In fact, some Egyptian populations may have been experimenting with plants as early as 12,500 B.C. Exactly this sort of intensive attention to food resources preceded the eventual emergence of agriculture in southwestern Asia.

But these prehistoric Egyptians did not continue toward farming. For about 500 years beginning around 10,000 B.C., a series of catastrophically high floods swept through the Nile Valley. They may have discouraged planting and brought a return to wandering ways. Fewer settlements show up, and no grinding stones. Instead, specialized stone tools and bone harpoons suggest greater emphasis on fishing. As late as 5200 B.C. Egyptians persisted as fishermen and hunters, and as gatherers of wild foods. This was some 2,000 years after farming became common in Asia and at least 1,500 years after herders had begun to wander with cattle, sheep, and goats through the moister highlands of the Sahara. By modern standards, these Egyptians would have been described as unprogressive.

Herding folk had by then reached the Libyan oases not far from the Nile. This suggests that the valley people did know about herding and even agriculture in general, but that they deliberately chose not to change their way of life. Agriculture provides a larger food supply and can support greater populations on smaller territory than can hunting and gathering. But it requires more work. Under seemingly little population

pressure, these late hunter-gatherers of Egypt may have preferred to preserve their traditional life-style.

Agriculture did—finally—establish itself in Egypt. But the change came about through infiltration of new populations. About 5200 B.C.—the date now used to mark the beginning of Egypt's Predynastic Era—the new people began to settle along the lakeshores of the Faiyum depression and next to the western Delta. They kept cattle, pigs, sheep, and goats, and they cultivated emmer wheat, barley, and flax. These farmers, who may have drifted to Egypt from oases in Libya or farther west, had already adapted a series of Asian agricultural inventions to North African environments.

The newcomers also brought a stone-working tradition unlike the microlithic culture then prevalent along the Nile. Their style emphasized large, leaf-shaped knives and arrowheads. Significantly, this style was quite different from anything known in the Sinai or southwestern Asia. It was an African technique, probably derived from a fine-tool culture, the Aterian, widespread in North Africa some 20,000 years earlier. Its exact origin cannot yet be pinpointed.

No evidence suggests that the newcomers' penetration was warlike. Instead, the local hunter-gatherers began to switch to farming—first in the Delta, then in the south. We know little about this transition, which was quite intricate and took about 1,000 years.

Thus, by 4000 B.C. at the latest, predynastic Egypt from Aswan to the Mediterranean coast had evolved into a single culture complex. That culture was to maintain its identity until Christianity became dominant during the fourth century A.D. It withstood repeated contacts with other parts of the world and periodic immigration of new settlers from Asia, the Libyan desert, and Nubia. Even its language reflected its tenacious identity. Ancient Egyptian was a distinct tongue that separated from the Afro-Asiatic family during the fifth millennium B.C. or even earlier.

Predynastic Egypt shaped this culture from several origins, all pre-eminently African. It was a mixture of

the best of each. The mix found agriculture, herding, and the imported stone tool-making tradition dominant, though a strong component of fishing and hunting remained. In time, metalworking and copper were introduced from southwestern Asia or the Sinai. And the stage was set for emergence of the Egyptian civilization recorded in dynastic times.

How did the landscape appear at this dawning period of 3100 B.C.? See it with the eyes of a traveler going by boat down the Nile from the Nubian frontier to the Delta. We embark at the rocky gorge below the cliffs of Gebel Silsila, on the edge of the Kom Ombo plain. We skim northward with the current. The Nile is a cooperative stream for boating: Current and broad oars can carry us swiftly downstream; prevailing winds blowing from the Mediterranean will let us sail against the stream on the way back—though when the breeze fails the crew may have to pull with tow ropes stretched ashore. Now we glide between riverbanks lined by thorny acacia trees and a scattering of long-fronded willows or towering sycamore figs. At a stop to barter for food, we can look across the high levees onto a maze of small fields and pastures and, only a little farther away, the low desert.

Going northward again, we encounter villages more frequently. We are farther from the frontier now, and the danger of Nubian raids is well behind. More people find it safe to settle; their villages nestle among groves of trees every few miles. Fishing craft are more common too. Near Edfu one of the sailors points out a desert valley—a wadi—stretching to the east. That, he says, is one of the routes to gold mines in the hills.

A few miles beyond Edfu we disembark to visit the capital of Upper Egypt. Its people call the town Nekhen; Greeks who will come in later millenniums will label it for the world to know as Hierakonpolis. Nekhen doesn't stand on the Nile's floodplain, but sprawls on the edge of the desert. Here several hundred houses cluster, some of them well-built of adobe,

Mediterranean Sea

[Alexandria] o •[Rosetta]
• Buto
• Sais
        • Busiris   • Tanis
Naucratis •

Delta

LOWER EGYPT   Abu Roash •   •• Heliopolis
                    Giza □   • [Cairo]
                   Abu Sir •
                   Saqqara •
                   Dahshur •   • Memphis

Wadi Natrun

Qattara Depression

SINAI

The Faiyum
Lake Moeris   • — Meidum
(Crocodile Lake)
Herakleopolis •

Siwa Oasis

LIBYA

Nile

Bahariya Oasis

Western Desert

• Beni Hasan

• Akhetaten (Amarna)

Eastern Desert

Red Sea

Farafra Oasis

Asyut •   • Badari

Dakhla Oasis

Thinis •
Abydos •   • Qena
            • Coptos
   Dendera •
   Naqada •   *Wadi Hammamat*
UPPER EGYPT   (Karnak)
Valley of the Kings →   Thebes
Qurna •   (Luxor)

Kharga Oasis

Hierakonpolis •

Edfu •

+ *Gebel Silsila 525 feet*

Kom Ombo •

Elephantine Island —   • Aswan
Philae Island —   First Cataract

Beit el Wali •

(Continuation of the Nile)

≈ *Third Cataract*   *Nubian Desert*

UPPER NUBIA (KUSH)

≈ *Fourth Cataract*

Napata •

Fifth Cataract ≈

LOWER NUBIA (WAWAT)

Abu Simbel •

≈ *Second Cataract*

Nile

≈ *Third Cataract*

Nubian Desert

A bountiful river, a prodigal god

Hapi, the deity in whom Egyptians saw the Nile brought to bodily form, appears as a male-female figure—symbolic of bounteous fertility. He often wore the clothes of a swamp fisherman; his colors were the green and blue of the waters. To him Egyptians penned hymns of praise and erected shrines for each of the seven-mile-long towing stages into which they divided their part of the Nile. At 4,132 miles the world's longest river, it nurtures a path of green between hills warding off the desert. Egyptians named their country *Kemet*—"Black Land"—after the color of the alluvial soil. Greeks called it *Aigyptos*. And Egypt it has been ever since. The map traces the Nile's course about 2000 B.C.

others with wooden frames and reed matting. A stockade of branches, thorns, and wattle-and-daub, sturdily anchored in a mud-and-stone foundation, surrounds the town. A small temple, built on an earthen mound, shows above the town wall. Guards are posted in front of a gate decorated with gay pennants; atop it two tall posts fly ornate banners. One is the insignia of the king, the other is the standard of the province—the double plume of the vulture goddess. We see the king's residence, a rambling, half-subterranean, mud-brick building in front of which stand sentinels with spears. Other retainers hold palm branches, ready to shade the king should he appear.

Beyond the town, the desert presents a not-so-barren vista. The occasional rain of these predynastic times is enough to support a scattering of umbrella-shaped acacias, tufts of grass, and low shrubs on the floors of the dry watercourses. As night approaches, herdboys drive small bunches of sheep and cattle down the desert valley toward circular stock pens. Then, in the very last light, a knot of tired huntsmen comes into view. They drag several slain antelope and carry bags of ostrich feathers.

After a few days we continue north, passing through some of the most fertile lands of Egypt. An almost unbroken string of villages and towns rims the shaded riverbanks. Ripening stands of wheat and barley lie beyond, between lines of palm trees. Here and there large tracts of thorny bush interrupt the cultivated fields. At some points the farmers have cut small sluices through the riverbanks. These let in floodwaters when the river begins to rise. They can be blocked with reed matting and mud after the flood basins fill—to help keep in the water until the fields, covered with five feet of muddy Nile, are thoroughly soaked. And coated with a sheet of fresh, fertile, reddish-brown silt. But the river is at low stage now, and women come to its edge with large jars to fill for household use. Drovers drive whole herds of cattle down for a drink.

Here and there a peasant has planted beans, chickpeas, lentils, and onions right on the banks. Laboriously he carries water to them in large containers made from hides. The desert lies farther back now, at the foot of steep limestone hills that radiate white light at noon but cast long shadows over the valley at sunset, when the skyline glows pink.

About halfway to the Delta, below Asyut, the capital of the Viper Tree province, the countryside becomes very wild. We see little cropland, but many herds of cattle in the rough pastures and bush country. That terrain stretches for miles toward desert hills in the hazy distance. Several days later the sailors tell us we are passing through Naret Tree province, near the northern frontier of Upper Egypt. Now we will meet fewer villages—because of recent warfare with a confederation of provinces of Lower Egypt. Nearby a branch of the Nile threads through the desert to nourish the forest of palms, willows, and figs in the Faiyum. And to feed its strange Crocodile Lake that has no outlet.

Passing the Giza area, we see nothing but low sandstone hills on the horizon, for the pyramids have not yet been dreamed of. And then the great water of Hapi divides into two main branches. Our boat glides down the right arm into countryside that seems ever wetter. Villages often sit on low rises of sand that crop up here and there; the riverbanks are too soggy and brush-covered to make good living sites. In some areas verdant pastures unroll as far as the eye can see; countless cattle graze. Elsewhere great ponds lined with tall reeds and papyrus and other sedges—and partly filled with blue and white lotuses—adjoin the river. Hippos and crocodiles are plentiful now, and the crew takes caution while harpooning some of the huge perch and catfish found hereabouts. At times the sky darkens with swarms of ducks, geese, ibises, and other water birds; in every shallow stately flamingos stalk. Then the riverbank forest begins to thin out. We have come 730 weary miles from our starting point, and before us a flat expanse of reeds extends to the horizon. Beyond them lies a belt of salty lagoons. Were we to go any

farther, we would have to switch to one of the seagoing vessels that sail the Mediterranean—hugging the shore on timid voyages to the cedar land of Lebanon.

Egypt had a population of probably half a million in those days. The people lived, as we have seen, in a valley where land was plentiful. Perhaps two-thirds of it was unimproved pasture or untouched wilderness—bush, thickets, and stagnant backwaters in Upper Egypt, lotus ponds and papyrus marshes in Lower Egypt. Much later, in 2000 B.C., records indicate the usable land was still evenly divided between cropland and pasture. Probably, therefore, in predynastic times farming took only a small fraction of the arable land. Even less, perhaps one or two percent, was artificially irrigated—to water gardens on high ground or to improve the wetting down of small accessible flood basins. After all, the Nile provided *natural* irrigation.

The valley was organized into a score or so of provinces, or nomes. These coincided with tribal units—themselves shaped by natural subdivisions of the floodplain. Most villages lined the Nile, with direct access to a permanent supply of drinking water and with indirect claim to a broad hinterland of cultivable basin, pasture, and bush. Village headmen organized the peasants in case of emergency and in turn owed allegiance to the tribal chieftain. He resided near the temple or shrine of the nome's patron god or goddess.

Around the middle of the fourth millennium, Upper Egypt began to transcend the small political units of the nomes. Strong leaders organized confederations. Eventually a single leader achieved control over all of Upper Egypt. In time, one became strong enough to weld his kingdom with the loose grouping of nomes that made up Lower Egypt. Little tangible information lights the process, which preceded the invention of an effective system of writing. Later traditional accounts are shrouded in allegory. Some Egyptologists doubt that a politically unified Lower Egypt existed, even that wars led to unification. However, a series of fragmentary records hints of at least nine Upper Egyptian

rulers whose major activity appears to have been campaigns against various confederations of Delta nomes or towns. And we know that unification finally was achieved around 3050 B.C. by a king called Narmer or Menes or perhaps Aha. Thus began Egypt's Dynasty 1.

Whatever the way he gained power, this new king soon amassed considerable wealth. He shared some of it with his supporters, and a small elite class grew. So did the king's power, along with his recognition as intermediary between gods and people. The development of an elaborate political system was well under way; it would serve the pharaohs for millenniums.

Community affairs continued to be organized at the grass roots level by village headmen. The king's court presumably linked a strong military caste and a priesthood serving local deities—whose shrines were decisive unifying points for the common people through Egypt's long history. So anchored, the state remained visibly unshaken except in times of unusual crisis.

Under pharaohs of Dynasty 1, unity and political control seemed firmly established. Nubian tribes between Gebel Silsila and Aswan were conquered, and forays reached even farther south. Massive architecture appeared—elaborate tombs, paneled brickwork, inscribed commemorative stones called stelae, sculptures. There is also, in royal tombs, grisly evidence of the sacrificial death and burial of retainers.

But amid this increasing kingly pomp, natural forces were undermining Egypt's economic base. Between 3000 and 2800 B.C. rainfall in eastern Africa decreased significantly. Average Nile flood levels dropped three to five feet—a drastic reduction of almost 30 percent. What the impact must have been can be guessed from the poor flood of A.D. 1877. It was 6½ feet below average and left a third of the valley completely dry. The simple irrigation of the early dynastic period would have been of next to no avail against such a calamity.

Little wonder that great unrest beset Egypt, that desert folk began to attack the frontiers or infiltrate the

Eternal sustenance on the walls of a tomb

Painted 4,500 years ago for a princess' chapel at Meidum, a frieze of geese magically assured food for the owner. This masterwork shows how early the Egyptians strove for symmetry in art.
Overleaf: In a timeless scene along the Nile, morning's mist tones the silhouettes of palm trees and of villagers bound for the fields.

valley, that Nubia was partly depopulated. Shortly before 2700 B.C. the crisis shook the very foundations of the state. Details are few, but armed rebellion spread, and the ruling dynasty barely survived.

Somehow the rulers of the Old Kingdom, which begins with Dynasty 3, restored the prosperity of Egypt. In part, agriculture may have adjusted to the new ecological realities. In part, the pharaohs in this age of the pyramids helped with expanded irrigation works, canals, and development of the Delta. Egypt's population probably grew to more than a million. But by 2250 B.C. a new crisis began. Lakes in the source areas of the Nile shrank rapidly. Some almost disappeared. Repeated famines are recorded from about 2250 to 1950 B.C. Literary works allude to scarcity of drinking water, mass deaths, rotting corpses, suicide, cannibalism, widespread plundering, anarchy.

In a society where the pharaoh was responsible for want or plenty and stability of the cosmic order, an unbroken succession of poor floods and bad harvests would spell more than economic disaster. It would threaten royal authority. Indeed, the Old Kingdom dynasties came to an ungraceful end with a chain of ineffectual and almost nameless kings. As the laments of the scribe Ipuwer tell us, even the social order experienced upheaval: "Behold, nobles' ladies are [now] gleaners, and nobles are in the workhouse. [But] he who never slept on a plank is the owner of a bed."

Middle Kingdom pharaohs took credit for a return of consistently good floods and good times after 1950 B.C. They reorganized irrigation and reclaimed the Faiyum. But they probably couldn't deal effectively with a new hazard: repeated excessive Nile floods that began about 1840 B.C. and continued for at least 70 years. These phenomenally high levels were recorded by inscribed marks visible today on the rocks of the Second Cataract, near the border with Sudan. Comparable floods in A.D. 1818-1819 wiped out whole irrigation networks, washed away 20-foot dams, razed entire villages. Quite possibly such unusual floods, recurring

three to five times per decade, again undermined the economic foundation. Contemporary records are mute, but during the 18th century B.C. Egypt slid into political impotence. By 1670 B.C. the capital of Memphis had fallen to Asian intruders, the Hyksos.

The New Kingdom saw substantial advances. The shadoof, a bucket-and-lever device that could lift water to higher-lying fields, was introduced. Grain was stored on a large scale, mainly in temples but also in big granaries administered by high government officials. Such innovations suggest a systematic effort to mitigate between the proverbial seven fat and seven lean years. Nonetheless, another period of dwindling African lakes and poor Nile floods impoverished the Egyptian countryside about 1170-1100 B.C. Another crisis, coinciding with an ineffective government, thus contributed to the downfall of the ruling Ramesside dynasty, and the end of the New Kingdom.

Through all this thread of economic history the close dependence of Egypt on the Nile and its behavior becomes strikingly obvious. Egypt *was* the gift of the river. With a whole range of projects Egyptians attempted to extend cultivation, to control excess floods, and to compensate for inadequate ones. Slowly, over the millenniums, they converted plain and Delta into a cultural artifact. The Black Land of the Nile was both home and handiwork of the Egyptian, in contrast to the Red Land, the unassailable desert. In this confined environment, Egyptian culture evolved with both an unprecedented self-sufficiency and a disdain for radical change. Where other ancient river-valley civilizations remained loose collections of city-states, Egypt became a nation that endured for 3,000 years.

"Hey! I'll whack you . . . on the rump!"

Donkeys rambling a village street and ranging the walls of an Old Kingdom tomb hint how strikingly today's Egypt echoes its past. And herders' remarks in many a hieroglyphic epigraph add a humorous postscript: The sturdy but stubborn beast of burden also has changed little through the millenniums.

Donkeys in Egypt had been domesticated by dynastic times—as had cattle, sheep, goats, and pigs. Wiry animals that can endure hard work with a minimum of food and infrequent water, donkeys stemmed from wild asses native to northeast Africa. Egypt didn't have the horse until it was introduced by the Hyksos around 1750 B.C. Nor the camel until the Persian conquest about 525 B.C. Oxen and donkeys plowed fields and carried loads. And, as in this 4,500-year-old bas-relief from a noble's tomb, threshed grain.

Prodded into a line by their drivers, the beasts walked around the hard-packed surface of the threshing floor, treading the grain beneath their hooves. The line swept a circle like the hand of a clock.

Men with sticks held horizontally slowed animals near the hub while others urged outer ones at a faster pace. The grain—usually barley or a kind of coarse, hard wheat called emmer—was piled knee deep; treading separated kernels from husks. Now and then an ass might reach down for a permitted nibble—for, as the Bible would later say: "Thou shalt not muzzle the ox when he treadeth out the corn."

Overleaf: Aging sails in an ageless land

Often a skimming swallow, sometimes a moth with tattered wings, feluccas on the Nile catch sunset's sheen. The ubiquitous boats carry passengers and cargo on the river highway, where in ancient times the common words for "travel" were *khent*—"to go upstream"—and *khed*—"to go downstream." So tuned to the river were people's ways that the words were used even when they meant travel by land. Today nimble crewmen climb the soaring yards, holding the hems of their tentlike galabias in their teeth to keep from tripping while handling the sails.

48

Pots—and maybe potsherds—for people

Plump, graceful, and with a design that goes back to the times of the pharaohs, clay pots still play an important role in everyday life in Egypt. Women fetch water in them for household use, though now the balancing trip may be to the village faucet instead of to the banks of the Nile. Potters in the region of Qena, where the town of Ballas gave its name to an Arabic word for the jars, turn them out in two minutes apiece. Feluccas freight them—pyramided on deck or slung in nets atop the gunwales—to users all along the river.

49

"The fields laugh"

And "the visage of men is bright." Thus sang the words from an ancient Egyptian paean to the Nile. Today, as then, the river's enlivening waters flow through checkerboard plots, greening cropland worked in venerable ways. Fellahin till with simple wooden plows pulled by patient cattle. Farmers dip up the Nile with a shadoof—a bucket levered by a weighted pole; in a dawn-to-dusk stint its user can water only part of an acre.

In ancient times fields produced one crop a year. Seed was cast in mud left behind when the Nile's flood ebbed in the fall. Plants matured during winter and were harvested in spring. More intense cultivation—with quick-growing summer crops that need less irrigation, or plants that can thrive on flooded land—spread after Greek rule came in 332 B.C.

New machines and methods slowly erase the old in Egypt's agriculture. But the soil still keeps the look that Gustave Flaubert, 19th-century novelist, called "India ink on the solid green."

"I can make something good out of them"

Date palms, growing here on the Nile's floodplain where levees (foreground) mark the desert's edge, gave much to the early people of the river. Trunks offered lumber; fronds supplied thatching and splints for basketry; fruit provided food, sweetening for beer, even medicines and mouthwash. Pits served as vegetable ivory for making buttons, beads, and rings.

Today's countryman finds the tree no less useful—even praising its pollen as a guarantee of fertility. Palms edge the river and outline plots where farmers winnow grain or plant maize. The latter provides a staple food—and stalks by the donkeyload for fodder and fuel.

Overleaf: "Let us make brick"

Patterns from the past shape mud-brick walls in sun-touched villages along the Nile. Using techniques old before history began, barefoot brickmakers tread a mix of clay, sand, water, and chopped straw, then press out bricks by hand in a mold. Ancient Egyptians let blocks dry in the sun; some that have come down to us still bear finger swipes of their makers. Today bricks may be baked in round kilns like the two here; heat comes from burning maize stalks. But old ways die— dams block silt that once replenished raw materials; use of cement block spreads.

Living and youthful forever and ever

Statues placed in tombs magically helped assure eternal life for the occupants. But they also give us insights into how early Egyptians looked. Though poses followed inflexible artistic rules and convention decreed red-brown paint for men's bodies and yellow for women's, the sculptors' skills caught individual character—idealized, perhaps, yet real. No matter that death might find them aged, the subjects were depicted at full prime of successful life. And thus they would be through eternity.

These examples date from the Fourth, Fifth, and Sixth Dynasties—a time when nobles began to have elaborate tombs, a privilege once reserved for the pharaoh. Portly Kaaper's image has eyes of quartz set in copper. Seneb, shown with his normal-size family, hints of royal fascination with dwarfs; he had a court post and 62,000 head of stock. Rehotep, seated near his wife, was a prince and a general. For the couple at right, time and termites have erased the names that on most statues helped ensure immortality.

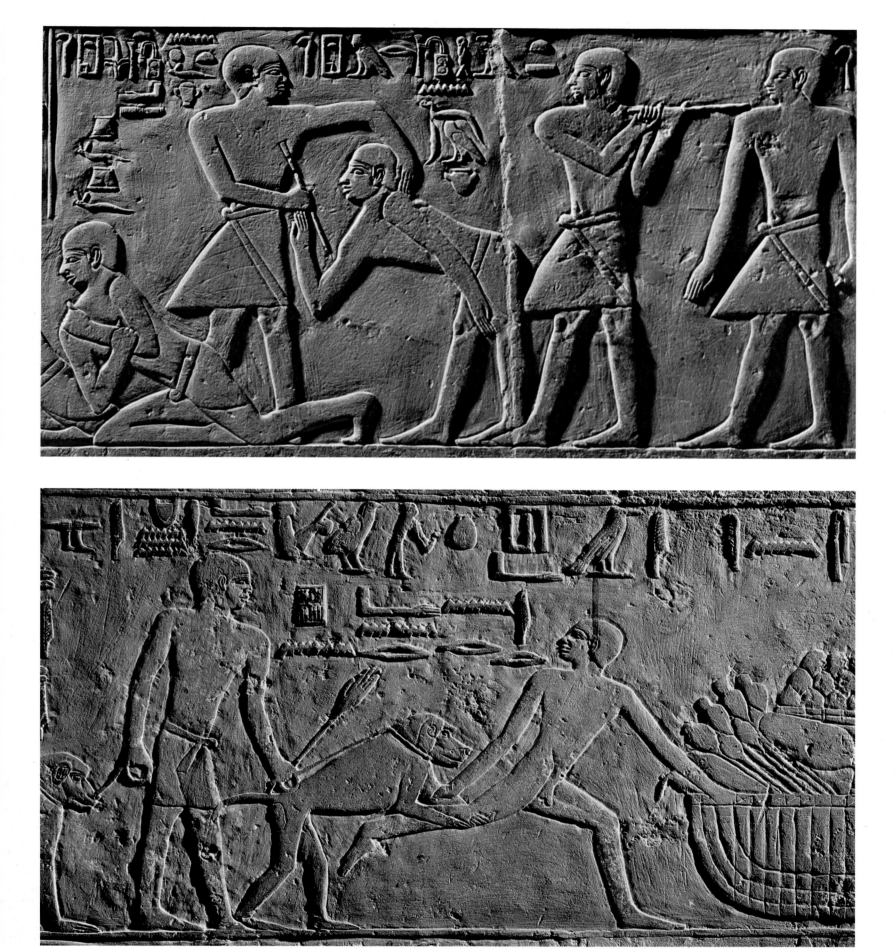

"Little men going this way and that"

The tomb had long before been plundered and emptied. But the archeologist's conscience prodded him: at least clear the fallen rubble and make a plan of the room. During the task, chips and dust kept dropping through a crack at the base of a wall. On his stomach, H. E. Winlock peered in. His flashlight bared "a little world of four thousand years ago," he wrote—a "busy going and coming . . . in

uncanny silence, as though the distance back . . . was too great for even an echo to reach my ears." Winlock's find came in 1920, and the statuettes he saw in the tomb of Meketre have proved the finest examples of a funerary custom that peaked in early Middle Kingdom times: stashing away models of everyday scenes to ensure their continuance through the afterlife.

This, the largest of some two dozen made for Meketre, shows the wealthy chancellor inspecting his herd. Egyptians used

cattle for meat, milk, and hides, and by the dynastic period had developed several breeds. This five-foot-long tableau of painted wood bore fingerprints of those who laid it away. Other models hint of being used—perhaps, surmised Winlock, as toys by children in Meketre's house. They give us a remarkable look at everyday scenes, as do these reliefs from Old Kingdom burials. Tax delinquents (top) are dragged before a court; keepers grouse at having to care for tame baboons.

"And small birds they eat also"

Egypt lies on a major migratory route for water birds shuttling between Europe and central and southern Africa. Twice each year great throngs pause on Nile marshes and lakes, resting after flights across the Mediterranean or the Sahara's wastes. In predynastic days incredible numbers—along with local wildfowl—gave Egyptians such a handy supply there was little incentive for domesticating flocks.

Old Kingdom tomb paintings show teams of men with huge nets hauling in catches. Clap traps and snares also took birds. Those captured went to the table or to fattening pens. Fluttering geese (top) and pigeons and ducks (opposite) on wall reliefs dating from about 2400 B.C. are so detailed that sometimes we can even identify the species. Like the crane at left, the fowl might be force-fattened with food crammed down their throats.

The birds' flesh was eaten roasted or boiled. Organs and extracts went into medicines—papyri give prescriptions: goose-fat potions "to treat the belly" or salves "to keep flies from biting."

Birds figured in sacrifices to the gods; Ramses II alone offered 360,000 during a 31-year period. Geese were sacred to the Nile god, yet still were eaten—a contradiction which perplexed Herodotus. He also noted that Egyptians ate small birds uncooked, "merely first salting" (pickling) them.

"He who tends his crop will eat it"

Cultivation of grains in Egypt traces its beginnings far back beyond the dawn of recorded time. Barley husks have been found in the intestines of predynastic mummies. Kernels of wheat have turned up in Stone Age storage pits dug in the desert's edge and lined with basketry. Egypt's land was superbly suited to such crops, and the nation became an envied granary. It was a breadbasket of the Roman Empire.

Tomb paintings give precise details of how the grain was grown. After seed was scattered over the Nile mud, sheep driven across the field trampled the grain into the ground. When the crop ripened, inspectors came with measuring lines (bottom) to set the government's quota; wheat was heavily taxed through all antiquity. Farmers seeking to curry the officials' favor offered refreshments and gifts. Then men with sickles lopped off the grain heads and hauled them in baskets and nets to the threshing floor (middle). Laborers might catnap or play a flute for a restful moment; girl gleaners might fall into a hair-pulling spat over territorial encroachments.

Oxen or donkeys, prodded by shouts and sticks, threshed the grain; men with wooden pitchforks (top) kept adding the heads underfoot from stacks around the floor. Then winnowers, their hair shielded from the dust by linen cloths, tossed the grain with wooden scoops to separate kernel from chaff. Samples of the cleaned grain went to the master for inspection, the rest to tallying and the granary.

63

"Supply my needs of bread and beer"

Staple foods of the poor, the rich, and the gods, bread and beer played such a fundamental role that in Ramesside times the words even became an occasional phrase used like our "hello." Preserved loaves and jars with beer residues have been found at predynastic sites.

In a model from the tomb of Meketre (top), scribes seated in a courtyard record measures of grain being brought from the threshing floor. Laborers carry sacks up stairs and empty them into granary bins. To make flour, the grain was pounded with mortar and pestle or ground with a roller on flat stones. Dough in big batches for a great household might be kneaded with the feet instead of by hand. Loaves were baked inside an oval oven; flat bread was cooked by putting dough on the outside, or on flat hearths such as those used today.

Barley and bread grains, worked into a mash in earthen jars (left), fermented to become the drink that neither the living nor the dead could do without.

"I made vineyards without limit"

Ramses III might have been exaggerating a bit, but it's a safe bet he needed extensive arbors to supply his demands for wine. His accounts show that he gave 20,078 jars as offerings to the god Amun, and contributed 39,510 more for use at temple rites. Then, of course, there were the requirements for palace feasting.

Beer was brewed almost daily in the average household, but wine, because of the time and care involved in its making, was a costly drink enjoyed mostly by the rich. Royal tombs from the earliest dynasties held caches of jars, and wall reliefs and paintings in burials of later nobles show wine making—and drinking.

Vines grew best in northern Egypt, particularly in the Delta region. They yielded grapes for half a dozen kinds of wine, though it's hard to tell from names the Egyptians used how they equate with modern types. Red wines seem to have been favored in early periods, whites in later dynasties. Most vineyards lay within walls of estates, with the plants trained to trellises; gardeners watered them from earthen jugs and shooed away birds with slingshots and shouts.

At harvest time, pickers carried the bunches of grapes to crushing vats, where barefoot workers stomped out the juice. while holding overhead straps for balance. For extra pressing the must went into sacks—twisted and levered with poles. An agile workman might add his bit by bridging the press (top). Juice fermented in open urns; finished wine went into jars. Lumps of clay sealed the reed stoppers.

Markings put on the bottles gave as much information as modern labels—often more. They bore the name of the estate, its location, the vineyard, the name of the vintner, the date, and an assessment of the quality—"good," "twice good," "three times good," "genuine," "sweet." One from an Amarna tomb was downgraded as "for merrymaking." Gourmets note: 1344 B.C. rated a great vintage year.

They labor on the river

In a simple one-man skiff made by tying together bundles of papyrus reeds, a fisherman poises a club for the catfish he has caught on a hand line. Behind him, balanced on the stern of a larger boat fashioned in the same way, a seaman poles his craft through the crowded waters.

Egyptians ate fish from early times; hooks made of shell and ivory, bone harpoons, and fish remains have been unearthed in prehistoric middens. Ebbing Nile floods left fishes stranded in low spots, easy to gather when the waters receded. Tomb inscriptions tell of that bounty. The reliefs also record the sculptors' concern with accuracy—we can identify some 24 present-day species of Nile fish in various wall carvings.

Light, easily paddled papyrus craft had shallow drafts well suited to the marshes and channels of the Nile. No one knows when man first learned to sail, but the earliest record of ships and shipbuilding occurs in Egyptian drawings. Large papyrus boats developed logically from bundled rafts in a land where wood was scarce. The trees, mostly scrubby acacias, yielded planks only a few feet long. As wooden ships evolved there, they were made of short boards lashed together much the way reed bundles were. The tradition stuck; millenniums later Herodotus likened Egyptian shipbuilders to bricklayers. But by 2500 B.C. Egypt's craft could barge great stones down the Nile for the pyramids, her traders could ply the Mediterranean, her shipyards could turn out a 100-foot boat in 17 days.

High sterns helped the crews push their craft off sandbars. Awnings served as cabins, and cargo was stowed on deck. Bipod masts—slim, twin poles tied at the peak—developed because only the gunwales of reed boats could support spars. On big boats rowers stood to dip oars, stroked by plopping backwards onto benches—oarsmen's kilts had seat pads sewn on. Even figureheads had unusual touches, facing aft instead of forward.

Ships slowly changed from these Old Kingdom beginnings, but Egypt remained a land for those who labored on the river.

Overleaf: Strata and sail on a tired Nile

Beneath stark cliffs near Beni Hasan the Nile sweeps by, "weary of endlessly murmuring . . . that it has traveled too far." Broad-bottomed, cargo-carrying naggars and slim feluccas coursing the river argue that here still lives the age of sail.

Pyramids: Building for Eternity

I.E.S.Edwards

May you cause to be enduring
this pyramid . . .
for ever and ever
                    Pyramid Texts

The ancient Greeks numbered them among the Seven Wonders of the World. Early Christian tradition identified them as Joseph's granaries, built, according to the Book of Genesis, in preparation for the seven years of famine. Arab historians linked them with the Biblical flood, suggesting that the written wisdom of mankind, or even the human race, found refuge in the imperishable pyramids of Egypt.

Today we count some 80 major and minor pyramids dotting the west bank of the Nile, most of them in the 55-mile stretch between Abu Roash and the Faiyum. In my four decades as an Egyptologist I have visited many of them, sometimes crawling like a snake through dark corridors choked with the rubble of centuries. I have clambered up a heap of stones to get a handhold on the entrance to a pyramid—and found myself clinging helplessly to the ledge when the heap collapsed under my feet. I have walked in chambers and passageways where the rock all around me was so decayed that the slightest touch brought down a shower of loose stone upon my head.

Today most of the rubble has been cleared, and most of the pyramids have been explored, studied, and documented. We know they are tombs, yet still they fire our imagination. Some say that such colossal structures could not have been built with the simple tools of ancient Egypt; the builders must have levitated the huge stones into place by magic, or watched in awe as

"There was constructed for me a pyramidal tomb out of stone"

A phrase from the "Story of Sinuhe" recalls the Pyramid Age. Such words might have been spoken by Djoser; his Step Pyramid was the first tomb in Egypt built entirely of stone. Restored buildings stand amid the rubble of others as if expecting their monarch's return. And so does his pyramid; through 46 centuries it has awaited his tread on its magical stairway to the stars.

visitors from outer space lent skills that our scientists have yet to discover. Others see in the myriad measurements of the Great Pyramid of Cheops at Giza a key to events past, present, and future. And some recent writers claim to have detected a mysterious force in the pyramidal shape itself. Inside even a table-top pyramid of cardboard, they say, a razor blade keeps its edge, and fruit and milk stay fresh.

But to Egyptologists, there are no "mysteries" about these great structures, only questions we cannot yet answer. For example, we do not know with certainty how the pyramids were built. But we do know something about ancient Egyptian building methods. What seems the most probable method for the pyramids unfolds in the paintings at the end of this chapter.

Using techniques that were known to the ancient Egyptians, we might duplicate the pyramids today. Our chief problem would probably be the mustering of a work force large enough to undertake such a project. But the Egyptians had little trouble assembling the necessary manpower. Farm workers by the tens of thousands had to be idle for three or four months of the year, due to the inundation of the Nile. Food was cheap, the labor force was enormous, and the efficient Egyptians knew how to mobilize both.

There is another question that is seldom asked, and to me it is a more intriguing one: Why? For what reasons did the ancient kings choose to be buried in tombs of pyramidal form? To understand the answer, we must remember that a pyramid is an expression of evolving religious ideas. In its purest form it is, almost literally, a sunburst turned to stone.

Before we consider the purpose of this design, we should look at what preceded it. For new ideas did not usually sweep away older notions; they were simply superimposed. Some elements persisted long after their purpose was forgotten.

One concept that never changed throughout Egyptian history was the need to preserve the dead body from decay so that the spirit of its owner could re-enter

"Is there another like Imhotep?"

It was well-earned praise, this passage from a New Kingdom text. By 600 B.C., Imhotep—architect and chief minister of King Djoser—had become a demigod. His devotees offered countless images like the bronze statuette below. Greece and Rome saw in him their god of healing until Christianity swept him away. Time all but swept away the great wall that stretched more than a mile around Imhotep's masterwork, the Step Pyramid complex at Saqqara. A restored section of the wall (opposite) suggests the grandeur of this monument for Djoser, whose limestone image once gazed with crystal eyes from a cell at his pyramid's foot.

it at will. In the Predynastic Era, before about 3100 B.C., and later in the case of all but the elite, bodies were placed in shallow graves in the desert, where preservation occurred naturally by the desiccating action of the warm, dry sand. Such graves were covered with low mounds of sand and gravel—and were soon eroded to oblivion by the desert wind. By the end of the Predynastic Era, more substantial mounds of sunbaked brick and rubble were built. These gave better protection from the ravages of jackals and marked the grave more clearly for relatives bringing offerings. But burial at greater depth prevented natural desiccation. Thus, in time, the art of mummification was invented.

Survival after death was too important to entrust to body preservation alone. And so an effigy of stone, wood, or other durable material became accepted as a "second body," especially when inscribed with the owner's name. I believe that this idea, more than any other factor, led to the rise of the art of sculpture.

Funerary customs, whatever their nature, needed magic to make them effective. Magic could be imitative: Make an image of something, then endow it with reality by magical rites. The size of an image did not matter, nor whether it was freestanding, carved in relief, or simply painted on a wall. Actual boats buried near the pyramids of Giza were intended to bear their owners upon the waters of the next world, but for a queen of about three centuries later, wooden models were considered enough.

Spells were another form of magic. Hundreds of them were uttered by priests from predynastic times until long after the Giza pyramids were built. The whole repertoire would have been lost had they not been inscribed on the walls inside the pyramids of the Fifth-Dynasty ruler Unas and his immediate successors. Known as the Pyramid Texts, they often referred to conditions long outmoded. "Throw off the sand from your face!" one of them tells a king buried in a pyramid. No identifiable predynastic royal tombs have been found, but such spells—though transcribed cen-

"As though heaven were within it"

The New Kingdom visitor rhapsodized over the little temple at the Old Kingdom Pyramid of Meidum (opposite). There was more within the pyramid than he knew: a seven-stepped monument inside an eight-stepped structure inside a true pyramid's sloping triangles. Shorn of its smooth facades by generations of stone-hungry builders, the towerlike ruin shows portions of its two stepped phases (bottom diagram). The base of the pyramid that may have soared 300 feet above the desert now lies buried under a circlet of sand. When—and if—it was completed, it may have been the first true pyramid in the world. The Bent Pyramid, begun earlier, could have been the first, but halfway up the builders blunted it to a rhomboid (third diagram).

There may be more within the Meidum ruin than *we* know. Perhaps it began as a mastaba, the tomb whose basic design (top diagram) outlasted the Pyramid Age. The Step Pyramid at Saqqara (second diagram) began with a structure that suggests a mound, a throwback to burials before the dynasties began.

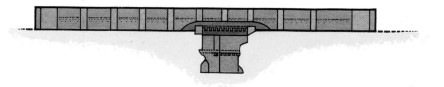

First Dynasty: Mastaba resembles a palace, though rooms lack doors. Sand mound covers burial pit. Middle chamber is for the body.

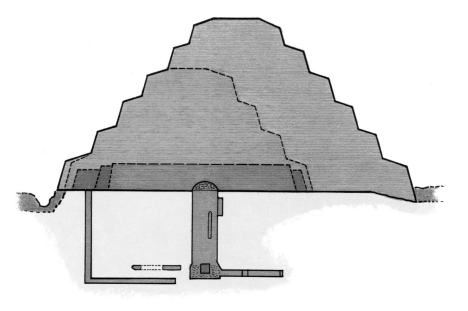

Third Dynasty: Djoser's men hewed deep burial chamber, enlarged its superstructure several times to create Step Pyramid.

turies later—show that the early kings were buried, like ordinary people, right in the desert sand.

The tombs of nearly all the kings of the First and Second Dynasties have come to light at Abydos; possibly some of these kings also had mastaba-tombs at Saqqara. "Mastaba" is a modern Arabic word for the low bench outside many an Egyptian door; there the man of the house likes to take his ease and sip coffee with his friends. Like the bench, the ancient mastaba was a boxlike structure. Its outer walls, in early examples, resembled the walls of a royal palace, with simulated doorways recessed between towerlike projections. Inside, it was divided by brick walls into cells containing funerary equipment. Beneath it was a pit hewn in the rock; this too was divided into compartments, the central one being the burial chamber. And over the pit rose a low rectangular mound of sand cased with brick, hidden from view by the superstructure.

The brick-covered mound had no structural function. In fact, its sloping sides were a source of weakness. The tomb-builders probably realized this, for in later First Dynasty mastabas they built brick mounds with stepped sides. But why include a mound at all?

It is not difficult to recognize in the mound a survival of the sand-and-rubble mound of a predynastic grave. The ancient Egyptians were always reluctant to discard anything once it had become a part of the funerary paraphernalia. But in this case there may also have been a more esoteric reason. Each year, the Egyptians saw patches of high ground appear from the waters of the Nile as the flood began to recede; from this sprang the belief that the world began as a mound rising from the waters of chaos. So, the mound of the predynastic tomb could have been regarded as a replica of the primeval mound, the source of all life, and by imitative magic its life-giving powers would have been imparted to the person buried beneath it.

Apparently there was no radical difference in the first two dynasties between the tombs of kings and those of the nobility. The divergence came at the begin-

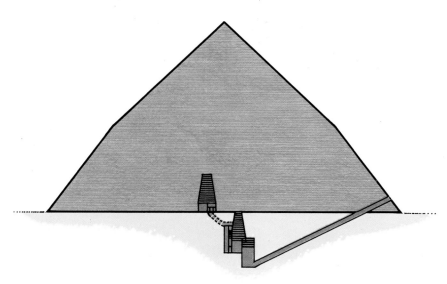

Fourth Dynasty: Bent Pyramid's northern shaft aims at circumpolar stars. Western shaft (not shown) leads to upper chamber.

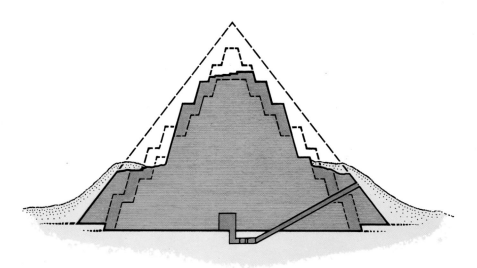

Fourth Dynasty: Snefru achieves true pyramid at Meidum. Dashed lines show its stages, shaded areas its remains. Diagrams look west.

ning of the Third Dynasty, about 2650 B.C., when Imhotep, the vizier and architect of King Djoser, built for his sovereign the famous Step Pyramid at Saqqara. This massive monument eclipsed anything the Egyptians had yet built. More than a thousand years later, their descendants were visiting it in admiration; eventually Imhotep became a god, one of the few ordinary mortals promoted to divine status.

Hewn stone had already been used in isolated parts of tombs, but this monument was the first to be built entirely of it. We can see that Imhotep's workers were inexperienced in cutting and handling building stones, for they built most of the pyramid complex with blocks that were much like mud bricks. Later generations would quarry larger blocks and drag them on wooden sledges. But as Imhotep's project took shape, the site probably swarmed with sweating laborers heaving stones into place by hand.

The pyramid itself dominated a large assemblage of buildings amid open courts in a walled enclosure. The buildings, like the pyramid, were faced with fine white limestone brought in by boat from a quarry at Tura in the hills east of the Nile. But many were dummies, solid masses of small stone blocks. One group, a double row of chapels on opposite sides of an oblong court, imitated the temporary chapels erected at Memphis by kings celebrating a *heb-sed*, or jubilee festival, usually after reigning for 30 years. Equipped with these replicas, and aided by magic, Djoser could celebrate any number of jubilee festivals during an endless afterlife. It didn't matter that such buildings had no interiors, just as it hadn't mattered that the mastabas lacked doorways and corridors. Only the living needed these conveniences; the spirit of the deceased could pass through walls unhindered.

One building which had to be real was the mortuary temple, for here the priests conducted regular services on behalf of the dead king. Nearby stood a small chamber known by the modern Arabic word *serdab*, mean-

ing cellar. Inside was a seated limestone statue of the king. But the sculptor's skill was never intended to be admired, for the building's only openings were two small holes in the front wall, intended either to let the statue look out or to let the smoke of incense in.

In its final form, Djoser's pyramid rose in six steps to 204 feet. But the original plan was not nearly so ambitious. Imhotep may have intended at first to build a large square tomb resembling a mastaba; we can glimpse such a structure embedded in the pyramid's base. It may, however, be a replica of the predynastic mound. A series of additions transformed it into a six-step monument. Was this simply an architectural design, or did it too have a practical function?

According to Egyptian ideas, the stars were divine beings and the dead king, as a god, could claim a place among them. The most desirable location for the king's afterlife was among the circumpolar stars, the "Imperishable Stars" that never set or "died." But before the celestial ferryboat could take him there, he must make his own ascent to the sky. One way was by ladder. "This king goes to his double, to the sky," says one of the spells in the Pyramid Texts; "a ladder is set up for him that he may ascend on it. . . ." Another spell addresses the king: ". . . a stairway to the sky is set up for you among the Imperishable Stars." No doubt the spells alone would have been considered sufficient to enable him to ascend. But they were not written down until long after Djoser's death; in his day their power depended on oral recital, which was subject to human caprice. The Step Pyramid overcame that risk by magically providing the king with a permanent substitute for the invisible ladder. On the symbolic steps of his pyramid he could ascend at will and return to partake of offerings and participate in ceremonies.

The last of the major step pyramids was built at Meidum, some 33 miles south of Saqqara. Today this pyramid resembles a high rectangular tower with its base engulfed in sand. At first it was planned, and probably completed, as a pyramid with seven steps cased with dressed Tura limestone. It was then enlarged to eight steps and again probably completed. At this stage, it showed no innovation to suggest new ideas about the requirements for the royal afterlife. But then its steps were filled in and the whole exterior was cased with limestone to make it a geometrically true pyramid.

Before its first stones were laid, a burial chamber had been built on the bedrock; as the courses rose, the room became accessible only by a corridor sloping downwards from the north face of the pyramid at about 28°. The burial chamber was surrounded with compact masonry which may have been intended both to strengthen the structure and to represent the traditional mound. But no clear instance of the mound has been recognized in any subsequent pyramid; it may at last have been discarded.

At the desert edge, east of the pyramid, stood a small temple where the dead king's body would have been mummified. Linking this lower temple with the wall of the pyramid enclosure was a causeway 235 yards long. A mortuary temple and a small subsidiary pyramid were built within the enclosure. For the next six centuries the kings included all these elements in their pyramid complexes.

Who built this trend-setting pyramid? A thousand years after it rose, a visitor scribbled on a wall of the mortuary temple that he had come "to see the beautiful temple of King Snefru." The sight moved him to rhapsodize: "May heaven rain with fresh myrrh, may it drip with incense upon the roof of the temple of King Snefru." Other graffiti from as early as the Sixth Dynasty also mention Snefru, first king of the Fourth Dynasty, who began his rule about 2600 B.C.

We know that Snefru built the unique Bent Pyramid at Dahshur, 27 miles north of Meidum. This odd pyramid begins at an angle of 54°31'—then, about halfway up, it "bends" to a shallower angle of 43°21', perhaps because cracks appeared while it was being built.

Snefru may not have built the Meidum pyramid as a whole. It is quite possible that he merely converted a predecessor's step pyramid by filling in its steps. When finished, its sides sloped at 52°, the typical slant of true pyramids from then on. But why did Snefru fill in the steps that would take him toward the stars?

When the true pyramid superseded the step pyramid at the beginning of the Fourth Dynasty, the sun cult of Heliopolis was establishing itself as the official religion. Such changes usually depended on politics and the favoritism of the kings. We cannot trace the various causes by which one or another priesthood gained dominance, but we can see the effects.

In the sun cult's conception of the afterlife, the dead king either accompanied the sun god across the sky or became identified with the sun god. The king would thus need a different way to mount up to the sky: He would ascend on the rays of the sun. "May heaven strengthen the sun's rays for you, so that you may ascend to heaven as the eye of Re," the king is told in a spell from the Pyramid Texts. In another spell, the king addresses the sun god Re in these words: "I have laid down for myself those rays of yours as a stairway under my feet on which I will ascend. . . ."

From time to time in Egypt, as elsewhere, the rays of the sun may be seen shining down to earth through a break in the clouds. There can be little doubt that it was this very striking phenomenon which was reproduced in the true pyramid. Through imitative magic, the stone pyramid possessed all the attributes of the intangible sunbeam. But, unlike the actual sunburst that came and went according to daylight and atmospheric conditions, the sunburst-in-stone would always be there "as a stairway" under the feet of the king. Significantly, the temple of the true pyramid stood on the east side, the side of the rising sun, while the temple of the step pyramid was placed on the north side, the direction of the Imperishable Stars.

Just as the mound of the predynastic grave had been embodied in the mastaba, we should expect that the step pyramid would be embodied in the true pyramid.

"Cheops is one belonging to the horizon"

So he named his pyramid—and so it perpetuates his name as it dominates the desert horizon. Largest of the group at Giza, the Great Pyramid of Cheops contains 2.3 million stone blocks, some weighing up to 15 tons. Here Chephren's, in the center, appears taller because it stands on higher ground, though each dwarfs the tomb of Mycerinus and its three subsidiary pyramids. The peak of Chephren's pyramid (above) still retains remnants of its original casing of fine, dressed limestone.

The major pyramids of the Fourth Dynasty at Dahshur and Giza are still largely intact—though stripped of most of their outer casings—so that we cannot be sure of the pattern of their internal construction. But the less well-preserved subsidiary pyramids at Giza show that a true pyramid does indeed mask an inner step pyramid. Another feature retained from the step pyramid was the sloping entrance corridor with a horizontal continuation, running from the northern side to the burial chamber. And in several true pyramids a small chapel stood at the entrance, probably a relic of the temple located in that position in the step pyramids.

No sooner had the true pyramid evolved under Snefru than it reached its zenith under his son and successor, Khufu, who began his reign about 2570 B.C. Khufu is better known to us by his Greek name, Cheops, and remembered as the builder of a pyramid that was never surpassed either in size or in architectural perfection: the Great Pyramid of Giza.

Profiting from the practical experience gained at Dahshur and Meidum, the builders of the Great Pyramid erected a massive monument whose base covers 13.1 acres. When complete, it rose to a height of 481.4 feet; today the top 31 feet are missing. Skilled masons and stonecutters fitted its casing stones to each other with clearances of hundredths of an inch. And the difference between its longest and shortest sides was less than eight inches, on lengths of more than 750 feet.

The accuracy of the squareness of its base seems all the more remarkable when we remember that an outcrop of rock, which was left unleveled in the middle of

Theirs was the greatness of Giza

From the sands around the pyramids of
Giza have come images of the kings who
raised these tombs. Ironies of fate link
the images and their namesakes' mighty
monuments. A tiny ivory figurine about
three inches tall (above) survives as
the only known statue of Cheops, builder
of the greatest pyramid of all.
Chephren's tomb stands second to Cheops's,
yet his life-size image in diorite (left)
ranks first in artistic merit among Old
Kingdom statuary. It shows the ruler on
a lion-legged throne adorned with the
lotus and papyrus of the two Egypts.
A falcon symbolizes the king as the living
god Horus—and perhaps braces a weak point
in the statue's construction as well.

In a triad (opposite) from his temple,
Mycerinus appears less formal and aloof
than his predecessors. He strides between
the cow-horned goddess Hathor and the
chief deity of the seventh nome, or province.
Many such triads, each with a different
nome god, may have lined the temple to affirm
the king's dominance over all of Egypt.

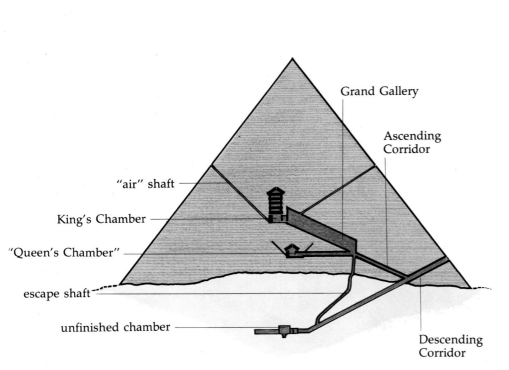

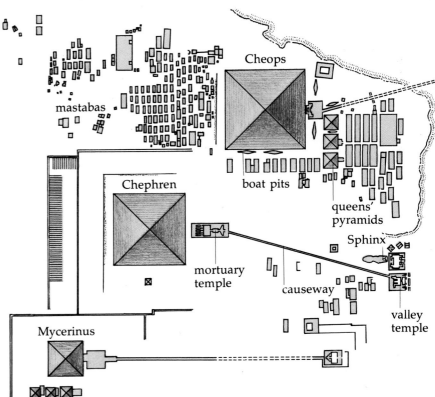

The Grand Gallery: wonder within a wonder

No other Old Kingdom monument has a chamber to compare with the lofty, upsloping passage aptly named the Grand Gallery in the Great Pyramid of Cheops. Above benchlike ramps at each side, polished walls rise seven and a half feet above the steeply pitched floor. Then seven courses of blocks, each offset three inches, rise in a corbeled vault to a ceiling 28 feet above the floor. A modern stair eases a climb that appears level to the camera's eye. Longer than half a football field, this impressive void pierces the pyramid to its heart—the King's Chamber, itself an engineering triumph with its five weight-relieving chambers. Shafts and corridors vein the mighty mass. The Queen's Chamber and a bedrock tomb were never completed. A causeway, temples, mastabas, and two more pyramid complexes lie outside.

the site, would have prevented the ancient engineers from making diagonal checks. Probably this rock was not removed for practical reasons; it reduced the amount of core material needed. But perhaps it was also kept because it constituted a natural central mound, an evocation of one of the oldest and most persistent of Egyptian funerary customs.

The pyramid's four faces were oriented almost precisely toward north, south, east, and west. In order to achieve this, surveyors made sightings on stars in the northern sky. Accuracy was vital—in fact, so important that the sightings would be reenacted in a religious ceremony by the king himself. A Fifth-Dynasty relief shows just such a ceremony, and in a much later text we can read the words that might have been said: "I take the stake and I hold the handle of the mallet. I hold the (measuring) cord. . . ." The royal surveyors knew the king was merely going through the motions, much as a modern dignitary would turn over the first spadeful of earth at a construction project, or lay a cornerstone with a silver trowel.

Externally, the Great Pyramid appears to have been completed without undergoing any significant changes in its original plan. But internally, great changes were made as construction proceeded. From an entrance in the north face, a descending corridor runs in a southward direction, first through the core of

the building and then through the rock bed, for about 345 feet. It then continues horizontally for another 29 feet, where a large chamber was hewn in the rock. A second chamber would probably have been added, but before the first chamber had been finished, the whole plan for an underground burial was abandoned.

Instead, an opening was cut in the ceiling of this descending corridor near the entrance, and from there an upward-sloping corridor was constructed. From its upper end, a level passage leads to what was then intended to be the new burial chamber, a room built of limestone blocks. Today this room is commonly, but incorrectly, called the Queen's Chamber.

But this plan also was abandoned. The ascending corridor was then extended in the form of a magnificent gallery with a corbeled vault, known as the Grand Gallery. It is undoubtedly one of the most remarkable architectural achievements of the Old Kingdom.

At the southern or higher end of the Grand Gallery, a level passage ends in a chamber of red granite called the King's Chamber. In order to reduce direct pressure from the weight of masonry above this chamber, five separate compartments were constructed above its ceiling. Four have flat roofs and the uppermost has a pointed roof. But in spite of these precautions, all nine ceiling blocks of the chamber itself—which together weigh about 400 tons—and some of the roofs of the relieving compartments are now cracked, perhaps as a result of earth tremors. The king's granite sarcophagus, though missing its lid, still lies intact in the chamber, near the west wall. It is an inch wider than the mouth of the ascending corridor and thus could not have been installed after the pyramid was built. It must have been placed in the room as the chamber itself was being constructed.

Kings had long been aware of the need to protect tombs from robbers, and so they took elaborate precautions with their own "houses of eternity." Entrance corridors were usually closed after the burial by heavy portcullises and filled with large blocks of stone. In

"I drive away the wicked one from . . . your tomb"

Quarrying stone from a nearby knoll, Cheops's builders left it a ragged outcrop. But Chephren's sculptors shaped the outcrop into the huge and brooding Sphinx. A royal beard and a royal headdress with its symbolic cobra once marked the head as that of a king, probably Chephren himself. A lion's body evokes an ancient belief that lions were guardians of sacred places. The words above, from a later and far smaller sphinx, may well speak for all of its kind.

Sprawling 240 feet from haunch to forepaw, the colossal image probably was once plastered and painted. Time and sandstorms have gnawed its flesh; from antiquity, benefactors have cleared engulfing sand and patched the monolith with blocks of stone.

Cheops's pyramid, the builders installed three granite portcullises in the level passage leading from the Grand Gallery to the King's Chamber. But it was difficult to block the ascending corridor that led to the gallery's lower end. How could the workmen push large stone blocks up the sloping floor, and how could the blocks be secured so that they could not be removed?

The only way to plug the corridor was to store the blocks in the Grand Gallery as the pyramid was being built and, after the funeral, push them down into the corridor from its upper end. But the workmen behind the blocks would then have been trapped forever inside the pyramid if a way of escape had not been provided. Although the retainers of some of the earliest kings had been buried with their masters to continue their service in the afterlife, the burial of living persons was not practiced by the time of the pyramids.

Imagine the scene as the workmen pushed these great stones into place. It was no mean feat, since the plugs fitted the ascending corridor very closely. The clearance at the sides was less than half an inch!

At the bottom, the mouth of the corridor was about an inch narrower than the plugs, thus preventing them from falling into the descending corridor. Three plugs are still in position; they can be seen from a passage cut by robbers in the softer limestone alongside.

When the last plug was in position, the workers returned up the corridor to the lower end of the Grand Gallery. From there a steep shaft had been sunk through the pyramid and the bedrock to a short passage that opened into the descending corridor near its bottom end. One by one the men lowered themselves down this narrow shaft in pitch darkness, feeling for footholds in the rough-hewn sides.

When all the men were out, masons sealed the lower exit, masking it with slabs identical to those of the corridor walls. The descending corridor was then filled with blocking material and the pyramid entrance covered with limestone like the rest of the outer face.

A problem of a different kind was created by the decision to make an upward-sloping corridor the only way of approach to the burial chamber. Custom dating back to the middle of the First Dynasty required that entrance corridors should slope downwards, generally from the north side of the tomb. When the burial chamber was located underground, a downward slope was inevitable. But even when the chamber was on ground level, as in the pyramids of Meidum and Dahshur, the custom was retained, though it would have been less laborious to construct a corridor running horizontally direct to the chamber. Moreover, such a corridor could have been blocked more easily.

The Great Pyramid, as it was first designed, also had a descending corridor. Even when the two upper chambers had been decided upon, it would have been possible to build corridors descending to them. This method, in fact, had been adopted in the Bent Pyramid when a second chamber was built at a higher level than the first. In the Great Pyramid, however, a different solution was found.

In the north and south walls of the King's Chamber, about three feet from the floor, there are small, almost square openings. They are the mouths of shafts that run horizontally, at right angles to the walls, for about five feet and then slope upwards to the north and south faces of the pyramid. It is not possible to tell whether they originally had outlets in the casing of the pyramid or were covered up by it. Similar shafts were planned and begun for the Queen's Chamber, but work on them seems to have stopped when it was decided to build the King's Chamber.

These narrow shafts have often been referred to as air channels, but that was not their purpose. The northern shaft was evidently a replica in miniature of the traditional downward-sloping entrance corridor. And so we see yet another example of an architectural element being reproduced out of its original context. It would certainly not have been retained unless a special significance had been attributed to it.

Although the entrance corridors of pyramids vary by a few degrees in their angle of incline, all except the western corridor of the Bent Pyramid are oriented toward the circumpolar stars. The northern shaft of the Great Pyramid slopes at about 30° and therefore must have been very nearly in alignment with the star Alpha Draconis, which was the pole star in the time of Cheops. So, there can be little doubt that the northern shaft, like the entrance corridors of earlier pyramids, was regarded as a way of ascent to the Imperishable Stars. These passages thus served the same general purpose as the step pyramids, and likewise depended on magic for their effectiveness.

The circumpolar stars, however, were not the only stellar group in whose midst the king would wish to spend part of his afterlife; the Pyramid Texts often mention the constellation Orion as another desirable locale. "O king," says one spell, "you are this great star, the companion of Orion, who traverses the sky with Orion." Another spell assures the king "you will regularly ascend with Orion from the eastern region of the sky, you will regularly descend with Orion into the western region of the sky." Here we find the explanation of the southern shaft, which slopes at about 45°. Once every 24 hours, three stars in the constellation passed directly over the axis of the shaft. With its aid, the king could make his ascent to their celestial region and return at will to his tomb.

Like every other pyramid, the Great Pyramid was part of a complex of buildings. The principal elements were the valley temple, the causeway, the mortuary temple, and three subsidiary pyramids for the queens, all to the east of the main pyramid.

Near the northernmost subsidiary pyramid, a Boston-Harvard expedition in 1925 discovered an underground chamber. Imagine their excitement when the room was found to contain the alabaster sarcophagus and rich funerary equipment of Queen Hetepheres, the mother of Cheops. Perhaps these objects had been

moved there from Dahshur after her original tomb had been violated and her mummified body stolen.

Another remarkable discovery was made in 1954. Egyptian workmen were clearing sand at the south side of the Great Pyramid when they came upon a rock-cut pit. Inside it was a fine wooden boat, 140 feet long. A second pit awaits excavation; three others were long ago robbed of the boats they once contained.

On all sides of the pyramid, except the northern, are rows of stone mastabas. These are the tombs of members of the royal family, nobles, courtiers, and their descendants, so placed that they might continue to serve their king in the afterlife. In return, they could expect to receive a share of the produce of the royal estates which the king had bequeathed forever to the priesthood of his pyramid.

Membership in such a priesthood carried with it both privileges and obligations. Living quarters for the priests were constructed near the pyramid complex, and its residents were usually exempted from certain taxes. But they were expected to maintain the complex in good repair and to conduct the appropriate ceremonies on a regular basis. Thus motivated—at least in part—by self-interest, they and their descendants would continue to look after a dead king's tomb for many generations.

Cheops's second successor, Khafre—whom we know by his Greek name, Chephren—raised a pyramid at Giza that was comparable in size to the Great Pyramid. Its sides at the base are only about 48 feet shorter and its original height was some 10 feet less. After one change of plan, its interior design consisted of a burial chamber reached by a relatively short corridor sloping downward from an entrance low in the north face, then leveling out in a long horizontal continuation cut in the bedrock.

Menkaure—better known to us as Mycerinus—succeeded Chephren and built the third and smallest pyramid of the Giza group. His design reverted to the long sloping corridor and deep burial chamber. The unfin-

ished mortuary temple contains blocks estimated to weigh up to 200 tons.

Without wheeled vehicles, how did the Egyptians move such great weights, and how did they raise them to the heights of the pyramids at Giza? In an experiment not many years ago, a French investigator obtained a one-ton block of limestone. The block was positioned on a track of moist mud taken from the Nile, and a crew of about 50 men was assembled and instructed to pull it with ropes. When they started pulling, the block slid along as if it were almost weightless. With half as many men, the block again ran away. The experimenter soon found that one man, with no difficulty, could push the ton of stone along on the wet mud. In ancient records we see Egyptian crews dragging great weights on sledges while water-bearers wet down the surface ahead.

To raise heavy weights above the ground, Egyptian builders constructed ramps of mud bricks. They knew how to compute the volume of a ramp; in one text, a scribe challenges a rival to calculate the number of bricks that a ramp of a certain size would require. In my first visits to Egypt, I saw a mud-brick ramp still in position against the unfinished first pylon of the temple at Karnak. It has since been removed, but it showed that the Egyptians were familiar with the ramp in practice as well as in theory. No matter how massive the ramp, disposing of it at the completion of the project was no problem. The bricks could be simply thrown back into the Nile. Being sunbaked and not kiln-dried, they would soon soften into mud again.

The workmanship in the pyramid complex of Mycerinus strongly suggests that he met an untimely death. Buildings begun in stone were completed in crude brick or simply left unfinished. Logs were used to roof the causeway. Some of the pyramid's casing stones were smoothed, but others were left in the rough.

Shepseskaf, the king who is believed to have succeeded Mycerinus, probably saw the project through to its hasty completion. He was the last king of the

Fourth Dynasty, and he seems to have had other ideas about the nature of the royal afterlife, for he and his queen, named Khentkaues, departed from precedent and built tombs with superstructures that were shaped like huge sarcophagi.

The pyramid returned to favor with the advent of the Fifth Dynasty in about 2490 B.C., and continued to be the resting place of every king until the end of the Old Kingdom in about 2130 B.C. Only one ruined pyramid dating from the unsettled period that followed the Old Kingdom has yet been found; probably very few of them were built.

The pyramidal design was revived in the Middle Kingdom, but the architects' chief concern by then was to devise ingenious ways to thwart the tomb robbers. Changes in religious ideas, and especially the growth of the cult of Osiris as god of the dead, had deprived the pyramid of much of its significance. And yet it was retained. In modest form and made of sunbaked brick, the pyramid survived the troubled times from Dynasty 15 to Dynasty 17.

Finally, sentiment yielded to prudence. For the next four centuries almost all the kings were buried in tombs hewed into the rock of the Valley of the Kings at Thebes. But I think it was not only seclusion that led to the choice of this remote valley. Here the most prominent feature was an outcrop of rock resembling a vast pyramid and now known in Arabic as El Qurn, "The Horn." A landmark dominating the whole necropolis, it is a last link with the ancient pyramids of Egypt.

"Being hard and difficult to be worked"

Quarrymen of the Pyramid Age would have accused Greek historian Strabo of understatement as they hacked at the stubborn granite of Aswan. Their axes and chisels were made of copper hardened by hammering. Tools of bronze were introduced in the Middle Kingdom. Esprit de corps toughened the stonecutters; inscriptions still visible on stones of the pyramids immortalize the "Vigorous Gang," the "Scepter Gang," the "Enduring Gang." For these were craftsmen, laboring on the project all year while the seasonal flood of farmhands receded with the Nile.

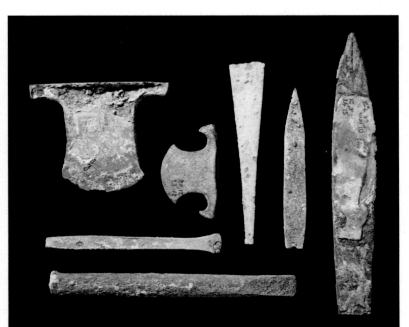

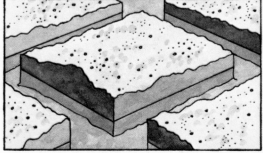

Builders begin on a sunburst in stone

Laboring willingly for their god-king,
swarms of men begin a typical pyramid.
Peasants clear away sand. Masons cut
channels in the bedrock—perhaps twice
as many as this painting can clearly show.
Filled with water, the grid is a gauge
(left, lower) for leveling the base. North
and east must now be pinpointed, for the
tomb must face the Imperishable Stars and
the rising sun. Inside a circular wall—
one way the Egyptians might obtain
a level "horizon"—a surveyor sights a
star with a notched *bay*. A helper marks
where the star rises and sets (upper).
Halving the angle gives a north-south line;
right angles then give east and west.
By canal and causeway, supplies arrive
in a procession that may last a generation.

Across the Nile, quarrymen hollow a hill

Working away with copper chisels and sledges of wood, stonecutters and hauling crews move countless tons of stone a block at a time. From the quarry wall they cut each block's sides, then crawl over the top to chisel down the back. Wooden wedges, hammered in along the bottom line, split the block free. Later, masons will use copper saws to shape and fit the blocks. Outside, workers drag the rough blocks to waiting boats. One inscribes a stone, another pounds his chisel to sharpen it. A scribe keeps tally. Other workers make bricks by the thousand. No such menial tasks dull the sculptor's senses; with artful strokes he draws a monarch from a stone.

As years pass, a timeless tomb rises

Course upon course, the pyramid is laid down—probably, as here, from the center outwards. Toward the north side, the walls of a downward-sloping passageway jut above the core blocks. At its end, in the pyramid's center, the burial chamber takes shape. Earlier, when its floor was finished, the great sarcophagus was moved into place. As the courses rose, so did the chamber's walls. Now, ready for a roof, the room is filled with sand (left, upper). Workers strain at wooden levers to position huge ceiling slabs; the sand helps to hold each until it rests against its opposing slab (lower). Finally the sand is removed.

Rising courses drown the chamber as if in a pool of stone. Now the room's pointed roof relieves the pressure of masonry above it and spreads it to the sides. Chinks show here between the core blocks, for they need not fit tightly against those at their sides. But on top and bottom, each block must be absolutely flat.

Stones skid skyward on a mountain of bricks

On a massive ramp of sun-baked bricks and rubble, teams haul
the heavy blocks to the rising pyramid. Some laborers carry water
to slick the mud surface; others carry timbers to brake the wooden
sledges lest they slip back when haulers pause. Stonecutters fit
the blocks in a staging area below. Then masons position them above,
aided on outer courses by a brick catwalk that jackets the structure
as pyramid, catwalk, and ramp rise together. A gilded pyramidion
tops off years of work. Months more remain as workers—some
on scaffolds—smooth the slant-faced casing stones. As they work
downward, ramp and catwalk are returned brick by brick to the Nile.

A pyramid begins an endless vigil

The monument is finished and the king is laid to rest. Now the priests take up their duties. Boats bring produce from estates bequeathed by the king to mortuary priests for his own sustenance and the maintenance of the pyramid. At a columned temple, offerings arrive which the dead king will consume in spirit and the priests will devour in fact.

Stone slabs now roof the causeway; a ceiling slit admits light and allows painted reliefs on the walls to be seen. A mortuary temple lies between causeway and pyramid. Outside an enclosure wall, courtiers who served the king in life remain in attendance in their mastabas of stone. Inside the wall, his queen lies in a subsidiary pyramid, a replica in miniature of the gleaming monument that shelters the mummy of the king and its lavish funerary equipment. Time has run out for a monarch of ancient Egypt. But for his tomb, it has only begun.

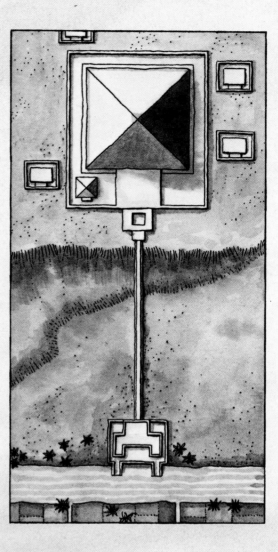

The Pleasures of Life

Barbara Mertz

Spend the day merrily!
Put ointment and fine oil to your nostrils
And lotus flowers on the body of your beloved. . . .
Spend the day merrily
And weary not therein.
Lo, none can take his goods with him.
Lo, none that has departed can return again.

This charming song, inscribed on the wall of a tomb, has always seemed to me to typify the essential quality of ancient Egyptian culture. No other ancient people enjoyed life as much as they did; and no other people, ancient or modern, spent more time and money on the equipment of the dead.

This seeming paradox, a poem praising the pleasures of life hidden away in the musty darkness of a tomb, is not really a paradox at all. For if life is enjoyable, we want it to go on as long as possible—even, we hope, after the change men call death. The Egyptian's afterworld, if he had prepared the way properly and won a favorable judgment in the awesome tribunal of the gods, was just like this one—only better! Despite all advice to the contrary—such as the line in the song quoted above—the Egyptian believed you *could* take it with you. So he furnished his tomb with all the things he enjoyed in life—pots of beer and wine, fine clothing, games, comfortable chairs. He hired artists to paint the tomb walls with scenes showing his favorite amusements. From the scenes that surround the dead we can learn the desires of the living—the pleasures they hoped to enjoy forever in the next life.

"As I love life and hate death"—so swore the ancient Egyptian. No wonder that a nobleman of the elegant 18th-Dynasty reign of Amunhotep III was reluctant to leave his luxurious existence. New Kingdom conquests had spread Egypt's sway from Nubia to the Euphrates. Tribute and trade goods poured into the palace, where Amunhotep and his imperious Queen Tiy reigned in splendor. Just under the divine pharaoh himself stood Ramose, vizier of the realm and governor of the royal city of Thebes—"a doer of truth, a hater of deceit . . . just judge . . . 'master of secret things of the palace.' " We read these epithets in the tomb that Ramose built for himself and his family at Thebes. The tomb was never finished, but the vizier's handsome figure is still there, frozen for all eternity by the skilled artists who carved the delicate bas-reliefs on the tomb walls.

Let us imagine we see the great vizier Ramose on a certain day more than 3,000 years ago, when he stood leaning on his staff watching the workmen carve out his House of Eternity. It was 1375 B.C., give or take a few years. The sun beat down out of the cloudless sky of Upper Egypt, and the sweat trickled down Ramose's forehead from under his elaborate wig. Its shoulder-length curls framed a thin aristocratic face. His household slaves had shaved him that morning with a bronze razor. Ancient Egyptians might find a narrow mustache or a goatee acceptable at some periods, but a bushy beard never. Excessive body hair was the mark of a barbarian—which Ramose surely was not.

His white linen shirt and long pleated skirt were as sheer as gauze. Even so, he would have been a lot more comfortable in the loincloth or short kilt of the stonecutters and masons. But a high official could not enjoy the workingman's freedom of seminakedness except in the privacy of his home. The jewelry that gave color to Ramose's plain white clothing weighed hot and heavy on his limbs and body, but such ornaments signified status and high office. His wide gold collar, with its rows of turquoise and carnelian and lapis lazuli beads, covered his breast like a piece of armor. The broad gold bracelets on his arms gleamed hot in the sunlight. Gifts from the king, the bracelets bore the donor's name in incised hieroglyphs. Even Ramose's sandals, made of flexible leather and adorned with bits of semiprecious stone, symbolized his rank. They would show little wear. Commoners walked. Noblemen rode in their own chariots. In earlier times they were carried in litters high above the dusty ground.

Yet Ramose was no man of leisure. He held the highest administrative post in the land. The list of the vizier's duties is staggering. He was responsible for everything, from the administration of justice to the regulation of canals and crops. We can be sure he had no time to waste at his tomb. He had already completed a full day's work, beginning at dawn. Now he had to hurry home. That evening he would give one of those banquets for which he was famous in Thebes.

Yet the vizier lingered, his eyes narrowed against the blowing stone dust and the glare of sunlight on the pale limestone cliffs. The square dark hole of the tomb entrance gaped like a great mouth. As he watched the workmen vanish into the blackness, Ramose must have thought upon that day when his mummy would be carried into the dark and his soul would face a greater darkness. His face would not betray those thoughts, not to the subordinates who followed him, but perhaps he was just a trifle brusque as he turned to the secretary at his side. The pillars in the tomb's central hall were clumsily shaped. Let the master stonecutter be told. Also, the design sketched on the left-hand wall was not to his taste. The secretary took notes as his master spoke, scribbling rapidly on a papyrus.

Time now to prepare for the evening's entertainment. Ramose had invited all his old friends and rivals, and he meant to put on a good show. Everything necessary for the party came from his own estate. His country home was like a small village, with gardens and fields, with a butcher shop, bakery, dairy, and space for a variety of crafts. His fields produced the grain for bread and beer, his vineyards yielded fine vintages. His herds of cattle and his flocks of geese supplied meat and milk and eggs.

All that day servants had sweltered in kitchen and bakery to cook roasts and bake bread and prepare dozens of sweet cakes, sticky with honey. Ramose did not need to trouble himself with supervising the details; he knew his trained household staff had matters under

Royal finery, agleam with "the flesh of the gods"

In the shops of Amunhotep III, whose reign became an endless pursuit of pleasure, a scribe weighs out gold—the divine metal that shines with the sun's fire. A bronze bull's head measures the heap; Maat, goddess of truth, crowns the scale. Artisans in this tomb painting shape *djed* pillars that signify stability, a sphinx, a vase, an inlaid box. Two men bear finished wares for inspection.

The gold-sheathed djed, buried with Tutankhamun, invoked a spell to revive the dead pharaoh. "I have brought you a djed pillar of gold," reads the inscription. "May you be pleased with it."

control. He paused to pray at the small household shrine by the front gate, then entered the house.

The mansion was cool and shady inside. High clerestory windows admitted thin rays of sunlight which illumined the birds and flowers painted on the walls in brilliant shades of orange and green and blue. The elaborate palm columns that supported the ceilings were also painted, and trimmed with gold. Woven mats covered the floor of the great reception hall. Servants ran back and forth setting up the small tables at which the guests would sit. The butler, a slave from Asia, cuffed a servant girl for breaking a fine glass goblet. Her howl of pain rose over the babble of voices, the patter of running feet, and the strains of music from the orchestra practicing in one corner of the hall.

A capable man, that butler. Before long, he would earn his freedom. He had already married the daughter of the overseer of Ramose's cattle. Like other foreign captives in the New Kingdom, he had found that serving the powerful opened the door to advancement. Some household servants enjoyed better prospects than the native peasantry.

In his own suite of rooms at the back of the villa, Ramose stripped off his sweat-stained garments. As he stood on the stone bathing slab, servants poured jars of cool water over him. Fresh robes had already been laid out in the dressing room, where beautifully painted boxes and woven baskets held his extensive wardrobe. The amenities of the villa included a toilet as well: a removable pot under a seat supported by bricks.

Cooled and refreshed, Ramose sipped wine while his servants dressed him in his most elaborate pleated robe and his finest jewelry. The massive, inlaid pectoral that hung at his chest like a breastplate was another gift from the pharaoh.

Ramose went to call on his wife, Meritptah, in her suite. The place was in turmoil. It always took Merit hours to dress for a banquet. The smell of the sweet oil of lily with which her body had been anointed reached her husband's nostrils as he stood in the doorway. She wore the filmy white linen favored by the nobles, men and women alike. The wide pleated sleeves of her gown billowed out as she turned to greet him and ask his advice on the jewels she should wear.

Ramose approved her bracelets, made of the red gold which had recently become popular, and the earrings he had given her—hollow loops of gold soldered together and covered with minute granules of gold set in geometric patterns. They matched her wig ornaments, short golden tubes that had been threaded onto the braids of hair. The wig was placed on her head, and gilded sandals were strapped onto her feet. Then she was ready to greet the guests.

The guests were also dressed in their best. Gold glittered and turquoise glowed softly. The white robes were clasped by girdles of precious metal or by fringed, embroidered sashes. As each person entered the house, a servant placed on his or her wig a cone of sweetly scented fat. This would melt as the banquet proceeded, enveloping the head and shoulders in trails of sticky perfume.

A soft ripple of background music accompanied the feasting. At first the diners' voices were equally soft; however, as jar after jar of wine was emptied into goblets of glass and alabaster, voices rose and laughter became more strident. Servants trotted in with loaded platters. The diners ate with their fingers—whole roasted ducks, haunches of beef, grapes and figs, washing it all down with wine. Finally the inevitable happened; one woman leaned over and was thoroughly sick. A serving girl ran to hold her head and clean up. (This messy scene is not invented; an artist painted it in graphic detail on a tomb wall at Thebes.)

Servants came around with bowls of water, which they poured over the sticky hands of the diners, and then the entertainment began. The orchestra struck up a cheerful tune. The simple pipes and arched harps of earlier periods had been augmented by new musical instruments borrowed from the conquered territories of Asia. Ramose's musicians had the oboe and double flute, lyre and lute, and several kinds of harps. The master of the musicians, old Nakht, was blind. So many children lost their sight from sickness of the eyes. Nakht was one of the lucky ones, having the skill to learn music and find a haven in a wealthy household where his talent was appreciated. The old man's sightless eyes closed and his lips curved in a faint smile as his fingers rippled over the harp strings.

A chorus of girls burst into a wailing chant—"Spend the day merrily. . . ." Dancers whirled onto the floor. They were slim young girls, naked except for strings of blue beads around their waists and hips; wreaths of lotus flowers crowned their long black hair. They stamped and kicked in a vigorous chorus line, swinging their hair and clicking clappers as they moved.

A troupe of acrobats followed. They were also young women. Their oiled brown bodies seemed as boneless as eels. Ramose leaned forward with shining eyes as they did cartwheels and handstands. The guests were delighted. Egyptians enjoyed seeing feats of strength and agility. Wrestling was widely popular. A modern fan would recognize the ancient Egyptian double-leg takedown; the repertoire included other holds which have evolved into some used today. Surely spectators cheered, as we do, at the sight of a wrestler flung to the ground. Occasionally a loser had to be carried out.

So did a few of Ramose's guests, when it was time to leave. We will leave too; Ramose has to get to bed. His workday begins at dawn, and it is a long, hard day.

"Ointment is the prescription for her body"

The sage spoke well; a freshly anointed body made life more bearable in a hot, dusty land. Even the humble prized oil as a daily necessity, as vital as food. The wealthy could find added delight in beautiful cosmetic accessories. A nude girl swims behind a duck that bore unguent in its hollowed back; hinged wings covered the bowl of the spoon. Clad only in a necklace and bikini-size girdle, the Nubian maid thrusts out a hip to support a heavy unguent jar. Front and back views show how the carver tried to portray the tensed body by twisting the upper torso and legs. Rare in Egyptian art, the technique—called contrapposto—was widely used in classical Greece and later in the Renaissance.

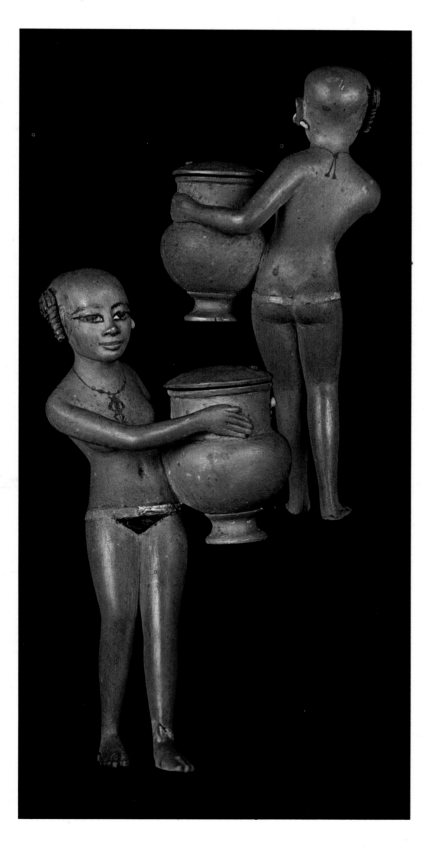

The Egyptians' entertainments were not always so extravagant. They loved to eat and drink, but they also appreciated more subtle domestic pleasures. Ramose's profile shows the refinement of a sophisticate and an aesthete; we can be sure he appreciated the quiet hours in his walled garden, beside the cool blue pool under the shade of tamarisk and persea trees. Here Ramose would sit as the shadows of evening lengthened, enjoying the soft music of the harp or playing the popular board game called *senet* with his wife.

The garden was a private, family place, where the children played and the household pets romped with them. I feel that only a sophisticated culture domesticates animals for pleasure rather than for utility, and the Egyptians were certainly pet fanciers. They adorned prize cattle with ribbons and gave them pet names; they mummified monkeys and horses and buried them with their masters. But, as in our culture, the household pets par excellence were cats and dogs.

The Egyptian word for cat was *miu*. We need not wonder how it was pronounced! Modern experts believe the cat probably was first domesticated in Egypt, being descended from the African wild cat *Felis libyca*. Originally Egyptians may have tolerated cats because they kept down rodents—an important job in an economy based on grain. But it was not long before cats wormed their way into the affections of their owners. A sculptor named Ipuy had a very spoiled puss; on the walls of his tomb Ipuy sits with a kitten on his lap while mother cat turns her head toward us so we can admire the silver earring her doting owner gave her.

In Ramose's time Queen Tiy had a pet cat which sat under her chair during dinner and, no doubt, received occasional goodies from her mistress' plate. King Intef II of an earlier dynasty preferred dogs. Five of them share immortality with him on his tomb stela. Two had names that are self-explanatory: Blackie, and the Gazelle. A third name has been translated as the Cook Pot—obviously a canine gourmand, like so many we know. Its owner, Intef, was one of the warrior rulers

of Thebes during a struggle to reunify a divided nation, but the humorous affection of his pet's name tells us more about the man than any of his warlike deeds.

Dogs assisted their masters in hunting, a favorite sport during the 18th Dynasty, and cats went along on bird-hunting expeditions. These latter trips, commemorated in numerous tomb paintings, often have the appearance of a family Sunday in the country. The marshy regions along the Nile were full of wildfowl, and the nobleman who poled his light skiff through the reed thickets took the wife and kids and servants along. The ladies picked water lilies while the head of the household knocked down the wildly fluttering birds with a throw stick. This skill must have required a lot of practice. A man who could equip his tomb with such fine paintings didn't have to forage for food. He hunted for sport, and the whole family, including the cat, obviously enjoyed it.

Many wild species abundant along the Nile in ancient times are no longer found in Egypt proper. In 1350 B.C. hippopotamuses wallowed in the marshes, crocodiles infested the river, and the lordly lion prowled the deserts on either side. Lion hunting was the royal sport. Ramose's master Amunhotep III commemorated his hunts on numerous scarabs which told how he killed more than a hundred "savage lions" during his first decade on the throne.

Mounted in a light horse-drawn chariot, a king pursued his prey armed only with bow and arrow. An entourage of alert courtiers followed along, ready to step in if things got out of hand; even so, it must have taken skill and courage to excel at this sport.

If we can believe their boasts, the Egyptians were among the great archers of all time. The bow served in war as well as in hunting. Boys probably began practicing at an early age. "Span your bows to your ears," says an instructor to the young prince who became Amunhotep II. None of his courtiers would have been tactless enough to challenge this king's claim to be the greatest of all bowmen: "There is no one who could

draw his bow, not among his own army, [or] among the rulers of foreign countries . . . because his strength is so much greater than [that of] any king who ever lived." He could shoot an arrow straight through a copper target three inches thick—at least that is what he said he could do. He may not have exaggerated too much; he was taller and more muscular than most pharaohs, and in fairly good health when he died at about 45. He had his favorite bow buried with him. It was a composite bow, of the kind introduced by the Hyksos, the Asian invaders who ruled in Egypt just before the New Kingdom began in the middle of the 16th century B.C. Made of layers of wood and horn and sinew, the composite bow had much greater range and power than the simple wooden bow of earlier periods.

Among the pleasures of life in ancient Egypt was a family's delight in its children. It continues today. Once, when I visited a modern Egyptian family, I was joined by my host's young children, a boy and a girl. They sat beside me on the divan while I showed them photographs of my own children, and we shared sticks of gum. Their father stood beaming at us with candid pride. One cannot call love of children a specifically Egyptian trait; it is common to all people. But the ancient Egyptians expressed their parental affection more openly than did other ancient peoples, whose love of children was expressed most often in the epitaphs of their young. An Egyptian father needed a son, not only to support him in his old age, but also to supply the necessary food offerings after death. However, he loved his daughters also.

Akhenaten, the so-called "heretic" pharaoh whom we will meet again in a later chapter, was a particularly fond father. He was often shown hugging and kissing his daughters. When one died prematurely, her father allowed the court artists to depict him in poses of abandoned grief over the pathetic little mummy.

Egyptian fathers even took their young daughters hunting with them, a display of parental affection rare in any period of history. But children had plenty of time for their own amusements. They had dolls and fancy mechanical toys, and played games with stuffed leather balls that resembled our baseballs.

Children assumed adult responsibilities earlier than modern youngsters do, and for a boy above the peasant class the first cloud in his sunny life came with the first day of school. We don't know as much about the schools as we would like, but we do know that children hated them as much as children do today—with better reason. Classes went on for long hours, and there were no rules against corporal punishment: "A boy's ears are on his back, and he hears best when he is beaten," says one adage. The lunches of bread and beer brought by mothers must have been the only bright spot in the day. Anyone who has studied Egyptian writing must feel a pang of sympathy for the poor boys who had to fathom its mysteries with no textbooks, no grammars, and the teacher's stick hovering over them. But writing was a key to advancement.

Some girls may have learned to read and write too. For the most part, however, a woman's place was in the home. From her mother she learned the domestic arts, and from mother nature she learned the lessons which are as old as Eve—how to make herself beautiful and please a husband. Our museums possess excellent collections of toilet articles, since these feminine necessities were often buried with their owners. The Egyptian lady had a wide assortment to choose from. When she was done with her toilette—the combs and tweezers, the oils and face paints—she not only looked ravishing but also smelled pleasantly of myrrh or oil of lily. And her lover obviously found her irresistible:

> *If I embrace her and her arms are open,*
> *I am like a man in the land of perfumes.*
> *If I kiss her and her lips are open,*
> *I am drunk even without beer.*

It is impossible to translate Egyptian love poetry literally; the admittedly free translation of this verse gets the point across, I think.

Some scholars believe that marriages in ancient Egypt were arranged by the parents of the bride and groom. Perhaps such theories are influenced by what was common not only in Egypt a century ago but also in European society until recently. Egyptian poems strongly suggest that boys and girls had their own ideas about love and marriage. We find hints of genuine love matches even in the royal family. The poems have an openly sexual element, but they are not erotica. They express physical desire naturally, and mention other feelings that can only be called romantic.

In one poem a young man boasts that his sweetheart's love gives him courage to defy a crocodile to reach her side. The lover who moans about an illness which the doctors cannot cure—an ailment which has afflicted him since he last saw his beloved—is lovesick in the most literal sense. The girls in the love poems express their feelings as openly as do the boys—an indication that, at some periods at least, Egyptian women enjoyed considerable social freedom.

The ancient Egyptian woman was also certainly better off than a wife of Periclean Athens, or a medieval European noblewoman, or a lady of the Victorian period in England. At some periods she could own property—which the Victorian wife could not—and she could dispose of it as she wished. In a divorce she was entitled to a third of the goods the couple had acquired during their marriage, which is a third more than the 19th-century American wife received.

Two quotations, from texts widely separated in time, demonstrate that an Egyptian woman could expect fair and loving treatment from her husband.

"If you are a man of means, able to establish a household, love your wife at home. . . . Fill her belly and clothe her back. . . . Make her happy as long as you live, for she is a profitable field for her lord. Don't judge her, or let her gain control. . . ."

These words are from the writings of the Old Kingdom sage Ptahhotep. The second quotation comes from a period about a thousand years later.

"When you . . . take a wife . . . remember how your mother gave birth to you, and how she raised you. Don't give your wife cause to blame you. . . . Don't supervise your wife in her house if you know she is doing a good job. Don't say to her, 'Where is it? Get it for me!' when she has put it in the proper place."

The admonitions of the later text are particularly attractive. Women had legal rights at this period, but the text goes beyond them into an area of ethical sensitivity which is rare in any age. The pangs of childbirth and the years of maternal care lay an obligation on the son, which he can repay by treating his wife with the same consideration he owes his mother. It is an astonishingly modern view, and the most charming touch of all warns the husband to let his wife manage the house without interference. Marriage counselors might well offer the same advice to nagging modern husbands.

Polygamy was permitted but rarely practiced, perhaps because of the expense. To clothe the backs and feed the bellies of two or more wives—not to mention the cost of ointments—might strain a poor man's income. Although marriage was a civil, rather than a religious, contract, marital infidelity by either partner was frowned upon. Sages such as Ptahhotep warned young men not to seek out prostitutes. When a man faced the last judgment and declared his purity from sin, he specifically mentioned that he neither committed adultery nor had sexual relations with a boy.

One has the feeling that Egyptians were basically monogamous. Couples expected to spend eternity together; the smiling tomb statues of husband and wife, their arms around one another, are attractive testimonials to marital love and fidelity.

As chief minister of the realm, a vizier such as Ramose had to do a certain amount of traveling—south to Aswan to supervise the quarrying of granite, north to check on the royal estates. Naturally he traveled by boat, along that handy road, the Nile. At times the river must have been as crowded as a

modern superhighway, filled with boats carrying bureaucrats on business journeys, barges loaded with produce, and innumerable private vessels.

The Egyptians traveled for pleasure as well as business. They were the first tourists of whom we have record. This is not surprising when we remember that to a man of Ramose's day the pyramids of Giza were already a thousand years old. When the Egyptians visited these wonders of the distant past, they scribbled all over the walls, just as uncouth modern tourists do.

Like medieval pilgrims, the devout Egyptians visited such popular shrines as that of Osiris at Abydos. And although religious piety was their ostensible motive, surely they enjoyed the excursion as much as the Canterbury pilgrims did, picnicking along the way, buying cheap trinkets and souvenirs from vendors.

A man of Ramose's wealth could enjoy any activity he liked, limited only by lack of time. He was exceptional, of course. Very few could afford jewels and servants, rich food and wine, dancing girls and harpists. But the humbler people had their own amusements.

We know very little about the peasants, the mute masses who made up the great majority of the population and left no written records. They must have led very hard lives, filled with unremitting labor from daybreak till dark. The Egyptian ethical code promised justice to all men, even the humblest, but a peasant often suffered from the bullying of petty officials, from bureaucratic corruption and indifference, from heavy taxes, and from the grim handicap of poverty itself. For many, the temple and tomb projects served as a kind of public works program, supplying jobs to tide them over the slack season, when their little fields were covered by the waters of the inundation.

However hard the life of the peasant serf, he was as anxious for survival as was his lordly master. Even the poorest graves contained a pot of food, a cheap bead necklace, or a child's cherished toy. And the serf enjoyed his simple pleasures. In the heat of noonday, when the overseer had gone home for lunch, he could

At times it looked like a topsy-turvy world

It's your move, lion. The antelope plays a board game with the king of beasts; hyenas and cat herd gazelles and geese. Animals playing human seemed to delight the people of the Nile, but this comic papyrus from the 20th-21st Dynasties may have the satiric bite of an editorial cartoon: Prey and predator ignore their natural roles. Chaos reigns. It was thus with Egypt in that dismal age. Inflation sapped its wealth, crime in the tombs soared unchecked, terrorists roamed the Nile Valley, and the pharaohs grew feeble.

loaf in the shade of a tree while a companion played a tune on a homemade reed pipe.

After his long day's labor his wife would await him with a frugal supper of bread and beer, lentils and onions. And surely he must have gathered with his friends in the blue twilight, for gossip and storytelling. Egyptian peasants were illiterate, and the storyteller is a figure often encountered in such cultures. Although there is no documentary evidence of his presence in ancient Egypt, I feel sure he was the central attraction of many a village gathering as he held his listeners spellbound with stories of wonder and magic and adventure. Such tales, found in Egyptian literature, represent a folk tradition—tales told around the hearthfire for generations before they were committed to writing.

Ancient Egypt had no middle class, in the modern sense. However, between the peasant and the aristocrat stood a sizable group of craftsmen, scribes, priests, and petty officials who made up what Professor John A. Wilson called the "white kilt" class. Like the snowy shirts of a modern white-collar worker, the clean white kilt showed that the wearer lived by his skill instead of by manual labor. A great nobleman of Egypt would have found a craftsman's home mean and comfortless; yet the latter's life-style compares favorably to that of many modern men.

On one of my visits to Egypt I had the good fortune to be entertained by a gentleman who worked for one of the archeological institutes of Luxor. He was a quiet, smiling man of indeterminate age, who wore his snowy white turban and long, flapping robe with

For the New Kingdom man of means the good life flourished on a mini-estate fitted neatly into a three-quarter-acre lot. From the guarded main gate a path angled by the family chapel to the house. At the porch, chiseled hieroglyphs gave the owner's name and rank. Cool, high-ceilinged, brightly painted, the central room comprised the heart of the house. Adjacent sleeping quarters varied—tiny cubicles for women and children, a luxury suite for the master with anointing room, shower stall, and contoured stone toilet seat.

Good design stands out. Prevailing winds blew away kitchen heat and stable odors. Servants climbed steps to fill the grain bins at the top and emptied them through trapdoors below. Passageways enabled grooms to feed the horses from outside the stable stalls.

Unlike stone tombs, mud-brick homes crumbled. This model derives from ruins of an Amarna suburb. Mud patches marked garden sites—mud borne from the Nile to defy the desert sands.

natural dignity. After we had visited several tombs, he suggested that we stop by his house for tea.

He lived in Qurna, a village on the west bank of the Nile, across from Luxor. Qurna is a fantastic town; its houses huddle among the ancient tombs of New Kingdom dignitaries. In the last century of our era the men of Qurna were notable for one accomplishment. They were the best tomb robbers in Egypt. Not all the villagers robbed tombs, but we can easily understand why some did. The terrible poverty of the fellahin contrasted painfully with the wealth of the Europeans and Americans who visited Thebes. The treasures rotting away in darkness seemed an irresistible temptation to people who lived on the ragged edge of malnutrition.

The men of modern Qurna do not rob tombs. They guard the shrines and guide the tourists, and some occasionally sell fake antiques to the unwary. Like many of his fellow townsmen, my host was a respected employee of the Luxor archeologists. He took as much pride in his national treasures as any trained scholar.

His hospitality was as gracious as any I have ever encountered, although the refreshments consisted solely of very black, very sweet tea, and slices of unleavened bread. The most prominent article of furniture in his living room was a long built-in divan, covered with cushions of faded chintz—and so high off the floor that only a tall man could sit on it with any comfort. It was meant, of course, to be squatted upon; but since sitting cross-legged was never one of my accomplishments, I had to let my feet dangle. A minor inconvenience. The visit will always live in my memory, not only for its intrinsic graces, but for a more poignant reason. As I sat swinging my feet and sipping my tea, I was conscious of an unaccountable feeling of familiarity. My host's home and domestic habits were familiar to me from my studies. In many ways they resembled those of his remote ancestors, the workmen of Thebes who had built the very tombs he guarded.

The tomb workers of ancient Thebes lived in a village about two miles from present-day Qurna. Their houses, like that of my host, were built of sunbaked brick and consisted of four or five rooms. The hall led into the living room, which had thick walls and small, high windows to keep out the sun. The main article of furniture was a built-in bench or divan.

A visitor to one of those houses would have been entertained in the living room, just as I was. He would not have seen the bedroom or kitchen, but he would not have missed much. Egyptian houses were sparsely furnished. Wooden boxes and skillfully woven baskets held the clothing, jewelry, cosmetics, and other personal possessions of the family. Aside from such storage boxes, the bedroom held only one other piece of furniture—the bed itself, a low wooden structure usually higher at the head than at the foot, with "springs" of woven cord or leather strips. Folded linen pads softened this hard surface to some extent, but there were no pillows. Egyptians used headrests instead. They look horribly uncomfortable, but a modern archeologist, who tried one, insisted it was not that bad once you got used to it.

The kitchen contained even less equipment than the bedroom. There were no counters, no tables, no cabinets; only jars and pots, grinding utensils, and an oven—a rough pottery shell with a lid on top and a shelf partway up one side. When the fire at the bottom of the oven had died down to a bed of coals, the loaves of bread were placed on the shelf to bake.

Such kitchens must have been unbearably hot. I feel sure that the ancient housewife ground her grain and cut up her vegetables out in the open, either on the flat roof of the house or in the courtyard, if her home boasted such an amenity. It was in the courtyard of the Qurna house that I met the ladies of the household— after I had been formally entertained in the parlor. They were amiable souls, swathed in dusty black robes; we had no common language, but our smiles and shared laughter spoke not only of our common humanity but also of that joy of living which has characterized the Egyptian for more than 5,000 years.

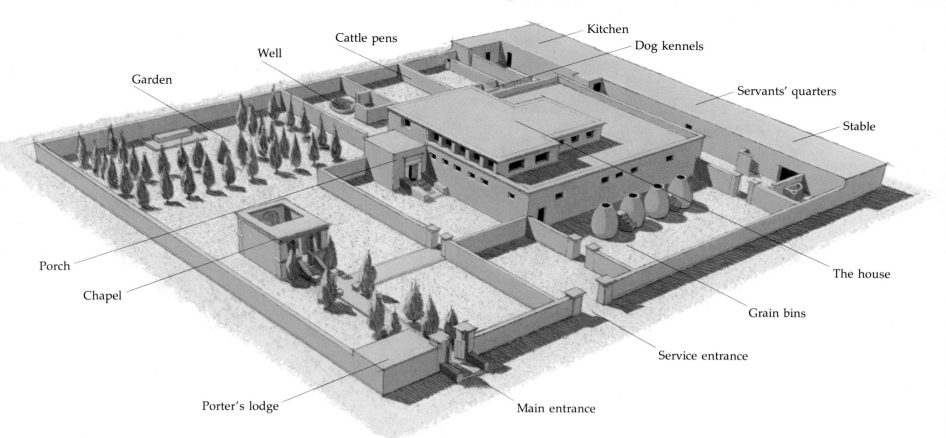

Well · Garden · Cattle pens · Kitchen · Dog kennels · Servants' quarters · Stable · Porch · Chapel · The house · Grain bins · Service entrance · Porter's lodge · Main entrance

Laughter is surely one of life's greatest pleasures, and the ancient Egyptian must have enjoyed a funny story. But we can't always be sure what he thought funny. One story, which depicts a great council of the gods bickering like sulky children, almost certainly was a comic tale—some of it quite bawdy. The literature includes many tales of entertainment, but it also committed to writing important information to help a person succeed in life or survive death.

W hen a man's mummy was safely stowed away in his tomb, his soul had to face the fearful ordeal of the last judgment, in which a divine tribunal would determine his right to enjoy immortality. We have a fairly clear picture of what a man had to do with his life if he expected to have it prolonged into eternity. With such high stakes as life everlasting in the balance, the Egyptians were perfectly capable of trying to bribe a jury; and since they believed in magic, they used it to influence the divine court. And yet there was a strict moral code. Whether the Egyptians actually lived by it is beside the point. It held as much validity for them as the Ten Commandments or Sermon on the Mount do for us.

> *I gave bread to the hungry, water to the thirsty,*
>   *clothes to the naked. . . .*
> *I was respectful to my father, pleasant*
>   *to my mother.*

Such statements appear in tomb after tomb, anxiously asserting the dead man's claim to virtue. He was not only supposed to abstain from wrongdoing, he was also expected to act positively—to succor the helpless and to render justice. Passersby were asked to testify to his good works and to pray for his soul.

One of the most revealing documents we have—a long text sometimes called "The Declaration of Innocence"—lists dozens of crimes which the dead man claims he never committed. These range from strictly ritual declarations ("I have not neglected the appoint-

ed offerings") to more profound ethical statements. I find myself grinning over some of them; they are so typical of the Egyptian fondness for order and method. "I have not killed," says one statement—but, unlike their Hebrew brethren, the Egyptians felt compelled to add, "I have given no order to a killer." A nice point, one that conjures up fantastic pictures of ancient hit men skulking through the alleys of Thebes.

> *I have not robbed. . . .*
> *I have not caused anyone suffering. . . .*
> *I have not falsified the grain measures. . . .*
> *I have not taken milk from . . . children. . . .*

In order to succeed in life a young man had to obey rules like these. Didactic texts, supposedly passing on the wisdom of ancient sages, taught a boy how to win friends and influence superiors. To us these texts seem a curious hodgepodge. They warn against wife beating—and also against talking too loudly in front of the boss. One of the most important enjoins a youth to listen respectfully to the advice of his elders.

Did the Egyptian boy listen? Of course not. He probably snickered to himself, and then went out and did all the things he had been warned not to do—drank too much, consorted with prostitutes, played hooky as often as he could get away with it, ignored his religious obligations. He was just as human as we are, and that is why we find him so sympathetic.

The Egyptian is an engaging character, really: spoiling his children, buying silver earrings for his cat, guzzling his beer and wine, puttering in his garden. These trivialities may not seem as important as a solemn religious ritual or an imposing temple. But they are the stuff of which the ordinary man's life is shaped. Perhaps in the long run they mean more than battles or treaties or state marriages. Human aspiration, human weakness, simple human pleasures. The Egyptians knew them all, and that is why they wanted to go on living in a world that was better than, but not essentially unlike, the world they knew.

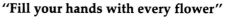

"Fill your hands with every flower"

"Make yourself a garden," advises an ancient text. "Plant trees . . . in every part of your home, and fill your hands with every flower which your eye may behold. One has need of them all." In the desert, where the "heat dries up the moisture in the mouth and the scorching wind consumes the very marrow of the bones," the garden is Eden—color and fragrance, green life and cool water wrung from the world of drab. But to make the desert bloom meant devoted nurture, endless watering. The bent little gardener, watched by a pet, lifts the shadoof from a lotus-filled pool to slake a garden of papyrus, cornflowers, and willow, and sycamore fig and persea trees. In the model garden from a Middle Kingdom tomb, a nobleman's verandah looks out on a grove of sycamores around a pool.

The arbor below teems with life— fish and fowl and flowers in the pool, flowers and herbs at the edge, grapevines and trees heavy with fruit crowding all around. In one corner appears a vision Egyptians hoped to see when they entered the world beyond—a welcoming goddess with food and drink, in the shade of a tree.

To modern eyes the painting looks odd, without perspective. But perspective hides detail. To show all elements, the artist combined several viewpoints. We see the pool in plan, as if looking down on it; but wildfowl, fish, plants, and trees appear in elevation—from different angles, as if seen by a moving observer.

A portable bedroom, fit for a queen

Incredible luck and workmanship that
46 centuries show us how a queen slep
in the Pyramid Age. Around the bed o
Hetepheres, mother of Cheops, curtair
hung from a canopy to ensure privacy a
provide protection from insects. Gold e
the wooden frame. Tenons and copper
sheathing braced its joints, yet it could
be easily dismantled. On the jambs gle
the names of the queen's husband, Sne
The detail above symbolizes his domair
sedge and bee stand for Upper and Lov
Egypt, as do vulture and cobra. The bo
stored curtains. Papyrus blooms adorn
the oldest chair in existence. Headrest a
sloping bed, typical then, strike one
modern scholar as "great for watching

In 1925 a camera tripod struck a patc
plaster near Cheops's Great Pyramid. U
the spot a shaft led down to Hetephere
tomb, a jumbled mass. Decayed wood
feel of cigar ash, but gold casings held
shape. For 14 years George Reisner, a r
Egyptologist, and his team sifted, reco
and restored the gilded boudoir for Ca
Egyptian Museum. The duplicate here
appears in Boston's Museum of Fine A

The queen? Gone. Reisner imagined
age-old cover-up: She may have been s
from an earlier tomb near her husband
Dahshur. Then a terrified bureaucrat go
approval for a transfer to the more secu
site at Giza—without ever telling Cheo
his mother's mummy was missing!

**Conversation pieces
from an eternal living room**

In Egypt of the pharaohs the poor sat on floors, as did many of the well-to-do; in desert heat, people did not stuff their homes with furniture. Yet a variety of chairs survive—chairs with slanted backs and woven seats, rigid and folding stools. The seats of the mighty were something else: intricately carved, ornamented with gold and stone inlays. These two graced Tutankhamun's tomb. On the deeply curved seat of the one at right a pattern of ivory inlaid on ebony gives the look of leopard skin—with colors reversed. Crossed legs, like those of a folding stool, end in carved ducks' heads, their beaks biting the crossbars. Vandals long ago ripped off part of the openwork grill.

The god of eternity, Heh, spans the back of the chair opposite. It was carved of reddish, cedarlike wood, perhaps for the king's coronation. A "life" sign hangs from Heh's right arm; his hands grasp palm ribs rising from hieroglyphic signs for "100,000 years" and "infinity."

Classical Rome and 19th-century Europe copied Egyptian styles, and Egyptian techniques serve us yet: dovetail, miter, and mortise-and-tenon joints. A coffin from about 2700 B.C. had thin wooden layers pegged together—perhaps the first plywood. Finely rounded furniture legs hint of a lathe, though none has turned up.

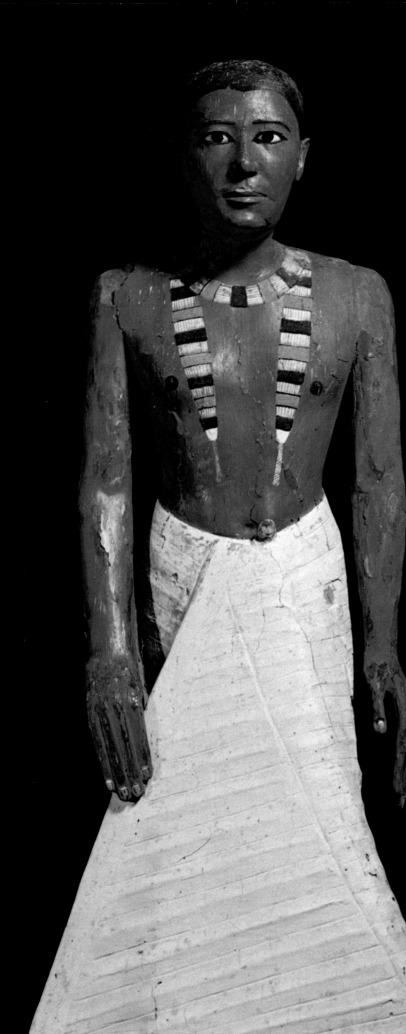

"That I may let you see my beauty in my . . . finest royal linen, when it is wet"

The poet in words, the sculptor in stone—each kindled New Kingdom senses with images still potent today. Sensuousness ripples across the lady in limestone; her pleated linen gown hugs every curve. She is thought to be the wife of Nakhtmin, an 18th-Dynasty nobleman.

Egyptians dressed lightly, mostly in white accented with rainbows of jewelry. A net of beads covers the white linen sheath of the offering bearer; her right hand pinions a live duck as the left steadies the drinking jars. She belongs to the charming troupe of wooden tomb models that livened the afterlife for the Middle Kingdom chancellor Meketre.

Children went naked; peasants wrapped a coarse cloth about their loins. A white kilt, modeled here by the Fifth-Dynasty overseer Methethy, symbolized status. Men wore kilts long or short, pleated or plain; one archeologist counted 40 styles. With a more complex society came more ornate clothing. By the New Kingdom the kilt had developed into a long skirt, and a nobleman's formal wear might include a shirt with wide pleated sleeves.

The masses walked barefoot, the rich in sandals. A king won a symbolic victory whenever he slipped them on. Royal sandals, such as these of Tutankhamun, had Egypt's enemies pictured on the inner soles.

**Beauty culture:
the treatment,
from head to toe**

The Lady Kawit, member of a royal house, sips milk while her hairdresser primps a ringlet. With her free hand Kawit holds the indispensable "see-face." Mirrors—made of bronze, copper, silver— never scribed a perfect circle; flattening gave them the look of the sun disk at the moment it sank from the sky.

Two thousand years before the pyramids, the Egyptians had cosmetics. They painted their eyes with green malachite or gray galena; the adornment served also to protect the eyes against harsh sun glare. In the time of the dynasties vanity could deploy a formidable arsenal—henna for toenails and fingernails; red ocher for lips and cheeks; myrrh and oil of lily and other scents to perfume the body; tweezers and razors to remove superfluous hair. And medical wizardry for not enough

hair: Fats of lion, hippopotamus, snake, crocodile, cat, and ibex made hair sprout.

Age need not wither. A lady past her prime had recipes for wrinkles and gray hair. She could resort to aphrodisiacs and to surgery for sagging breasts. With the proper medico-magic formula, she could turn a rival into a bald hag.

Artisans summoned proud skills to craft and package the toiletries. The restored chest of Princess Sithathoryunet, fashioned of ebony, ivory, faience, carnelian, gold, and silver, had the shape of a shrine. Her tomb also held razors, whetstones for honing bronze blades that dulled so quickly, the squat pot for eye makeup, the silver rouge dish, the three unguent beakers of obsidian, and a mirror like the reproduction shown here. The hardwood comb lay in another tomb.

The triumph of the *nuby* and the *neshdy*

Goldsmith and lapidary, creators of fine jewelry, reached the peak of their art in the Middle Kingdom. For Khnumet, a princess of the 12th Dynasty, they wove a diadem of delicate beauty—a scatter of tiny flowers, strung on threads of gold, gathered by crosses of papyrus blooms. The wreath blends hues of semiprecious stones: red carnelian, deep-blue lapis lazuli, blue-green turquoise—the "classic trio" of Egyptian lapidaries. Nile sailors inspired the design. When stiff winds tousled their hair, they wove weeds into headbands. From the "boatman's circlet" came Khnumet's dainty wreath—one of the loveliest pieces ever found in Egypt.

To Khnumet, also, belonged this pendant. On its medallion a cow rests against a background of blue frit (a fuse of ingredients similar to those of glass or faience, cheaper than the imported lapis). Its rosettes and stars are embellished by granulation, a meticulous technique which uses solder to fix tiny grains of gold to a golden surface.

With the New Kingdom came new riches, new styles. "In Egypt," wrote an Asian king, "pure gold is the dust on the highroads." Cascades of golden rosettes form this headdress for a wife of Thutmose III. She is not the model, and no one knows just how it looked originally. Tomb robbers of Qurna found it in pieces in 1916. The lady who wore it had $4\frac{1}{2}$ pounds of gold and stones on her head. "Beauty," concluded archeologist Herbert Winlock, "was taken seriously in ancient Egypt."

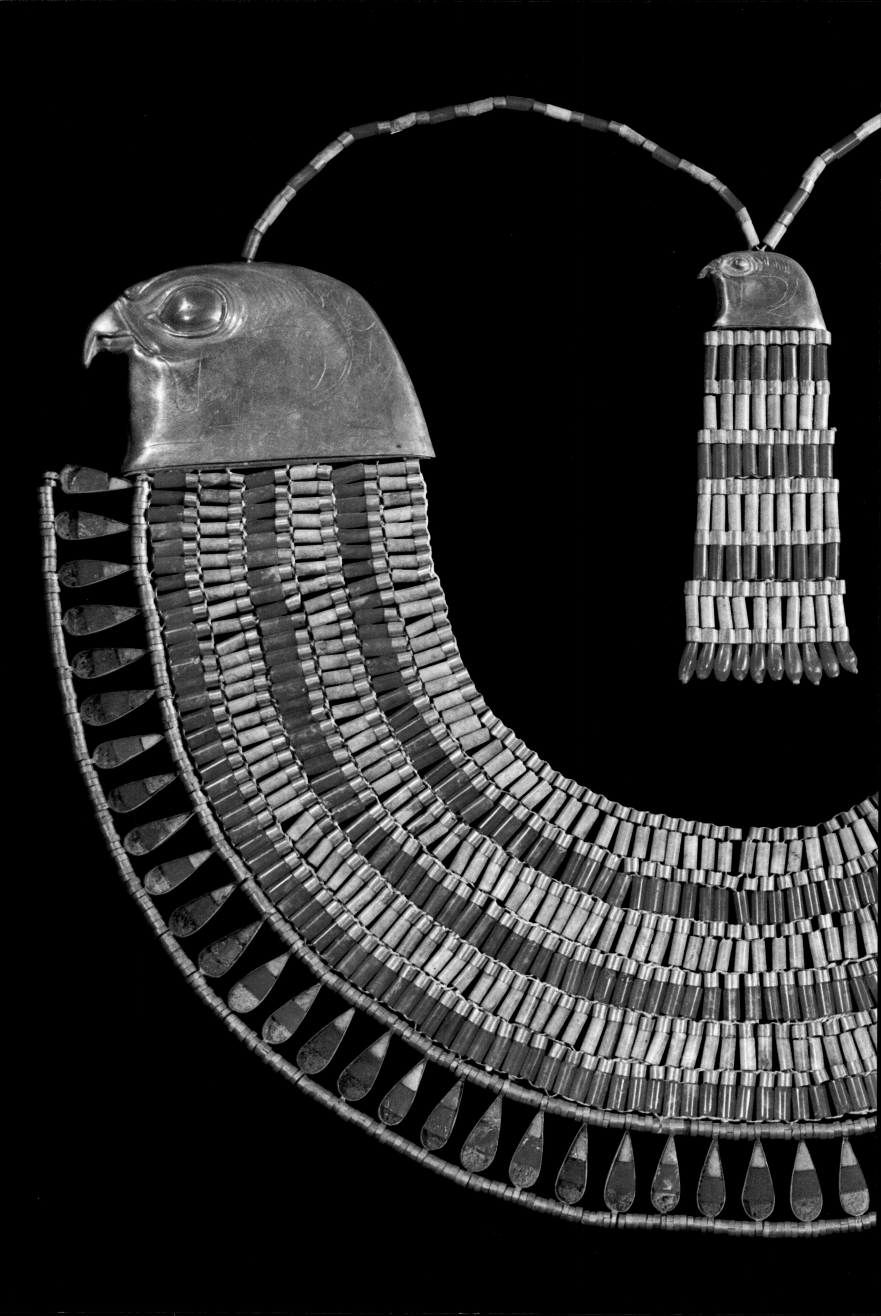

An ornament of enduring popularity

Ever in fashion, the broad collar appears
in every age, on men and women, living
and dead. Nefertari, beloved of Ramses II,
wears one in a painting; a serpent deity
squiggles through her pierced ear, and a
vulture goddess caps her head. For the
living a counterpoise tied at the back
prevented slipping; the dead had no need
of it. Hawks' heads form the shoulder
pieces of this collar strung with beads
of gold, carnelian, and feldspar.

Egyptian beads, unmatched in number
or variety by any other ancient culture,
exert a timeless lure. Long after the last
of the pharaohs, a guide for tomb robbers
bore the title *Book of Buried Beads and
Precious Treasures*. "Mummy beads," real
or fake, still dazzle the tourist's eye.

Jewels had magic: the charm of beauty
and the charm against evil. A mummy,
especially, needed protection. These three
rings, graven with gods, were among
15 found on the mummy of Tutankhamun

The golden filling in a mud pie

Petrie found her tomb in 1914, her body broken, the amulets that guarded it gone. But off in a recess, roiled by floods and finally caked in mud, lay the jewels Sithathoryunet had worn as a princess of the 12th Dynasty. Little golden tubes, a thousand and more, sheathed the plaits of her wig. And on it sat this crown, golden plumes flashing and quivering with every step the princess took. The plumes are a token of the goddess Hathor, whose realm included love and beauty, the desert where gold and bright stones were found, and the miners who gathered them.

The crown's rosettes are worked in cloisonné—the technique of setting stone, faience, or glass within gold *cloisons*, or cells. Cloisonné jewelry, wrote the British scholar Cyril Aldred, "is the chief glory of Egyptian decorative art."

Feathers of cloisonné fill spread wings of the chest ornament from Tutankhamun's tomb. Above a fringe of flowers the pectoral centers on a falcon-winged scarab, composite symbol of the sun god. Falcon claws grasp "infinity" signs; scarab forelegs uphold the left Eye of Horus, symbol of the moon. On the silver moon disk, gilded deities flank the king.

The New Kingdom brought rigid bracelets into style. These, crafted for Ramses II, display two-headed birds and fine gold granulation. Hinges with movable pins made it easy to slip them on the wrists.

**"Taking recreation,
seeing pleasant things. . ."**

Nakht the hunter is a crack shot; his
throw sticks unerringly knock birds out
of the sky as he prepares another fling
at the flapping melee. His left hand holds
a decoy above the papyrus blind; a nude
son, wearing the sidelock of youth,
and an attendant pass the ammunition.
Nakht the fisherman, by contrast, is only
going through the motions. He has no

harpoon, though the fish wait patiently
in the bubble of water at his feet.

Nakht the scribe of the granaries in
the opulent 18th Dynasty surely had no
need to hunt to put meat on the table.
The hieroglyphs make clear the purpose of
this expedition: It is pure pleasure, a family
outing—the women lending a hand to
steady the sportsman. The tomb painting,

never completed, retains an amazing
freshness of color after 34 centuries.

The scene appears often in Egyptian art,
the lord of the tomb afloat on the
marshes, doubling as fowler and fisherman.
There is magic in it, a symbolic conquest
of hostile powers. But also, it expresses
the ageless yearning for a happy hunting
ground, where the season never closes.

Senet, the national pastime

Everybody played senet. Menes, the traditional first pharaoh, knew the game. Nineteen dynasties and some 2,000 years later an artist showed Queen Nefertari sitting down to a game. A humble scribe who lived in her time was buried with the game board below, the playing pieces stored in the little drawer at the end. Tutankhamun must have loved the game; four sets went with him to the tomb. Temple workers scratched game grids on stone, schoolboys drew them on tablets.

The "blessed" ones could play on into eternity—so said the Book of the Dead. The senet board is also a hieroglyph, part of the word for "endure." Despite its enduring appeal, no one in modern times has discovered the rules of the game. The aim, apparently, was to move your flat or conical pieces through the 30 squares and off the board first. Moves depended upon the throw of "knucklebones" (on the board's left edge, below) or sticks. The scribe's board shows a 20-square game of Hyksos origin; the traditional version is on the bottom.

"Hounds and Jackals" vie on the ivory board in another popular game. Presumably the animal pieces raced from the trunk of the palm tree to the crown. By Coptic times an Egyptian die (bottom) had the array of spots we know today.

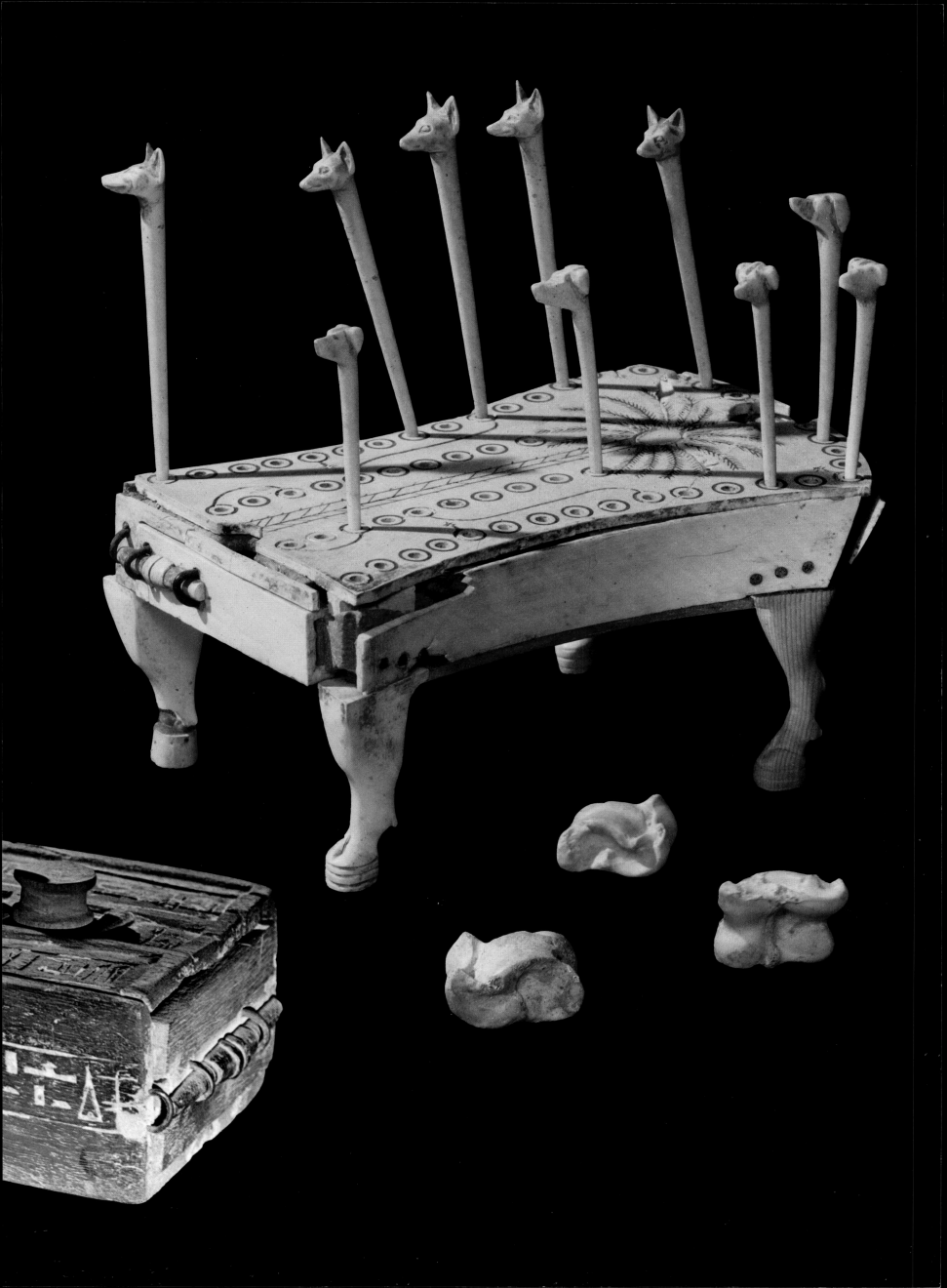

"For your soul. Make holiday."

A banquet begins. The alabaster table balances a pyramid of grapes, bread, meat, birds (some still unplucked), and a bowl of figs. Under the table stand jugs of wine. A maid offers refreshment, napkin at the ready to wipe diners' lips. Waiting ladies sniff each other's lotus flowers; streaked gowns may indicate melting of the greasy, scented cones on the women's heads—though no streaks mar their huge jeweled collars in this 18th-Dynasty scene.

The lotus also lent its beauty to Egyptian tableware; its petals cup the alabaster goblet bearing the names of Akhenaten and Nefertiti, and the gold-rimmed glass goblet. Its foot has been restored, but it is one of the oldest vessels of glass ever found, part of the tableware that Thutmose III gave to three "minor" wives; the sets included the gold bowl and cup, and the silver goblet. The white alabaster bowl and the slender blue bottle also date from the New Kingdom; artisans achieved the popular zigzag pattern by fusing glass rods of different colors into hot glaze. The flat faience dish held unguent cones. Diners did without silverware. Teeth and fingers served as knife and fork.

Partygivers besought the blessings of Bes, the jolly dwarf god of the household, ruler of merrymaking, guardian of women in childbirth, grantor of virility. Here he appears on a casket; more often his image graced the headboards of beds.

On with the dance.

Hand drums held face high, the dancing women in see-through gowns slap and step and bend and twist; plaited wigs flare out as heads snap around. A pair of adolescent girls, dancing in the nude, enrich the rhythm with hand clappers. Three rows of marching men approach, hands high as if cheering in unison. Are they leading a funeral procession, the sarcophagus close behind? Or are they celebrating a joyous event, word of royal acclaim for

their master? Probably no one will ever know. The bas-relief is incomplete, the tomb from which it came, destroyed.

Dancers performed at both funerals and celebrations, and at festivals and parties as well. Women predominated—trained servant or slave girls, lithe of limb, and professional troupers hired for the occasion. They danced in sacred ritual or for the delight of others. Social dancing, boys and girls together, was unknown.

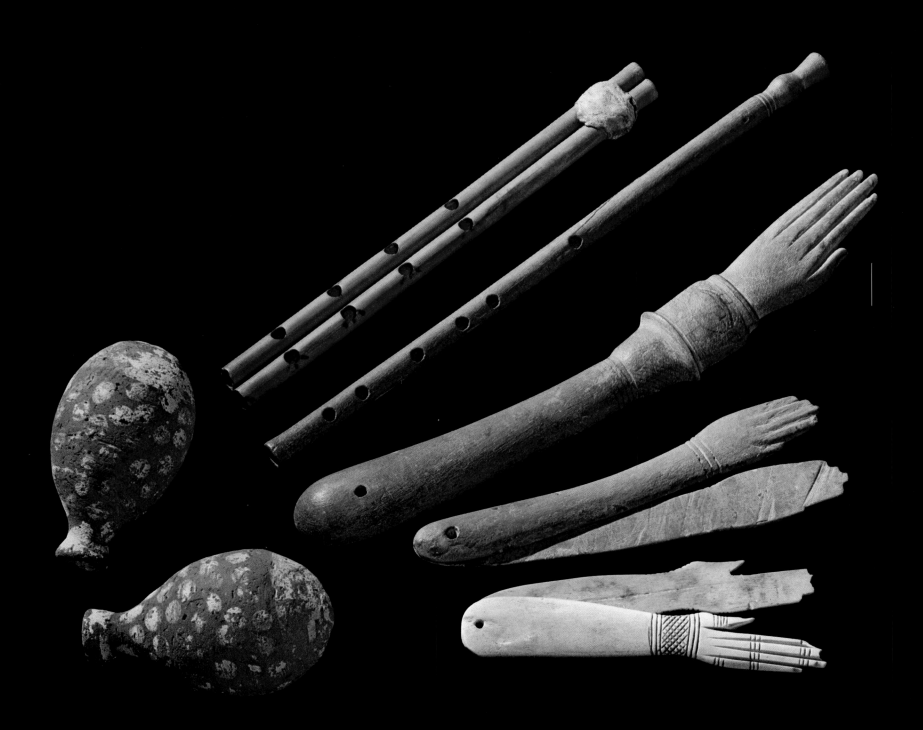

"Let there be singing and music before you"

Any Egyptian could name that tune. It was their all-time hit: the Song of the Harper, a favorite, in varied form, through many centuries. People heeded its lyrics. There was music everywhere—in the air, wafting through the garden on the cooling north wind; in the morning at a rich lady's toilette; at dinner, and long after. Clappers kept rhythm while vintners stomped the grapes; pipers whistled a tune while farmers worked.

The harp, prized above all instruments, was patterned initially after the hunting bow. Often, as in this relief from the 18th Dynasty, a blind man played the harp. With time it added strings and grew in size until—in the reign of Ramses III— one model stood nearly seven feet high. Strings were tuned by winding them more or less tightly around the neck—the pegs used merely as fasteners.

Clappers, the earliest instruments recorded in Egypt, also evolved from a weapon. The earliest clappers had the bent shape of throw sticks. Hunters stalked the marshes, whacked their sticks together to flush the game, then fired them off for the kill. In time clappers came to have the shape of hands. The three shown here were carved of wood and bone (lower). Tomb furnishings often included clappers to scare off evil spirits which, it was well known, had a phobia about noise. Clay rattles, such as those above, and the sistrum— often shaped like a cow's head and shaken in honor of Hathor or to soothe women in labor—added to the rhythm section.

Among the winds, the double clarinet (top), native to Egypt, has kept the same design for 4,700 years—from 2700 B.C. to the present day. The oboe next to it was of Asian origin. Oboes arrived in the New Kingdom, along with lyres, lutes, new harps—and skilled instrumentalists to play them. The New Kingdom orchestra must have been noisier, more exciting to listen to than the earlier ensembles. The melodies did not linger to our time. People played by ear, without notation. An Egyptian trumpet seems to be the only ancient instrument that sounds today as it did to the people who made it. The notes have been likened to a melancholy mooing. To Plutarch, 19 centuries ago, it sounded like the braying of an ass.

Heel over head for the goddess Hathor

Weighted pigtails swing down, arms and legs fly up—harem girls reach a delicate balance in an acrobatic dance, its beat set by clapping hands. The harem leader dances bottom row, center, according to the hieroglyphs. Time has leached some of the color in this relief from the tomb of an Old Kingdom vizier. In later times dances like this one highlighted rituals in the cult of Hathor. "The Pharaoh comes to dance," proclaimed the performers. "Sovereign Lady . . . look how he leaps!"

Pulsing rhythm, youthful bodies so supple and firm—ah, that such visions would never end! This was the driving hope of the ancient Egyptians, and they bet much of their lives and their treasure to fulfill it. Yet the hope remained only that, for who had ever returned from the "land of silence" to affirm the reality? Better to enjoy the pleasures of life now, sang the harper: *Spend the day merrily!*

139

The Gift of Writing

William Kelly Simpson

*It is to writings that you must set
your mind. . . . I do not see an office
to be compared with [that of the
scribe]. . . . I shall make you love books
more than your mother, and I shall place
their excellence before you.*

Thus the bureaucrat Dua-Khety admonished his son Pepy some 4,000 years ago as they sailed south to place the boy in a school for scribes. In so doing, he recognized a central fact of life in ancient Egypt: Though most Egyptians could not read or write, writing was an essential element in their society. Hieroglyphs—pictures of animals and the human body, plus myriad other signs—covered the walls of temples and tombs. And hieratic script, the cursive form comparable to our handwriting, pervaded daily affairs. It filled rolls of papyri in government and commerce and covered the stucco boards of students.

Writing already had a long history in Egypt by Dua-Khety's day, for hieroglyphs appeared in early dynastic times, around 3100 B.C. Scholars believe writing began with pictographs, in which, say, a picture of an ox meant an ox. Next came pictures that represented sounds and concepts. In English, a classic example of this rebus principle pictures a bee and a leaf to convey the idea of *belief.* Egyptians probably adopted the principle from Mesopotamia, where Sumerians had formalized a system of pictographs. There, pictographs evolved into cuneiform, cryptic wedge-shaped signs pressed into clay tablets. But in Egypt, formal hieroglyphs remained little changed for millenniums.

Meanwhile, cursive hieratic developed as the practical tool of communication—first as the script of accountants, with only slight modifications from the hieroglyphs. Then, as it found wider application on papyrus, hieratic assumed a more stylized form. Finally, around 700 B.C., it developed into a shorthand called demotic. Even when the Egyptians themselves eventually forgot how to read hieroglyphs, the demotic script never lost touch with its origins in the pictographs. Thus Egyptian writing preserved a language that, when rediscovered in the 19th century, revealed the history of a great civilization.

The writing also has a tie to us. Sinai workers, mining turquoise for Egyptian masters, put hieroglyphs to alphabetic use in their written language. Scholars tenuously trace some symbols from there into the Phoenician alphabet, ancestor of our own. So our writing, though not our language, has roots in the hieroglyphs.

The ancient Egyptians called their writing "words of the god," a gift of Thoth, the ibis-headed god of learning and writing. Later, the Greeks coined a word that preserved the meaning, hieroglyph—*hieros* (sacred), *glyphein* (to carve). To master the mysteries of the hieroglyphs was to be a scribe.

Scribal teachers poured scorn upon all other kinds of work. Students, usually the sons of officials who were expected to follow in their fathers' footsteps, were reminded that the tenant farmer saw the profit squeezed from his harvest by the landowner. The soldier had to go abroad and leave his family to the mercy of the tax collector. Dua-Khety, in the timeless manner of fathers counseling sons, hammered home the point. "The barber shaves until the end of evening. . . . The bricklayer . . . works outside in the wind with only a loincloth. . . . The weaver . . . is more wretched than a woman, his knees drawn up against his belly." But a scribe! He is, says one papyrus from around 1200 B.C., "the taskmaster of everyone."

Though many a boy might be trained at home by a tutor, the youth of means often went away to a scribal

Egypt's indispensable man

A scribe, still pinching a long-lost pen, sits in traditional cross-legged position, his tightly drawn kilt serving as a desk to hold a roll of papyrus. A masterpiece of Egyptian statuary found in a tomb at Saqqara in 1850, the limestone figure now in the Louvre dates from about 2500 B.C. It may represent Kai, a provincial governor during Dynasty 5 who, like many officials, sought to be remembered for his writing skills.

school. In the Old Kingdom, the schools would be at court in Memphis. In the New Kingdom, each department of the government probably had its own school with a department official as teacher.

Seated on the ground with his palette and inks, his water pot, his case with rush brushes, and his erasing stone, the student practiced some 700 signs that he had to memorize over the course of several years. With these, he wrote down texts prescribed by the teacher. The exercises might include difficult set pieces with the names of foreign countries, parts of chariots, and strange plants and minerals. Or famous stories of the past. Or model letters of correspondence with flowery salutations: "The priest Pramheb . . . inquires after the steward Seti. In life, prosperity, and health, and in the favor of Amun-Re, king of gods! . . . May you prosper, may you live, may I see you again in safety, and fold you in my embrace."

Scribes used various writing surfaces. Flat pieces of limestone from the desert and potsherds served for jottings, business accounts, and literary compositions. Popular with students were writing boards covered with gesso, a mixture of plaster and glue. These could be erased or resurfaced again and again for daily exercises. The standard writing material, however, was papyrus, a paper made by pounding strips from the *Cyperus papyrus* plant into sheets.

Ordinarily the writing moved from right to left. But, as with monumental writing on temples and stelae, it might flow left to right or even from top to bottom for symmetry's sake. It took the deft hands of special artists and sculptors to inscribe temple walls with monumental texts. In unsurpassed workmanship, figures and symbols march across the stone, chronicling a procession of kings and conquests.

After ancient Egypt's eclipse, this writing gradually fell into disuse. Then for more than 1,000 years it mystified visitors. It defied decoding by scholars—until Napoleon's expedition turned up the Rosetta Stone that would present to Jean François Champollion the key to the mystery. The rock slab uncovered near the Delta town of Rosetta bore writing in three scripts—hieroglyphic, demotic Egyptian, and Greek. That the scripts were versions of the same text was quickly confirmed by the stone itself. Scholars could translate the Greek text easily enough. It was a decree made at Memphis in 196 B.C. to commemorate the coronation of Ptolemy V. The priestly assembly that issued the decree resolved to set up copies in the "writing of the god's words" (hieroglyphic), in the "writing of the books" (demotic), and in the language of the Greeks.

The attempt to read the hieroglyphic text with the help of the Greek translation proved more difficult than expected. The word order and writing systems of the two languages differed widely. Imagine trying to understand Chinese if the only clue is a copy of the Declaration of Independence in that language. Some 18th-century scholars, in fact, had claimed that hieroglyphs represented Chinese ideograms.

The first person to find solid clues in the Rosetta Stone was Jean David Åkerblad, a Swedish diplomat. He knew both Greek and Coptic, a later version of the Egyptian language still used in Coptic church services but little understood except by scholars and priests. Coptic was written mainly in the Greek alphabet, supplemented by characters derived from demotic. Concentrating on the demotic script on the Rosetta Stone, Åkerblad succeeded in finding equivalents for some Coptic words, like "Greeks" and "temples."

A decade later Thomas Young, an English scientist who made a hobby of languages, picked up on Åkerblad's work. In 1814 he attacked the puzzle of the stone. Within two years he had broken the demotic into words by matching them with the Greek. He also established from other sources that hieratic was the cursive form of hieroglyphs. But his most important contribution dealt with the significance of the name-oval, or cartouche. He proved that groups of hieroglyphs enclosed by oval rings spelled royal names.

Proud professionals with simple tools

Early scribes plied their art with a writing kit—palette, water cup, and brush holder—similar to the one reconstructed below minus the writing brushes. Stylized as a symbol, the kit became the hieroglyphic word for "scribe." It identifies two workers in this scene from a Saqqara tomb of 2400 B.C. Hollows in the palette held inks of red and black. Pigments came from red ocher and from carbon, the latter often scraped from cooking vessels. Ground to a powder and mixed with gum and water, the material was dried into a cake and placed on the palette. Spare cakes were carried as refills. Much the same way we use watercolors, the scribe dipped his brush in the water, rubbed it on a cake, and made his stroke, averaging ten signs for each dip. He wrote in red for emphasis and to set off titles and headings.

guages, including Greek, Hebrew, and Coptic. In 1822 he startled the world by mastering the hieroglyphs on the Rosetta Stone. His discoveries ushered in the era of modern Egyptology.

Champollion had started out believing the signs were strictly symbolic. But as he matched the characters in the oval rings with the names in Greek, it occurred to him that certain signs must stand also for sounds, that the script was sometimes phonetic and thus in part alphabetic. Using a cartouche found on another text, he compared it to the Ptolemy ring on the Rosetta Stone. Transferring the P, O, and L to the other ring, he recognized the name Cleopatra.

Champollion deciphered other inscriptions and picked out more names—Alexander, Tiberius, Trajan. His final understanding of the Rosetta Stone came, however, with the help of Coptic. Through it, he could assign phonetic values to the signs. The Greek and demotic texts helped explain their meaning.

Although hieroglyphs did not provide signs for true vowels, by the Ptolemaic Period the consonant *aleph*, a glottal stop represented by a vulture, was used for the *a* sound. The noose symbol, representing *w* plus *aleph*, was used to convey the *o* sound. The vowels *i* and *e* were expressed by a reed symbol—consonantal *y*. The hieroglyphs for *d*, the hand, and *t*, a half circle depicting a loaf, were often interchanged, as the sounds are similar. The final half circle and an egg symbol in Cleopatra's cartouche form a feminine ending.

The absence of true vowels makes translation of the earlier writing doubly difficult. It is like trying to understand that "thmnwk" means "the man awoke." In a word like *nfr*—Egyptian for "beautiful"—therefore, scholars arbitrarily add vowels, making it in this case *nefer*, though the Egyptian may have pronounced it nofor or nifir or nufur or a combination of these.

It is not known what insights Champollion gained from Young's work. But in the hands of the dedicated French scholar, the "royal rings" proved instrumental in unlocking the hieroglyphs.

Champollion had a remarkable passion for languages. Born in 1790, he taught himself to read French by the age of five. At 11, shown fragments of papyrus and stone tablets with hieroglyphs, he was told that no one understood their meaning. Vowing to read them one day, he prepared himself by learning a dozen lan-

Individual figures and groups of signs in the Egyptian writing system may stand for more than one word or sound. Some signs are pictographs called ideograms—⊘ can mean "head" or indicate "first." Other signs are phonograms that carry a phonetic value and make up an alphabet of 20 or so single symbols. The picture of an owl 𓅓, for example, indicates the sound of our letter *m*. Some signs represent two or more consonants: a hoe ⌔ equals *mr*. Frequently the end of a word is marked by a special ideogram called a determinative. It designates a type of object or activity—the house enclosure ⊏⊐ which follows the names of buildings, or legs 𓂻 which follow a verb of motion.

For us the system exhibits an extraordinary degree of redundancy. The word "beautiful" can be rendered as the three signs ≋ *nfr*, but this is never done. Instead the sign 𓄤, which stands for the three consonants, is always used. Sometimes the second and third single consonants are added as if to reinforce the obvious. Thus the usual writing of the word appears as 𓄤𓂋. To show that the word applies to a man's name, the signs are followed by a seated figure 𓀀.

With such signs and symbols ancient Egypt left us a varied literary production. Among the earliest examples are the Pyramid Texts, chiseled inside pyramid chambers or painted on coffins. There are also hymns and prayers, rituals for king and temple, guidebooks to the underworld. An incredible amount of papyrus recorded matters as diverse as medical manuals, lawsuits, and trials of thieves. The Hekanakhte letters, written by an absent landowner around 2000 B.C. to his large household, offer a glimpse of business management problems: "As to any flooding on our land, it is you who are cultivating it. . . . I shall hold you responsible for it. Be very active in cultivating, and be very careful. Guard the produce of my grain—guard everything of mine. . . . if my land floods . . . woe to you!"

Generations of Egyptologists have studied this mass of material. From it has come a body of literature we can group as narratives, teachings, and poetry.

Narrative writing developed as a carefully structured craft during the first great age of literature, the Middle Kingdom. Many stories emphasize the virtue of the protagonist and his conduct according to *maat*, the principle of order and truth. Usually a high official, he exhibits the qualities of righteous conduct and the capacity to overcome hardships.

We see the principle at work in the story of "The Eloquent Peasant." Khunanup loads his train of donkeys with trade goods and sets out for the local capital. When he reaches the valley a misadventure befalls him: A low-ranking official covets his possessions and arranges to rob him. The peasant complains to the High Steward Rensi in a series of bombastic but eloquent pleas for justice: " . . . you are a father to the orphan, a husband to the widow, a brother to her who is divorced, a garment to the motherless; let me make your name in this land in accord with every good law—a leader devoid of rapacity, a magnate devoid of baseness, who destroys falsehood and fosters truth, and who comes at the voice of the caller."

The steward, impressed, relays the complaints to the king. Not only is the petty official arrested, but all his possessions are confiscated and given to the peasant. We learn something of Egyptian ethics here. Even a peasant can get justice—if he's eloquent enough!

The "Story of Sinuhe" was especially popular as a school text, copied and recopied for hundreds of years. It commences with the death of King Amunemhet. Sinuhe, one of his courtiers, fears political upheaval will attend the succession. Confused, he flees to Palestine, becomes the trusted aide of a local prince, marries his daughter, raises a family, and prospers.

"It was a wonderful land called Yaa. There were

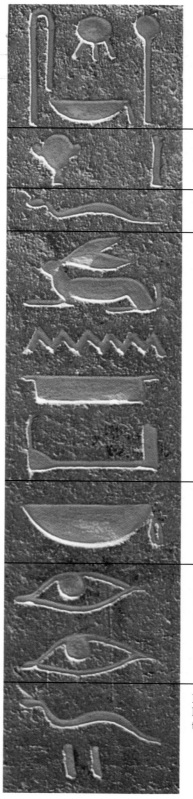

Spelling with pictures

Hieroglyphs usually combine ideograms (signs of things or ideas) with phonograms (signs that indicate sounds). A determinative—a sign to clarify meaning—is sometimes added. On this coffin lid from the fourth century B.C. (opposite), the name of a goddess can be found at the blue sign of the three-tiered throne in the far column. The throne is a phonogram, *st*. Adding vowels translates it into Aset, the Egyptian name for Isis. The half circle and the egg signify female. On the Dynasty 18 sarcophagus of King Amunhotep II (left), the throne resting on the kneeling woman's head readily identifies her as Isis. But in the column facing her, the same symbol preceded by an eye and followed by the seated "god" symbol changes the meaning to Osiris. The detail below, taken from the column behind her, spells out her prayer to the earth god Geb for the dead king: "Illumine his face, open his eyes."

Hook sign and long-handled mace, phonograms for *s* and *hd*, spell the word for illumine, *shd*. The sun is a determinative, the basket a masculine suffix for "you." Literally, "May you illumine."

Face ideogram has value of *hr* and also means *face*. Vertical rod signals "here symbol means what it depicts."

Horned viper is masculine suffix -*f* and signifies "he," "him," or "his."

Desert hare stands for the sound *wn*—the word for "open"—reinforced by the wavy water symbol *n*. Two determinatives follow: Door on its side indicates "open," forearm holding stick adds the idea of "force" or "effort."

Basket: masculine suffix for "you." Coupled with preceding group, it makes the five signs read, "May you open."

One eye is an ideogram that can stand for "see." But two indicate the "eyes" themselves. This pair have the phonetic value of *irty*.

Horned viper: "his." Diagonal strokes indicate the duality of "his eyes."

cultivated figs in it and grapes, and more wine than water. Its honey was abundant, and its olive trees numerous. . . . I spent many years while my offspring became strong men, each man managing his tribe."

But troubles interrupt Sinuhe's peaceful existence. He helps the prince against unfriendly tribes and at one point is challenged to single combat by an envious rival. The episode anticipates the Biblical story of David and Goliath: "There came a strong man of Retenu to challenge me in my tent. He was a champion without equal and had defeated all of Retenu. . . . He took up his shield, his ax, and his armful of javelins. . . . I made his arrows pass by me. . . . I shot him, my arrow fixed in his neck. He shouted and fell upon his nose."

Although successful in his new life, Sinuhe longs for home. He does not want to die abroad and be buried in a ram's skin instead of receiving the elaborate Egyptian burial rites and mummification. He decides to return to Egypt if the new king, Sesostris, will pardon his unauthorized flight.

The king welcomes Sinuhe back in a magnificent homecoming. "Years were caused to pass from my body. I was shaved, and my hair combed out. . . . I was outfitted with fine linen and rubbed with the finest oil. I passed the night on a real bed."

The king constructs a tomb for him with an inscribed and decorated chapel, and Sinuhe happily waits for the "day of mooring," his death. The story has many elements of interest: a description of Palestine around 1960 B.C., the resourcefulness of the Egyptian abroad, Sinuhe's touching homesickness and his reluctance to be interred far away with barbarous burial customs.

No group of literary works was more prized than the instructions of the great sages. In the maxims of the vizier Ptahhotep, the aging official begs the king to allow him to take his son as his assistant and successor. The king agrees but advises Ptahhotep to instruct his son properly: "Speak to him, for there is none born wise." Whereupon Ptahhotep writes: "If you find a disputant arguing, one having authority and superior to you,

Papyrus—creation of genius

Communication quickened in the ancient world with the invention of paper made from papyrus. Superior to the heavy, bulky, clay tablets of cuneiform writing, papyrus paper was thin, strong, flexible, easily carried, and conveniently stored. *Cyperus papyrus* (opposite), a marsh reed of the Nile, furnished the raw material.

First, workers harvested the stalks, as shown in the detail from the tomb of Nefer at Saqqara (above). Then papermakers peeled off the bark and cut the stems into foot-long pieces. Slicing thin strips lengthwise from the pith, they laid them—probably on a cloth—side by side and slightly overlapping (right). On these they superimposed more strips at right angles, covered them with another cloth, and with a mallet beat the assembled strips. The pounding interlocked cells of the strips, making a solid sheet. Then the sheet was set out to dry. A stone, shell, or piece of wood polished it smooth. To form rolls, sheets were stuck edge to edge with a flour paste.

On just what day some inspired Egyptian pounded out the first sheet of paper from papyrus is unknown, but scholars have found an unused roll in a Dynasty 1 tomb at Saqqara. Papyrus spread throughout the eastern Mediterranean, and for 4,000 years it fed the growth of civilizations. So vital was papyrus to the Romans that Tiberius rationed it during a shortage.

Conservation-minded Egyptians often scoured sheets clean for re-use. Their practice of recycling old paper into mummy casings proved a boon to classical scholars. In some casings they found early copies of Plato.

After cheaper pulp paper introduced from China became popular in the Middle Ages, Egyptians abandoned the making of papyrus and lost the art. But in 1962 Hassan Ragab, an Egyptian engineer and former diplomat, began experiments that led him back toward the original method. Today his Papyrus Institute in Cairo turns out papyrus similar to that of his ancestors. With only slightly modernized tools, institute workers hand-made the sample attached to this page from plants cultivated on an island in the Nile.

Ancient Egyptians found more than paper in *Cyperus papyrus*. In a land with relatively few trees, the all-purpose plant became a substitute for wood. People burned the root for fuel or carved it into utensils, and fashioned small boats from bundled reeds. They also plaited the inner bark into rope, and wove it into sailcloth, blankets, and baskets—perhaps one cradled the infant Moses. They even cooked and ate the plant.

Pliny the Elder reported that dried papyrus was used to heal boils, and that the ash from burned paper, "taken in wine, induced sleep."

Little wonder that Lower Egypt early made the plant its official emblem.

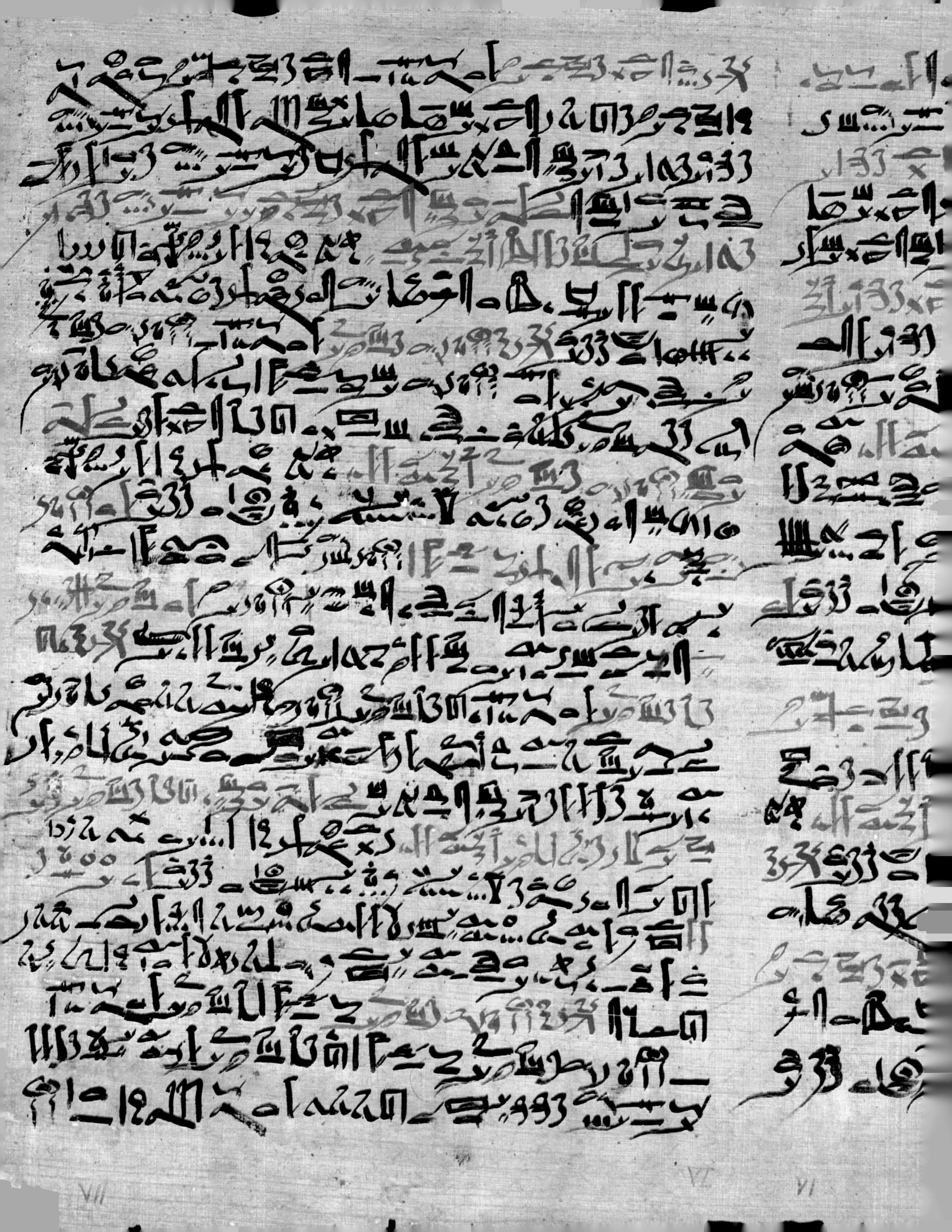

Hieratic: Speedwriting spreads the word

From earliest times scribes rounded off hieroglyphic symbols into a handwriting called hieratic. Using instruments similar to those below found in Tutankhamun's tomb—ivory palette with brushes and ink cakes, wooden brush holder, and ivory burnisher for smoothing papyrus—they employed the cursive script for commonplace documents. The folded letter (right) from Hekanakhte, a landowner of Dynasty 11, is addressed in hieratic to "The overseer of the Delta, Hrunufe." Hieratic also records early medical treatment in the Surgical Papyrus (opposite). Dating from 1700 B.C. but based on writings from the Old Kingdom, the cases were probably drawn up by an army surgeon: "One having a wound in his temple. An ailment which I will treat. . . .bind it with fresh meat the first day, and . . . treat afterward with grease and honey every day until he recovers."

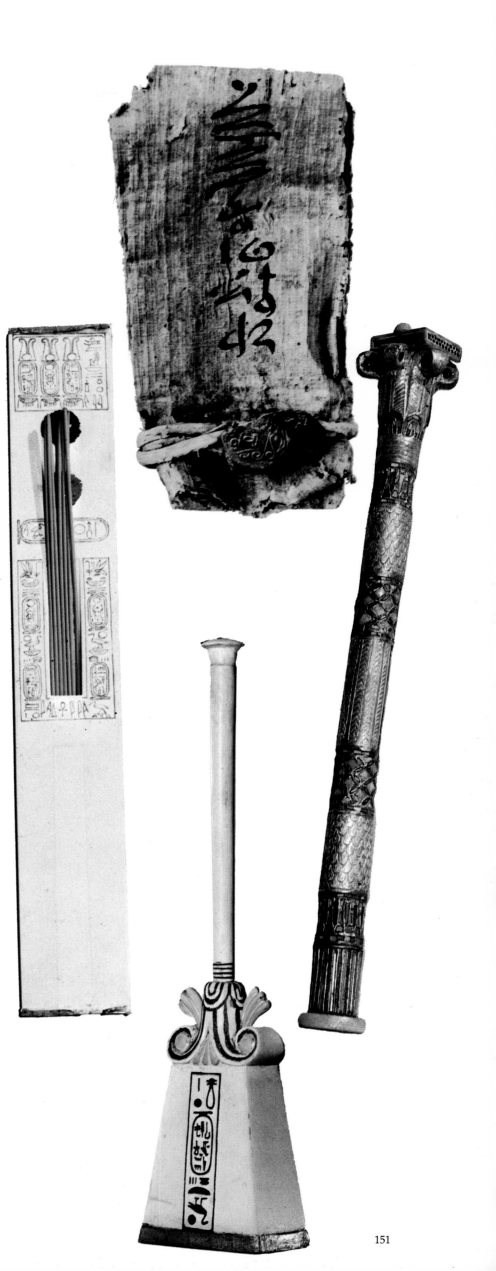

bend down your arms and bow your back; if you disagree with him, he will not side with you. . . .

"If you desire to preserve friendship in a home into which you enter, whether as lord or as brother or as friend . . . beware of approaching the women, for no good comes to a place where this is done. . . .

"If you desire your conduct to be good, refrain . . . from all kinds of evil. Beware of an act of avarice; it is a bad and incurable disease. . . . it alienates fathers and mothers . . . it drives wife and husband apart. . . .

"Do not repeat slander. . . . Repeat only a matter seen, not what is heard."

A thousand years later, the 30-chapter "Instruction of Amunemope" also emphasized proper conduct and ethical dealings. Some of the passages parallel those of the Old Testament's Book of Proverbs.

"Give your ears and hear what is said, give your mind over to their interpretation: It is profitable to put them in your heart." (Proverbs 22:17: "Bow down thine ear, and hear the words of the wise, and apply thine heart unto my knowledge.")

"Beware of stealing from a miserable man and of raging against the cripple." (Proverbs 22:22: "Rob not the poor . . . neither oppress the afflicted.")

Under the New Kingdom, Egypt entered upon an era of cosmopolitanism. Campaigns in Dynasties 18 and 19 penetrated the Levant to conquer or to maintain economic domination. Now, in literature, the soldier replaced the administrative official as a kind of cultural hero. In the tale of "The Doomed Prince," the theme, like that of Sinuhe, deals with the Egyptian abroad.

At the prince's birth several goddesses predict that he will be killed by a crocodile, a snake, or a dog. His father, the king, keeps him safe from these dangers in his youth. But when the prince grows up, he becomes restless for adventure and sets off in his warrior's chariot for the Land of the Two Rivers. At the court of the Prince of Naharain, he wins the hand of the nobleman's daughter by outdoing the sons of other princes in a leaping contest.

Wall-to-wall words of magic fill the antechamber of the Pyramid of Unas at Saqqara. Oldest example of the Pyramid Texts, these "Utterances" helped launch Unas, last king of Dynasty 5, on his perilous journey through the underworld to his place among the gods. Pyramid Texts—funerary literature inscribed in pyramid burial chambers of Dynasties 5 and 6—preserve Egypt's earliest known religious beliefs. Utterances describe the hereafter, offer rituals for the dead, and repeat spells, or incantations, against evil. Hieroglyphic symbols are sometimes altered to neutralize possible peril: the scorpion without its tail and humans lacking bodies and legs.

As a formal script, hieroglyphs changed little through the ages. A thousand years after the Pyramid Texts, Unas would have understood the characters on the Dynasty 18 steatite scarab of Amunhotep III (left). Medallions commemorating the king's latest project, scarabs were circulated like newsletters. This one, measuring more than three inches long, tells of an irrigation project created in honor of Amunhotep's queen, Tiy.

One evening as the young Egyptian sleeps, a snake appears. His wife has set out bowls of wine and beer; the snake drinks and gets drunk, and the wife chops it to pieces with an ax. Later, the youth's greyhound tries to bite him. He flees to the lake, only to encounter a crocodile, who tells him his life will be spared if he can overcome the crocodile's enemy, a water spirit.

Here the manuscript breaks off. Let's assume a happy ending for the "doomed" prince. Egyptians firmly believed that good could triumph over evil.

Mythology abounds in the tale of "The Two Brothers." Humans change into animals and animals talk. And again we find an incident that parallels a Biblical episode, the story of Joseph and Potiphar's wife.

Anubis and his wife live on a farm with his brother Bata. One day when Bata returns from the fields to fetch seed, his sister-in-law suggests they make love while her husband is still out working. Bata refuses and rejoins his older brother. When Anubis returns to the house, his wife tells him Bata tried to rape her. Angered, Anubis hides in the stable to kill Bata.

At sunset Bata returns with the cattle. "The lead cow entered the stable and said . . . : Look, your elder brother is standing in wait for you, bearing his spear to kill you." Bata flees. Eventually, Anubis learns the truth, kills his wife, and casts her body to the dogs.

From this point on, the storyteller's account takes one bizarre turn after another. Bata goes off to Lebanon and places his own heart in the top of a pine tree, having arranged with Anubis to put it in a bowl of cool water if evil befalls him.

In Lebanon, the gods fashion a beautiful wife for Bata. Soon the sea carries a lock of her hair to Egypt. Its scent becomes mixed with the pharaoh's laundry, and he sends out expeditions to find the owner of the hair. In due course, the wife deserts Bata for the pharaoh, who has the pine tree cut down. Bata dies.

Prompted by strange events at home, Anubis seeks out his brother's heart and restores Bata to life. Bata changes himself into a bull in order to kill his wife. She slays the bull, but Bata lives on in two trees that spring up from his blood. When she learns of Bata's new identity, she cuts down the trees, accidentally swallows a flying splinter, and becomes pregnant. Bata is reborn as her son, the crown prince. When the pharaoh dies, Bata ascends the throne, judges his mother/wife, and appoints Anubis his successor.

This story may have been invented to reflect an intrigue at court or to elaborate on the lives of the gods, for Anubis and Bata were familiar deities. Rich and vivid, it is also complicated, in sharp contrast to the simple directness of Egyptian love poetry, seen in these examples from New Kingdom times.

Seven days . . . and I've not seen my lady love.
A sickness has shot through me.
I have become sluggish,
And I have forgotten my own body.
If the best surgeons come to me,
My heart will not be comforted with their remedies. . . .
My lady love is more remedial than any potion;
She's better than the whole book of medical lore. . . .
If I see her, then I'll be well. . . .

Distracting is the foliage of my pasture:
The mouth of my girl is a lotus bud,
Her breasts are mandrake apples,
Her arms are vines,
Her eyes are fixed like berries,
Her brow a snare of willow, and I the wild goose!

This poetry from ancient Egypt, like the wondrous tales and the serious instructions, deserves to be better known. We are familiar with the pyramids, the great temples, the marvelous bust of Queen Nefertiti, the treasures of Tutankhamun. But few people know the enchantment of the stories or the insight into distant times provided by such literary works. The world of Egypt belonged to the kings and the gods with their tombs and temples. But it also belonged to the scribe and the written word, the hieroglyphs.

Pathways to the Gods

Virginia Lee Davis

Take to yourself the Eye of Horus
That you may gain power through it,
That you may gain peace through it
And become a living being, foremost of the gods.

That was the Egyptian formula for immortality. We may not recognize the reference to the eye of a god. But we can see here an idea: transformation. And we can see in "gain power" and "gain peace" the steps leading toward transformation. That inscription could also proclaim the Egyptians' faith in the durability of their monuments. They tried to make their temples and tombs into time capsules for eternity.

The buildings were meant to survive forever and maintain the proper conditions that would ensure fulfillment of the Egyptians' deepest belief. It was a belief we can translate into a bold declaration: "You have not gone away dead. You have gone away alive!"

We see the temple as a house of worship for a god and the tomb as a burial place for a mortal. To us, each building has a different sort of owner as well as a different purpose. Egyptians did not think that way. To them, the gods and human beings did not differ very much. Both had need of a tomb as well as a temple.

This is fortunate for the modern investigator of Egyptian religion. The temples and tombs of men are the more numerous and also the better preserved. Insights discovered in them can be applied to the few and usually battered temples and tombs of the gods.

To an ancient Egyptian, every temple was a miniature replica of Egypt itself and every tomb was a replica of the primeval mound of creation. Everywhere the people could see and feel their religion. And the gods were real, as real as mortal beings.

Enough stones still stand so that we can envision, in the ruins of temples and tombs, what was built by the religion of the Egyptians. But time has worn away the spiritual bridges between them and us. Our eyes are not their eyes, and our minds are not their minds. Yet, to understand the Egyptians, we must learn about the religion that was the center of their lives. We must try to span the gulf between their time and our time, between their thought and our thought.

When we compare our religions to Egyptian religion, we usually don't compare the right things. We want to compare our belief in God to their gods, our kings to their kings. We should compare our God to their kings and their gods to angels and demons.

They saw their gods every hour of the day and night, in sun and moon and stars, in the Nile and its cliffs, in flowers and in animals. And in human beings, for the goal of their religion was the transformation of human beings into gods—or gods into human beings.

Their religion was administered by a bureaucracy under the pharaoh. Officials of the central and local governments could have both political and religious duties. A director of public works might also be a chief of priests. The priests he directed would also be double jobholders. They might work tilling in the fields—and, when called upon, perform work in the temple.

The few ordinary people involved in services were servants, not worshipers. Most Egyptians participated in religion by labor or through "endowments," a kind of tithing with grain, cattle, or other valuables.

It was a living religion. And behind its complex theology lay basic beliefs not drastically different from some of ours. Most of us believe in a relationship between God and human beings. We read in the Bible that we were made in God's image and that we are the "sons of the living God." Noting similarities between Egyptian thought and ours does not detract from the Bible's teachings. We are merely making observations. What we personally believe is another matter.

We observe, for example, that, like us, Egyptians wondered how to deal with the environment. To them, mother nature was unruly and human civilization was orderly. The Egyptians saw this reality in terms of conflict. Heedless nature had to be controlled if people were to build, in the realm of nature, a realm of man: a social order, cities, a nation.

The Egyptians' religion gave them a way to reconcile nature and civilization. The gods had to be tamed and taught to look after the interests of human beings. And people had to learn to be wily enough to take care of themselves and cope with nature.

Temples and tombs were terminals in this ceaseless shuttling between divine and human. No being was complete until it had passed through both transformations as god and man. The transformation of man into god took place within the tomb; the transformation of god into man took place within the temple.

The tombs were the province of gods, who would free the dead from human limitations. The temples were places where people would school the gods in human ways. This idea of vice versa, of things working conversely, ran through Egyptian thought. In fact, one of their frequently used expressions can be translated as "vice versa."

Religion was a rhythm of faith. It resounded in the rituals of tomb and temple. It was a faith that could be seen in symbols and in realities, a faith that tried to achieve a balancing of the powers of heaven and earth. Religion became a veritable way of life, its influence extending to every aspect of human endeavor.

We cannot now "explain" that religion any more than we can fully explain the Christianity of the Middle Ages. Can we fully explain how the Cross symbolizes the entire Christian ethic? We try. And perhaps by trying to understand the Egyptian concept of a single important symbol—the Sacred Eye—we can understand a basic concept of Egyptian religion: the quest for the ideal person.

The ideal person was a composite of parts, and so was the Sacred Eye. Indeed, the eye's name, *udjat*, meant complete, in the sense of having all parts present and accounted for. People wore Sacred Eye amulets to help ensure that they would be complete, with all parts attached and all faculties in good condition. There is an echo of Egyptian thought about "parts" of a person in some of our slang expressions: "He doesn't

"Hail to you, O Eye of Horus"

The Sacred Eye, "which leads on the road of darkness," hovers over a dead man in his tomb. He will be ushered into the underworld by the eye, whose mystical hands hold a bowl of flaming incense. Torn from the great god Horus by his foe Seth, the eye was recovered by Horus's friend, the god Thoth, and became a symbol for things lost and found again, for things made more precious by having been restored. Symbols filled tombs, temples—and minds—of Egyptians. The hieroglyphic sign for Horus was the falcon, bird of all-seeing eyes. As a bird symbol, Horus soared back in time, for the oldest sky deities were falcons.

have all his buttons," "He's got a screw loose," and "She's just not all there."

The Sacred Eye, the most common and still the most mysterious of countless Egyptian symbols, owed its shape to visualizations of the powerful sky god Horus, who had the sun and moon for eyes. He was also what we call the Milky Way and was portrayed as an elongated human, a star-spotted cheetah, or a giant falcon with outstretched wings. So the eyes of Horus could combine the characteristic markings of all three species: the long eyebrow of a human being, the coiled "tear-stripes" on the face of a cheetah, and the tiny cheek-marks of a falcon.

According to a myth about the phases of the moon, the wicked god Seth plucked out the eye of Horus and tore it to bits. But the wise god Thoth stuck it back together again—as if it were just a cracked grain of barley. And so each part of the eye became a hieroglyphic sign for a fraction used in measuring out bushels of grain: ◁ for $1/2$; O for $1/4$; ⌒ for $1/8$; ⊅ for $1/16$; ↘ for $1/32$; ᑊ for $1/64$. When the fraction symbols are put together, the marvelously restored "sound eye" looks like the symbol shown in this paragraph. (Note that if you add up the fractions, your answer is only $63/64$. The missing $1/64$ was the bit of magic needed for cement, the miraculous stuff that makes a dead eye shine again with life!)

In the Sacred Eye, the Egyptians saw the six parts of a well-rounded personality, plump with every sort of power, both heavenly and earthly. This was a creature able to control heaven and earth. Neither the gods in heaven nor people on earth could aspire to such greatness, for the gods lacked earthly bodies and men lacked heavenly powers. Only one person could achieve such perfection: the pharaoh. Other people and the gods, however, could do their part by furthering his interests, for the benefit of all. So it was the pharaoh who shone out of the Sacred Eye.

Since the Sacred Eye with its six parts symbolized a complete person, it seems to follow that a complete

Egyptian should also be analyzed as a six-fold thing. We know that the human body—as well as the human personality—can be divided into as many parts as a physician or a psychoanalyst cares to name. The Egyptians likewise came up with a good many names for "parts." But six words for parts of a person stand out in texts by virtue of their frequency and importance: ⛢ *ka,* ⛢ *ba,* ⛢ ⛢ *khat,* ⛢ *ren,* ⛢ *shut,* ⛢ *akh.*

In what follows, I will be exploring the meaning and significance of these words, though I wish to stress that full understanding of them still eludes us.

There is, however, a beautifully simple approach. How do we recognize a person, an animal, or anything else? By sight, touch, hearing, taste, smell—or by plain old intuition. I suspect that, in Egyptian terms, each part of a being is whatever can be perceived by our five senses and that extra we call our sixth sense.

I suggest simply this: An Egyptian, contemplating a being, perceived its glowing color as its *akh,* its cool shadow as its *shut,* its name as its *ren,* the flavor of its flesh as its *khat,* its odor as its *ba,* and its inner and hidden nature as its *ka.*

Can the Sacred Eye stand for those six parts? I think it can. Using all six (!) senses in my study of Egyptian texts, I reach the following conclusions.

Let us start with the inner corner of the white of the eye, written as ◁. I think this symbolized the ka, the mold that begins the creative process. As this part of the eye cups and shapes the eye, so does the ka hold and guide the personality. For a pharaoh, his ka meant "My majesty has breeding." His lineage, then, by the value assigned to this symbol, was worth at least half of his personality. The first of Tutankhamun's five kingly names, for example, was "Strong bull, perfect of births." The many-worded name stressed the importance of the pharaoh's genetic heritage.

The pupil of the eye, ⬤, had a symbolic worth of one-quarter, an indication of how important to Egyptians was the quality they called the ba. The pupil does for the eye what the viscera does for the body: contains liquid. The ba, representing the inner power that determines the thrust of the personality, also said, in a way, "The pharaoh has guts."

The eyebrow, ⌒, with its one-eighth value, shelters the eye and bends to its every movement. So does the khat, the material substance that sustains the body. Flesh is a kind of khat, for it covers the bones, yet is always flexible. The khat shelters the pharaoh's personality. With their love of puns, the Egyptians would say of the khat, "The pharaoh is a weighty personage."

The outer corner of the eyewhite, ▷, moves with facial expressions, just as the lips move to the sound of a name. And so this eye part, with its one-sixteenth value, represents the ren, the name that characterizes the individual. Always it was said of the pharaoh, "He boasts a great name."

He also "casts a long shadow," and this is acknowledged in the fifth part of the personality, the shut—the dependent shadow that repeats its owner's proportions. The eye part that symbolizes this is the cheetah's tear-stripe, ↘, for, just as the tear-stripe traces the track of tears expelled from the eye, so does the shadow follow the profile of shade cast by its owner.

The vital spirit that animates the personality is the akh, symbolized by the falcon's cheek-mark, ◊. As the sharpness of the cheek-mark heightens the sharpness of the eye, so does the vitality of the spirit heighten the vitality of the owner. This sixth and final facet of the personality has the seemingly smallest value. But in this mere spark is the essence of life.

In these symbols-within-symbols—in the akh as well as in the ka, the ba, and other attributes of personality—Egyptians perceived still other symbols and imagery. Like modern psychiatrists with their probing of id (akh), ego (ren), and superego (ka), Egyptians searched for hidden meanings through wordplay and free association: Why is this word feminine and that word masculine? What does the moon make you think

In the dark of the tomb, life and light

The *ka*—what we might call our conscience or other self—seems to step through the wall of a House of Eternity. Egyptians believed that after death parts of the personality lingered in the tomb. At the feet of the ka were placed offerings on behalf of the body. Three parts of the deceased—the ka, the name, and the mummy—stayed close by. Other parts, such as the winged, soul-like *ba* and the black *shut*, wandered. We see them portrayed in tombs (right). The human-headed ba, a creature of night, flits across the sky with the stars. The inky black shut, shadow of the personality, stalks the dark halls of the mortuary temple. The shiny *akh*, spirit of light, follows the sun by day and returns at night to illumine the tomb with rays of hope.

of? What does the *word* for moon make you think of?

Take the ideas included in the akh, for example. The root-word has so many possible meanings that some authorities wonder if "akh" can even be translated. It may mean the act of being good, or effective, or agreeable, or sacred—or transfigured. The akh is even sometimes thought of as an adolescent girl! This is because akh and other words defining the personality have a connotation of kinship. The ka is "fatherly" and the akh is "daughter-like." From the akh, then, arose the image of an adolescent daughter. She is vital, passionate, sparkling with life—and subconsciously in love with her father.

Also locked within the akh is the idea of a controlling spirit. The idea can be seen by imagining a daughter being taken away from her father, for the good of both.

If you see this aspect of the akh as the stuff of myth and drama, you are beginning to think like an ancient Egyptian. The role-playing words that describe the personality do, in a mystical shorthand, act out religious myths. And from myth, from the magic of words—from the concept of the akh itself—comes the inspiration for Egyptian drama. It is a drama that swirls through the complex life-and-death world of Egyptian thought and religion. It is a drama we can recognize.

The Egyptians believed that a proper play should reflect universal truths. And, as sound dramatists, they realized that a play should be based upon events which ordinary people could understand. Dramatic enactments were basic to all Egyptian ritual. The enactments were associated with cosmic events. And to bring the cosmos down to earth, the Egyptians often used a theme everybody would recognize: robbery.

In the myth-filled drama of the heavens, robbery is what makes the universe go round. Just as a pharaoh loses his crown to a usurper, so does Venus lose its position near Sirius to the waxing moon. But the moon will be pushed aside by the immense sky. The Milky Way will dominate the sky. Then will come the sun, but it will be robbed by the clouds of twilight.

On earth, the drama is also give-and-take. The river in flood robs the banks, the towns and canals rob the muddy floodwater, the land robs mud from the water.

In the heavens and on the earth, events coincide. If everyone on earth performs his or her proper role in life, then everyone in heaven will—to use a favorite Egyptian expression—do likewise. Or, to use another one—and vice versa.

Temples and tombs, the theaters for ritual dramas, are the creations of an intellectual process rooted deep in the Egyptian consciousness. Before men built these stages of stone there was ritual itself—drama that inspired key details of temple and tomb. Before the ritual came the symbols that clothed even the sorriest actor with divine charisma. Before the symbols came the names that defined the character of every actor. Before the names came the images of the gods that filled the weakest actor with godly power. And before there were words or images, there was the source of it all: the primitive thoughts, the basic plots that assigned the roles to gods and people.

Inspiring the religion's complex, long-evolving drama was a simple desire: to solve all the problems and obtain all the comforts of life in this world and in the next. The favorable conditions of life in Egypt practically guaranteed satisfaction of at least part of this desire. And as long as such satisfaction repeated itself year after year, the Egyptians did not waver from belief in their religion. We can still see this faith in the complacent smiles on faces looking upon eternity: "You may rise like the sun, rejuvenate yourself like the moon, repeat life like the flood of the Nile."

The religion's ritual dramas varied little from time to time and place to place. Like the mystery plays of the Middle Ages, the Egyptian rituals were designed to instruct, not entertain. But, unlike performances of mystery plays, Egyptian ritual had no popular audience.

Its audience consisted of the gods themselves. The temple proper was off limits to ordinary people, unless they had been purified by the priests for the performance of specific temple duties.

The priestly actors, with the pharaoh at their head, impersonated such cosmic beings as the planets. But the events of the plays—as we can see in a papyrus "script" that survives—are simple human acts: from plowing and planting and reaping through hunting and fishing and warfare—and birth and death and embalming. The enactments anticipated the real events; the idea behind the play was to help shape these events for the benefit of all, both people and gods.

In what has become known as the Mystery Play of the Succession, the pharaoh enacts, in city after city, his assumption of office. It is a kind of coronation. But it is more than that. The pharaoh had to act out the drama in order for the real event to occur. In a description of a typical scene, the papyrus script sets forth the action in two ways—as a happening and as meaning:

It happened that barley was put on the threshing floor.
It happened that male animals were brought to trample it.
[Stage direction: The animals—sheep and donkeys —are beaten by the officiating priest.]
That means Horus avenging his father.

In Egyptian mythology, Horus, son of Osiris, battles Seth, the murderer of Osiris. Horus and Seth are rivals for the throne of Osiris. Though dead, Osiris is ruler of the world beyond and is resurrected as the seed that becomes grain, the river that floods, the moon that waxes and wanes. Horus avenges his father through an agricultural version of death and resurrection.

In the play, the pharaoh, portraying Horus, tells the animals not to trample the grain (a symbol of Osiris). The animals disobey. (The grain, after all, has to be threshed—sacrificed—if there is going to be any food.) Horus then symbolically beats the animals and, says the script, "Horus speaks to Osiris: 'I have beaten for you those who have beaten you.'"

Near the end of the play, the pharaoh passes out food. A stage direction in the script says: "A loaf of bread; a jug of beer." Thus does food and drink—both the products of "sacrificed" grain—come from the king-god to the people. Kings must die; grain must die. But sons come forth, as do beer and bread, the offspring of a successful harvest.

Only the initiated—officials, priests, royalty—were permitted near the pharaoh during a ritual. But the entire community participated in the feast and celebration as god—and king—paraded through town and country, renewing the intimate connection between heaven and earth and reaffirming the mutual dependence of the two realms.

Rituals everywhere became more and more similar as the priestly organizers improved their techniques and approached what they hoped would be the perfect ceremony. Not so the myths, however. The myths, in which the proper cosmic order is proclaimed, varied greatly from place to place and through the years.

Every important town had its own creator god and its own explanation of how he had made the universe. The environment had much to do with the explanation, and changes in the environment brought changes in the mythology. A gradual change in climate, a shift in political power—these were the typical forces that helped to reshape mythology.

In the marshy Delta area of Lower Egypt, where the perennial task was dealing with wetlands, the people generally turned for aid to the solar gods: the sun, the planets, and the dusty wind off the desert. In the arid valley area of Upper Egypt, where the problem was

A royal barge voyages through time

This 140-foot vessel, buried 4,500 years ago and discovered in
1954, is the oldest ship ever found. Such a ship probably bore
the body of Pharaoh Cheops from his capital at Memphis to Giza,
site of his Great Pyramid. Stowed nearby for afterlife cruising,
it was taken apart and some of its 1,220 pieces were marked with
shipwrights' directions for reassembly. In restoration, the ship
was virtually sewed together with thousands of feet of rope, per
direction. Its timber came from the Biblical cedars of Lebanon.

dealing with dry lands, aid was sought from the lunar
gods: the moon, the sky itself, and the Milky Way.

Politically, the historical pattern was for southerners
to unite Upper and Lower Egypt—the Two Lands—
and then to move north, reigning in a capital in the vi-
cinity of Memphis. There the southerners would come
under the influence of northern culture and would re-
spond to peculiarly northern problems until they
themselves turned into northerners. Or were replaced
by a new wave of rulers from the south.

A theological shift accompanied the political one.
The changeover from lunar to solar worship first developed in the Third Dynasty. The solar theology culmi-
nated in the Fifth Dynasty when it became a matter of
doctrine that all pharaohs were "sons of the sun." (Because of their love of—and reverence for—puns, Egyptians would enjoy the coincidence in the sound and
appearance of those English words.)

Famine and disorder in the First Intermediate Period
put solar worship into eclipse. The sun's prestige was
never quite the same. Not until the beginning of the
Second Intermediate Period did solar worship revive in
the Delta. The revival coincided with the coming of
Asiatics and a breakdown in authority at Memphis.

The founding of the 18th Dynasty and the beginning
of the New Kingdom brought a resurgence of lunar
worship. At the same time, the Valley of the Kings became a royal burial place and temples began rising at
Thebes. Not until the end of this dynasty did solar
worship once more gain precedence.

During later dynasties, Egypt prospered under the
protection of Re, the sun god, and Shu, god of the air
and bearer of the heavens. And it is from this era that
we get a rare and explicit statement about proper order
in the universe:

" 'As for Egypt,' 'tis said since the time of the gods,

"Imperishable Stars" sail the northern sky

Divine constellations cruise the lively night, painted on the ceiling of a burial chamber. Hippopotamus and crocodile precede the goddess Isis. Egyptians split the sky into southern and northern parts, with the Milky Way as the dividing line. They called some stars "untiring" because they ceaselessly rose and set on the horizon. Some were seen as sailors of The Ship, probably our Pegasus. Stars wheeling around the northern sky never set and were "imperishable." These (right) included the bull Meskhetiu, which corresponds to our Big Dipper. Some stars that form our Little Dipper appear in the falcon-headed human who, below the bull, tugs on the axis of the world.

'she's Re's only daughter, and he on the throne of Shu is his son, and no wits suffice to defeat her people, for every god's eye is after her spoilers; herself she'll defeat all her enemies,' say they who look to their stars and know all their spells from gazing on winds."

Egyptians looked to the skies for much of their symbolism. The moon was a white skull, the sun a red face. They saw the night sky as a milk-filled udder. But what we call the Milky Way they saw as an elongated torso. As writing developed, its hieroglyphic signs became sacred and often poetic symbols-for-symbols. The sign for the sun looked like one of their numerous pills. In the winding sign for Milky Way an Egyptian would perceive a writhing serpent. The moon sign resembled a scimitar to slit open the serpent's belly.

To symbolize a cosmic being with tiny hieroglyphic signs was to reduce his awesome powers to manageable earthly dimensions. And to symbolize an earthly being as a composite of all the cosmic entities was to magnify his feeble powers into cosmic dimensions. If the signs were well chosen and evocatively designed, the powers of the heavens would be captured in caricatures made by human beings. Belief in the potency of symbols was a basic tenet of Egyptian religion.

Though the symbols themselves did not often change, the things they represented did. The original eye symbol, for example, was called Iris ("the active eye") and represented the star Sirius. At first Iris was an eye at the edge of the lunar profile. When the moon's path took it near the star, the moon was said to have regained its lost eye. This produced the brilliance of the harvest moon in October.

With the shift to solar worship, all the same symbolism was transferred to the sun. Now it was the *sun* that took a path near the star, regained its lost eye—and attained the blazing power of the summer sun of June.

Eventually, as a pair of eyes came to represent these cosmic events, the symbolism underwent change. The left eye's inner eyewhite looked like the first crescent of the moon as seen in the west at sunset, heralding the beginning of night. The right eye's inner eyewhite looked like the last crescent of the moon in the east at sunrise, promising day.

The left eye, called *mehit* ("the full eye"), became the symbol of the moon; the right eye, *udjat* ("the whole eye"), represented the sun. They were then attributed to the sky god, Horus of the Two Horizons, "amidst the sky, with day his right eye and night his left."

Egyptian imagery was inspired by a belief that paralleled the faith in symbols: Something imagined could produce something real. A proper image reflected a being's power. And the best images, like the best symbols, were to be found in the heavens.

Our eyes see Egyptian images as beautiful and unfathomable. We look at things literally. Yet, hidden in our minds are perceptions beyond sight. We need only a prod from a psychologist to see fantasies in an ink blot. The Egyptian, with the double vision of religion, saw both the object portrayed and, beyond the portrayal, not fantasy but reality.

Look with Egyptian eyes—and see! A pair of swimming cows, only their curving horns visible? See the curves of both horizons circling the vast expanse of a watery blue sky. A pair of cobras, one rearing and one striking? See in their beady eyes and eye-like markings on their hoods the blazing disks of the rising and the setting sun. Now look with insight upon a sacred ibis of snowy plumage, poised to snatch a fish—and see reflected the pale sheen of the moon as it swallows the stars in its path across the sky. A great crocodile with hooded eyes glides through the swamps, evoking the Milky Way's shining grace as it sweeps through the night. Sharp-eyed falcons climbing or stooping in flight re-enact the motions of the planets in their strange wanderings.

Showing earthly beings with cosmic shapes injected the ordinary with mysterious powers. And giving cosmic beings earthly shapes infected the powerful with the weaknesses of their earthly counterparts.

One of the most powerful images is that of the fal-

con. The pharaoh is Horus, and his image is the falcon, which combines within itself the dark colors of the sky, the downy shadows of the earth, the soaring motions of the Milky Way, the swooping orbits of the planets, and a pair of shining eyes for the sun and moon.

Of all the changes that occurred in Egyptian imagery, the greatest was from purely animal forms, through half-human forms, to purely human forms. Such changes went along with the evolution of an urban culture and an increase in population. People competed with animals for space until finally man's only competitor was man and the animal world ceased to be of much importance.

Improvements in tools and technology also had their effect on the details and quality of the images. But no matter the era or the place, manufactured images always were accompanied by living images. These might be certain animals, such as bulls revered in their temple stables as living manifestations of the gods. Similarly, a pharaoh was revered in his palace, built near the site of his proposed mortuary temple.

Both divine animal and divine king were mummified at death and carefully stored away for all eternity. After earthly death, such creatures were believed capable of assuming any form at will.

In "spells"—texts found on coffins—we can read of such changes:

> *Being transformed into a divine falcon. . . .*
> *Taking shape as a falcon. . . .*
> *Becoming a human falcon. . . .*
> *Assuming all forms in the realm of the dead. . . .*
> *Taking shape as Hathor* [a sky goddess often portrayed as a cow] *in the realm of the dead. . . .*
> *Becoming Sobek* [a crocodile god], *lord of the Winding Waterway. . . .*
> *Taking shape as any god that a man may wish. . . .*

To Egyptians, much was possible because they believed in something that would sound familiar to us: "The word is father to the thought." And if one par-

ticular word was right, it would foster a rightness with the universe. That particular word was the name, the ren, of an individual. The feeling was summed up in an inscription: "I am hale and also my flesh; it goes well with me and with my name."

A name had to reflect the character of its owner, and the owner was expected to live up to the name. As usual, the place to look for the best names was in the sky, among the rightly named cosmic beings.

The wider-ranging a name, the greater the effect on a being's character, and the more double meanings or puns, the more power. A resounding example can be found in the name of the great god Amun. Now there was a name that echoed in the heavens!

Representing the hieroglyphic signs for "Amun" as the letters *i m e n* in our alphabet, we can take the god's name apart and look inside it, Egyptian-style. This means looking for anagrams. We find creator (*imen*), herder (*mien*), shelterer (*inem*), shouter (*nemi*), grasper (*meni*), and wanderer (*niem*).

At first nearly every province in Egypt had its own name for its creator god. As the country was unified, each successive unifier brought into prominence his own local creator god. The sun god Re of Heliopolis—"City of the Sun"—attained his greatest power during the Old Kingdom. His power radiates in the names of pharaohs: Khafre (Chephren) is made of signs that mean "Re is his glory," and Menkaure (Mycerinus) translates as "Enduring is the solicitude of Re." Two of the wondrous pyramids at Giza rose as monuments to the greatness of those pharaohs.

But Re faltered. The Old Kingdom fell, and the records lamented: "The wrongdoer is everywhere. . . . The robber is a possessor of riches. . . . He who possessed no property is now a man of wealth. . . . Jewels are fastened on the necks of slave girls. . . . The children of princes are dashed against walls."

In the Middle Kingdom, when order was restored by a centralized government from Thebes, the new era

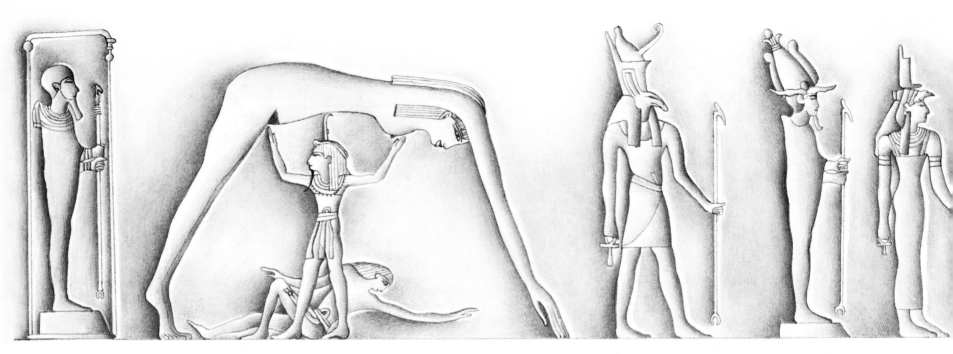

| Ptah | Nut | Shu | Geb | Seth | Osiris | Isis |

brought new gods to the fore. Again we can read the rise of the gods in the names of the rulers.

Pharaohs who bore the name Mentuhotep, for example, were saying, "Montu is content." As well he should be. Montu had been a local deity of a small town. When he became a favorite of pharaohs, Montu wore the falcon-head attribute of Horus and was worshiped as a war god.

Other gods were also arising. In Sobekhotep's royal name we see that "Sobek is content." And in the name of Amunemhet the message is that "Amun is in front." Sobek, a god in the form of a crocodile, began humbly as a divinity worshiped in a couple of places. Amun had been one of eight gods in a creation myth that had developed in a place called "the [town of] eight" in central Egypt. Linked to pharaohs, though, Sobek and Amun would become national deities.

Sobek's original cult center was Crocodilopolis in the marshy area of the Faiyum in Upper Egypt. As a god associated with the pharaoh, Sobek also joined company with the great god Re. Honored in a hymn as Sobek-Re, he soared out of the swamps and into the heavens, a sky god. The hymn hails him as "the great god whose eyes emit the two disks of light, whose right eye shines by day and whose left eye shines at night, whose two large eyes light up the darkness."

Amun too became associated with Re; Amun-Re was "the god who begat a place in the primeval ocean"—the creator of the primeval hill, the source of all life. Infused with such divinity, pharaohs bearing Amun's name could claim power over the Nile. They could also boast:

"I was one who produced barley and loved the grain-god. The Nile respected me at every defile. None hungered in my years, nor thirsted in them. Men dwelt [in peace] through all that which I wrought."

But the alliance of pharaoh and god could not prevail forever. Once more the realm fell apart and barbarians infiltrated Egypt; once more the old order gave way to

"Hail, you gods! I know you as I know your names"

With this salutation, an Egyptian worshiper might address these gods and goddesses—beholding them from right to left, the way illustrations and hieroglyphs were displayed on temple walls. These super-beings had many, often conflicting roles. But they sustained a belief of god and people: "You will not disappear."

"Amun-Re, king of the gods. 'Hidden' is his name as Amun. 'Approachable' is his name as Re." He began as Amun, patron of Thebes, and he rose with the princes of Thebes when they took the throne. Linked with the ancient sun god Re, he became the chief deity of the Middle and New Kingdoms.

"I am **Thoth** [the moon], who brings **Maat** [true order], and heals the Sacred Eye." Scribe of the gods, inventor of writing, math-minded reckoner of the calendar, Thoth was a god of many talents. As the moon, he helped rule time; as a magician, he knew the secrets of healing. And as lord of wisdom, he was associated with Maat. The administrator of justice, Maat wears in her headdress a lone feather, which embodies the delicate balance between order and chaos in the universe and in human souls.

Anubis, "claimer of hearts," had a jackal's head because, like those scavengers who roamed graveyards, he communed with the dead. But, as god of embalming, he helped the dead gain eternity.

Min, god of fertility, holds a flail that symbolizes kingship in Upper Egypt and wears a crown that ties him to Amun. Behind him grows stylized lettuce, a reputed aphrodisiac sacred to Min.

Hathor, motherly "queen of all gods and goddesses," originally was worshiped as a cow. (She wears cow's horns cupping the sun.) A special goddess of women, she blessed dancing and drinking.

Horus, "the great god, the lord of heaven," shared his divinity with the pharaoh. A sky god with falcon head, his eyes were the sun and moon. In one myth he is the son of **Osiris** and **Isis.** The myth, which spiraled through time in many versions, gave people hope in an afterlife. The basic story has royal Osiris killed by **Seth** and hacked to pieces. Isis finds them. Horus, fighting Seth, loses an eye. It helps restore Osiris, who reigns as god of the netherworld and judge of the dead. Seth survives as a god of violence. Isis becomes the divine symbol of a loyal wife.

A three-god tableau portrays creation. Re, solar father of **Nut,** the sky, decides to put a stop to her continual embracing of **Geb,** the earth. Re slips **Shu,** the god of air, between them, thus making space. But Nut managed to have children, including Osiris.

Ptah, "maker of substance," was at first a local creator god in Memphis. He gained prominence as his city did, becoming known as the ultimate source of all things—"the creator of gods."

Horus   Hathor   Min   Anubis   Maat   Thoth   Amun-Re

the new; once more new gods supplanted the old. New Kingdom rulers turned from lunar gods to solar gods, as shown by the changes in royal names. "Thutmose" celebrated the birth of Thoth, the moon or lunar eye and lord of wisdom. A successor, Akhenaten, chose a name that celebrated Aten, the sun-disk god. Akhenaten, whom we will meet in the next chapter, would fail as a religious reformer. A new dynasty, brandishing a new name, would revitalize the old god Re. In the name of Ramses was the message: "It is Re who bore him." And the gods indeed seemed to bless the Ramessides, who restored for a time the powerful state that had been weakened by Akhenaten.

The names of the gods themselves often merged—as in Sobek-Re and Amun-Re—with the lesser god borrowing prestige from the well established sun god Re. But there was something more at work in the name Amun-Re. Egyptians wanted to combine—and contrast—all important cosmic functions within a single god. Amun, originally "the hidden one," needed to get a solar attribute. So he became the hidden midnight sun, in contrast to the brilliant noonday sun, Re.

Atum-Khepri, like Amun-Re, was a merger. Atum, "who is in the evening," represented the vanished sun beyond sunset. Khepri, the sun of morning, emerged from the maze of Egyptian speculation about the cosmic connections between things. The god also can be traced to the Egyptian tendency to see the cosmos everywhere—even in the dung of their livestock.

Egyptians were fascinated by the scarab beetle. Standing on its front legs as if doing a handstand, the beetle churned dung with its back legs and formed a ball. The beetle, its gaze not on where it was going but on where it had been, propelled the ball backward toward a burrow. Surely, the Egyptians thought, there was something to this. They decided that what they watched was an enactment of the rolling of the sun, which moves from east to west while the heavens appear to move from west to east.

Beetles were also observed emerging from the earth as if they had come into existence spontaneously. (Actually, they had hatched from eggs deposited in dung buried in the ground.) Pondering this marvel, Egyptians saw it as self-creation and linked beetles with the creator god Khepri. He was also portrayed as the rising sun, and so, as "Khepri in the morning," joined Re.

By the kind of semantic coincidence that the Egyptians revered, the words for the name of the god and the name of the beetle—along with the words for regeneration, creation, and existence—all had similar sounds. In writing, the hieroglyphic sign representing such concepts was 𓆣, the beetle. Thus a single sign could stand for an idea as complex as "to come into existence by assuming a given form."

The beetle symbol, known as a scarab, became a popular object of many uses. It was a seal, a good-luck charm, a commemorative, a jewel tucked in a mummy's wrappings, even a kind of greeting card sent to a friend and inscribed with "Peace of heart is better than anger" or a wish for "A good year."

Just as Khepri could be the "divine beetle" and, as a scarab, become common, so could divine names enter the lives of ordinary people. A person might be named "Re is content" or "Amun is her riches." But quite often names were the vessels of parental love. "Beautiful morning" recalled the happiness of a boy's birth. A daughter would be wryly named "Ruler of her father." The dead came back in such names as "The brothers live" or "His father lives." Or in the plea of a grieving widower's name for his daughter: "Replace her."

Though death inspired grief, the mourners knew that life went on, even for the dead. There was a connection that spanned the now and the hereafter. Sometimes there was even a one-way correspondence. One widower felt he had suffered too much after his wife's sudden death. He suspected that somehow, from the grave, she had managed to produce his wretchedness. After having "lost all gaiety for three years," he wrote

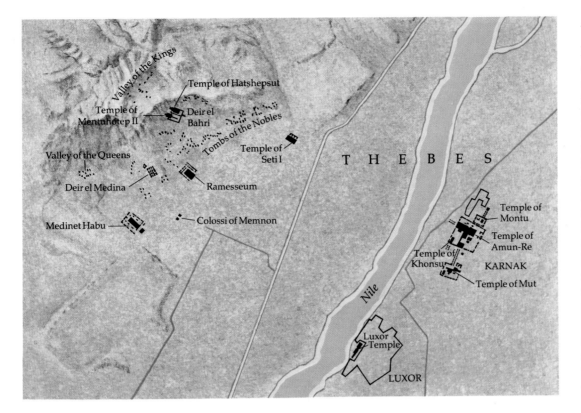

Labels on map: Valley of the Kings · Temple of Hatshepsut · Temple of Mentuhotep II · Deir el Bahri · Tombs of the Nobles · Valley of the Queens · Temple of Seti I · Deir el Medina · Ramesseum · THEBES · Medinet Habu · Colossi of Memnon · Nile · Temple of Montu · Temple of Amun-Re · Temple of Khonsu · KARNAK · Temple of Mut · Luxor Temple · LUXOR

"Thebes is a model to every other city"

Here on the Nile stood a proper kind of city: houses of the living on the sunrise side of the river, houses of the dead in the western desert. Processions could thus shuttle between temple and tomb, investing them with the mystique of the sun's own daily circuit. Dots indicate the tombs of New Kingdom pharaohs, queens, and high officials. Some tombs were cut in the side of a mountain that forms a natural pyramid over them. Mortuary temples, such as that of Ramses III, rose at the edge of the canal-laced cultivation belt. Thebes embraced the area from modern Luxor, built around an ancient temple, to Karnak, the site of massive temple ruins and colossal monuments.

Temple architecture (cutaway opposite) aided processions. No obstacles met the sacred bark on voyages from its chamber, through columned hall and courtyard to the thronged avenue of sphinxes.

her a letter and deposited it at her coffin. In his words we can hear the voice of an Egyptian who utterly believed in the existence of life after death.

"What harm have I done you that I should be the poor man which I am?" he wrote. "Why have you set your heart on weighing me down, I who was always your faithful husband?" He reminds her of the goods he rained on her, alive and dead. He ends with a threat of "evil action . . . if you do not let my heart gladden." For he believed he could manage to reach into the afterlife and give her a bad time too.

Bargaining with the dead and the gods was a basic part of life. The object was to incarnate the gods in human form and resurrect the dead as gods. The transfer points of this cosmic stock exchange were in temples and tombs. These were not merely structures but massive symbols proclaiming the mystic unity of the dead and the living, the divine and the human, the power of nature and the cunning of civilization.

Egyptians began building for the next life as soon as they were well established in this one. The work often continued through a lifetime, sometimes with many changes of plan. If the builder died before the job was finished, his heir was supposed to carry on. A New Kingdom pharaoh would have both a mortuary temple, located next to his palace at the edge of the cultivated land, and a tomb hidden several miles away in the Valley of the Kings. Lesser folk combined tomb and temple structures in a single monument, often no more than a simple grave with a place outside for offerings.

Royal tombs achieved their greatest splendor in the era of the Old Kingdom, when the great pyramids rose at Giza. The pharaohs' tombs then slowly declined in size and religious importance. Conversely, the temples for the gods, which started out small and comparatively insignificant, grew bigger and more magnificent, dazzling the New Kingdom. Though royal power also reached its zenith then, the pharaohs were never able to match the grandeur of the gods.

The temples and tombs, in their architecture and in the names of their parts, conjured up a symbolic landscape of the Nile Valley. The architectural imagery was designed to control the floods of the Nile. The temple's courtyards portrayed open reservoirs for the distribution of godly powers. The tomb's caverns symbolized sealed whirlpools in which human powers were concentrated. Each temple courtyard was built as a barren desert that would suck fluids from the heavens. The tomb was seen as a pool that would gather earthly floods. Thus the waters of heaven and earth were churned together in a flood beneficial to all.

As we enter the temple's hypostyle hall, it is relatively easy to imagine a fertile marshland, for the pillars are arrayed like reeds and carved and painted to resemble papyrus or lotus. The symbolic marsh itself symbolized perishable food that would make the gods dependent upon their human servants. Offsetting this idea, as usual, was a vice versa: The tomb's storage rooms symbolized dry, preserved food that would make the dead independent of the gods.

Similarly joined were the images of the temple shrine, built to suggest a lowland where the barley grew, and the images of the tomb shrine, suggestive of an open highland where wheat ripened.

The profiles of the buildings also contributed to the symbolism. The long, relatively narrow temple imitated a channel in which the godly spirit would be submerged and the coming flood of the Nile would be confined. The mound shape of the tomb suggested the boosting of the human spirit—and the image of heaps of river-borne silt that would be the seedbed of grain.

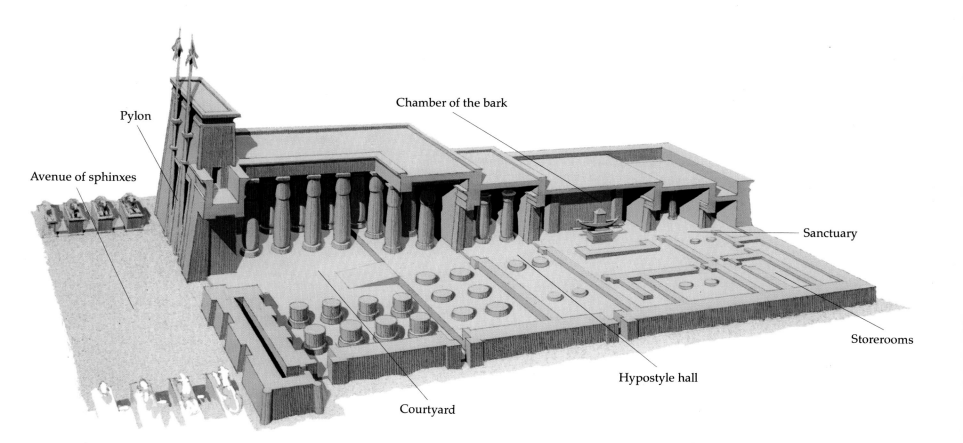

Avenue of sphinxes

Pylon

Chamber of the bark

Sanctuary

Storerooms

Hypostyle hall

Courtyard

Thus were the needs of field and stream clearly communicated to all the cosmos.

The symbolism was translated into words put into the mouth of the Nile. He boasted of his year:

> *The Floodtime's mine, the Slacktime's mine,*
>   *by me is runoff made;*
> *The water's tongues upon my mouth,*
> *The silt's my form at time of Flood,*
> *The runoff's sweat from out my flesh,*
>   *by me are month feasts made. . . .*
> *I am the whole, the whole I am. . . .*
>   *for I am Nile.*

To a modern reader, such elaborate personification of a river is merely poetic imagery. But the ancients took their metaphors most seriously. Indeed, they ran them into the ground, quite literally, in the form of colossal monuments. To them, the river was a living being and its surrounding landscape was another.

Temple and tomb were more or less stylized reproductions of that landscape—and so they must be living beings too, with doors for mouths and windows for eyes. (The word for door is in fact identical to the word for mouth.) Although modern skyscrapers are often described as phallic symbols, we do not call them that and do not ordinarily think of our buildings in that way. But for Egyptians, such thinking about inanimate objects was as normal as breathing.

The temple shrine originally was designed to suggest the profile of a jackal, with the door for a mouth, the gateposts for ears, and the sloping roof for a back. A later tomb shrine of more angular form, was described as a squatting jerboa (a small rodent that looks like a kangaroo), with the pointed roof for a sharp nose, the sloping sides for a slender body, and the broad base for powerful haunches.

Similar creatures in Egyptian myth are said to swallow up the Nile god and other dead things at the time of drought and famine before each new year's flood. An important part of Egyptian religion was devising ways and means to make these creatures vomit forth—like Jonah's whale—the precious things they had taken. Thus would the dead come up from the mouth of the grave and thus would the life-giving flood come forth from the mouth of the river.

There was magic in what they believed—the kind of magic that could tame the gods, that could hold the Sacred Eye together. And the magic happened often enough so that a civilization flourished. If we do not see gods today, we at least remember a people who believed they had potential for divinity. They proved, of course, how human they were, for ultimately their magic failed. In the portfolio that follows we will visit temples long in ruin and tombs long emptied.

The mortuary temple of Amunhotep III, probably the wealthiest pharaoh ever to rule, disappeared almost entirely. His successors stole the stones, the pavements of silver, the doorways of gold. We are left with hardly more than his claim that he had built "an everlasting fortress, a possessor of eternity."

We skeptical modern folk may scoff at his boast. Neither temple nor tomb succeeded in possessing eternity. But if we remember the Egyptian belief that the preservation of a name guaranteed the preservation of the being, we must conclude that something more than ruin has endured. One tomb was named, "Enduring is the beauty [of Pepy]." Pepy is no more; the rest does endure—as "Memphis." The name of one temple was the "Mansion of the ka of Ptah." The name was transcribed as *Aigyptos* and became our "Egypt." You, reading this, are keeping alive the Egyptians' eternity.

Stone sentinels for a mighty god

Ram-headed sphinxes line the processional avenue before the Temple of Amun-Re on the east bank of the Nile at Karnak. Here, adorned by temples, was the northerly part of Thebes, a capital of empire and city of Egypt's patron deity.

Amun, who evolved from a wind god to the king of gods, took the ram as his emblem. A symbol of fertility, the ram also projected power. When the pharaoh took his army into battle, one of his divisions carried the ram's standard.

The sphinx, a creature of parts, was usually a lion with a man's head. In this version, the sphinx honors Amun with its head. The rest of the body becomes "the celestial lion throne of Re." Thus the merged sun god Amun-Re gets homage from a merged animal. Between the lions' paws stand figures thought to be Ramses II, creator of the avenue of sphinxes. In its glory, 124 sandstone animals crouched along the great sacred way, which ran from a temple gateway to a landing quay on a canal leading to the Nile. Here processions could embark for the city of the dead.

Now some 40 sphinxes guard Amun-Re, "the teacher, the maker of things." But things made for him still evoke his majesty here, drawing pilgrims to Thebes and its monumental splendors.

Overleaf: A temple's mystic landscape

This pylon gateway, "the horizon from which Re goes forth," conjured up the sight of two mountains, between which the sun would rise. Such a temple was called the horizon of the god.

Ramses II built this entrance to the temple complex at Luxor, southern part of ancient Thebes. He preserved his colossal vanity in stone: six statues of himself and two obelisks inscribed with his accomplishments. He sits now in double majesty and, crowned but ravaged by time, stands amid the rubble of his granite clones.

Only one obelisk remains. The other was carried off to Paris in the 19th century and stands in the Place de la Concorde. The one here is 82 feet tall and weighs about 250 tons. Paired obelisks, each topped by a pyramidion, recalled an ancient solar cult. The tips were gilded to flash in the sun's light.

Holes in the pylon mark sites where "flagstaves reaching to heaven" bore brightly colored banners.

Symbols bloom in the garden of the gods

"Hail to you, Field of Offerings!" said those who walked in the temple courtyard. The only area of the temple open to the public, it was a place where offerings were deposited. Some were for the gods and some were for the dead. Other symbolic offerings appeared on the columns that towered like giant plants in the stone-floor field.

"Lilies," representing produce of the southern valley (Upper Egypt), grow from a pillar in the Temple of Amun-Re at Karnak (left). Papyrus flowers open atop columns of the temple colonnade at Luxor (right). Papyrus of the northern marshes symbolized Lower Egypt.

Ramses II, who completed the colonnade, sits before it on a throne, a symbolically tiny female relative below his elbow. He wears the double crown of the two Egypts and the uraeus cobra for the goddess of kingship. It came to symbolize the power of the pharaoh.

Inscriptions on the 52-foot columns, many of them too high for people in the courtyard to read, were instructions to the gods, who presumably could see them—and learn from human beings.

Another lesson tops the floral pillar (left). The name of Thutmose III is attached to the flower "at the very junction of heaven and earth." The pharaoh's name is in a cartouche. Once that symbol was circular, representing the sun and its heavenly realm. Stretched to an oval to enclose the royal name, it proclaims to the gods on high that the pharaoh reigns over "all that the sun encircles."

Overleaf: Tribute for a god "Great of Awe"

Ruins of the Temple of Amun-Re, largest columnar structure ever built, shimmer in the waters of its sacred lake at Karnak. Probably begun during the Middle Kingdom, the shrine was still being enhanced in the Ptolemaic Dynasty some 2,000 years later. Miles of painted reliefs covered the walls of the temple, which was 1,200 feet long. Its interior glowed with color: blue ceiling flecked with yellow stars, columns green, obelisks red, floors black, and walls white.

Etched in sky and water are, from left to right, remains of the monumental pylons leading to the courtyards; jagged remnants of the hypostyle hall; a 64-foot obelisk erected by Thutmose I, and a 97-foot one sponsored by his daughter Queen Hatshepsut.

The sacred lake provided holy water for priestly ablutions and rituals. The god's bark floated here on festival days. Symbolically, the lake recalled the fearful primeval flood "before men existed, before gods were born."

Reaching "to the height of heaven"

A field of columns thrusts to the sky in the hypostyle hall of Amun-Re's temple at Karnak. A colossal pharaoh stands nearby, his queen between his feet. In this fabulous world of giant metaphors, the hall is a field where dramas of creation take place. Here, say the tracts, the barley stands 7 feet high, the wheat 12 feet, and there are spirits of the afterlife tall enough to reap the great crops.

The real statistics sound awesome enough: The hall is 330 feet long and 170 feet wide, covering an area of about 56,000 square feet—big enough to hold the Cathedral of Notre Dame of Paris. The 12 tallest columns, each 79 feet high and 12 feet in diameter, raised the roofing slabs of the central nave above the level of other columns. This allowed light and air to enter through rows of stone-grilled clerestory windows, such as the one here. A total of 134 pillars supported the hypostyle hall.

The 32-foot statue in the courtyard stands as the "Unknown Pharaoh" while experts debate whether he is Ramses II and the miniaturized queen Nefertari. Some say he is Pinedjem, priest turned pharaoh, who put his name on a predecessor's sculpture.

Overleaf: Walls that tell royal tales

Great deeds of Ramses III emblazon his mortuary temple at Medinet Habu. Attendants with plumed sunshades and an incense burner lead a regal procession. In life, the pharaoh thus paraded here "to behold his father Amun-Re" on feast days. In death, the pharaoh still parades the stone. On the pylon beyond, he hunts the wild ass and antelope of the desert and (below this scene) the wild bull of the marsh. Archers guard him as, daringly poised on the tongue tree of his chariot, he drives his spear into his third kill of the hunt. Birds and fish dart in the papyrus thicket where the bulls fled for refuge. Such realistic scenes, by proclaiming the pharaoh's might, helped protect the temple, itself a refuge for Ramses after his death.

A mystic menagerie of beastly gods

Egyptians cherished animals and even mummified those deemed sacred. The cat portrayed Bastet, goddess of happiness. The pet *miu*—house cat—led a life blessed by Bastet. And when a miu died, its owners shaved eyebrows in mourning.

The falcon, sky-god image of mighty Horus, soared as the sign of the pharaoh. The stylized plumes and cobra-prowed uraeus of the falcon's crown join bird and serpent, symbols for the union of kingship and divinity.

Beast and man merge in the ram-headed god Harsaphes—"He who is on his lake." Name and image link the god to fertility, which popular notions associated with water and the virility of male sheep.

The hippo, here adorned with plants of its habitat, may have symbolized the struggle against the evil god Seth. Hippos were also sacred to Taueret, divine midwife and goddess of pregnant women.

The mongoose, here in bronze as a temple offering, was revered in some areas as a snake-killer but was hated for eating crocodile eggs in places where that animal was worshiped. The crocodile, as the ferocious god Sobek, wears ram's horns—and Maat's ostrich plumes, which show Sobek's link with order.

"Serve the god that he do the same for you"

The epigram helps explain why pharaohs took care of the gods. Rituals were performed in reality and in temple reliefs such as these. Amun-Re (opposite) gets clean clothes, and hieroglyphs record the helpful pharaoh's pun: "I have come not to dismantle the godly mantle . . . but to rehabilitate the godly habiliments."
The pharaoh (above) delivers a trayful of round bread, roast fowl, grapes, figs, and a pomegranate. As he perfumes another feast (left), incense pellets defy gravity to make a pleasing pattern. Wine jugs stand between four altar pedestals holding food offerings that include ducks and haunches of beef. Amun-Re, thus coaxed to give "all life," obligingly replies, "I have given you all that is splendid."

Overleaf: A cruise for father Amun

"Pharaoh conveys him who begot him," decrees another ritual performed by the ruler to honor his father the god. On the wall of a shrine in the Temple of Amun-Re at Karnak, a pharaoh obeys. Carrying an incense burner, he leads priests who bear a sacred bark. Its ram-headed prow and stern mark it as ancient Amun's. In processions, the statue of the god was taken from the temple and placed amidships in the bark. The shrine is hard to see on the wall, as it would be to watchers. Fine linen enwrapped the shrine, concealing the god who began as Amun, "the hidden one."

A shrine for rites of renewal

This exquisite sanctuary witnessed
a pharaoh's jubilee. Sesostris I had it
built for his *sed* festival, a rejuvenation
of his role as link between the human
and the divine. He ruled—"with his
strong right arm, a man of action"—from
1971 to 1928 B.C. At some time, probably
the 30th year of his reign, he had his
festival. "Come in peace, O Sesostris,"
says an inscription, "that you may see
your father, Amun-Re." Each pillar
illustrates, in finely carved reliefs,
rites that took place in the shrine, now
part of the temple complex at Karnak.
In the foreground, the pharaoh gives
cups of wine to Amun-Re, shown
in the guise of Min, god of procreation.
On the pillar beyond, the god is carried
before the pharaoh on a pedestal. The
god's statue was brought here aboard
the sacred bark. Priests dragged it
on a sled up the ramp to an altar
that can be seen between the pillars.

Archeologists reconstructed the shrine
from its limestone blocks, found inside
a pylon. Amunhotep III, some 500 years
after Sesostris, had used the stones as
stuffing, thus preserving a matchless
array of sharply etched hieroglyphs.
Those below are part of a message
to all the gods; the basket means "all."

"A procession will be made for you"

A fine funeral was something to live for, if you were an Egyptian who could afford the high cost of dying in style. The laments of family and friends were led by professional mourners who shrieked, sprinkled dust on their heads, and tore their clothes. These weeping women, lamenting that their "great shepherd is gone," mourn eternally on the wall of the tomb of Ramose, a vizier of the New Kingdom.

In his procession, moving men (below) bear furniture for after-living rooms. Four carry chests that probably would have contained clothing; their shape reproduces the outline of an Upper Egypt shrine. One man clutches a walking stick, another totes a pair of white sandals.

Next come a pair burdened by a bed with bedding and headrest; they also carry a checkered bag and a fan. Speaking via the hieroglyphs between them, the rear man impatiently tells the one in front, "Get a move on! Stir your stumps!"

In Thebes, where Ramose was entombed, the participants in the funeral boarded ships on the east bank and disembarked on the west bank, along with the bier, the body, and the goods needed for a happy afterlife. The procession of wailing mourners headed for the city of the dead, the necropolis where tombs and mortuary temples awaited.

A typically mystic anagram tells why mourners cry. The sun god, who wept at his own funeral, explained, "That is how humans [*romi*] came into being—as the humors [*rimi*] which came forth from my Eye."

Overleaf: Last journey—"the silent land"

Mortuary temples and tombs emerge from the sand and stone of Deir el Bahri at the necropolis of Thebes. To Egyptian eyes, the setting sun buried itself each day in these 1,000-foot cliffs and, in mystical imitation, so at death did the royal family and nobility. The temple of Queen Hatshepsut—its three tiers a monument to endurance—reigns over the city of the dead. Though often depicted as a kilted, bearded man, she did rule

in her own right. She took over from her male co-regent. After some 20 years in power, she died. Her nephew-stepson Thutmose III succeeded her, toppling her statues and effacing her name. But her memory still defies him.

She had a tomb in the Valley of the Kings, just beyond these cliffs. There New Kingdom pharaohs sunk tombs into the heart of a mountain, trying—usually in vain—to thwart thieves. Hatshepsut's burial chamber, 320 feet down into the rock, was among those robbed in antiquity.

"He who is yonder shall be a living god"

Like a window that opens to both life and afterlife, the wall of an artisan's tomb shows the double vision of Egyptian religion. Though the scenes portray life in paradise, they also give us a glance at a real landscape and its three seasons. Viewing from the bottom up, we see the wavy-lined Nile in flood, shrubs on the west bank, fruit trees on the east. In the next two seasonal registers, the deceased Sennedjem and his wife toil, wearing festive white, in the Egypt-like "Fields of the Blessed." They plow and seed (from right to left), pull flax, and (upper) take the grain of harvest. Each season had four 30-day months, for a 360-day year. The remaining five days became holidays for honoring gods depicted in the next register: Re, Osiris, Ptah, and two lesser deities; the couple kneels before them.

Atop all, Re in his bark is adored on New Year's day—around summer solstice—by sacred baboons. (Egyptians thought that baboons made such commotion at sunrise that they must have worshiped Re.) Inscriptions promise that Sennedjem will have an infinity of New Year's days.

If he tired of working in the fields, he had substitute figures called *ushabtis* or "answerers." A ushabti responded "Here I am!" when the deceased was summoned for labor. The figures here span dynasties and show changes in style; their inscriptions label them farm workers. A wealthy dead man would have one for each day of the year.

"You will live again forever"

The embalmer uttered this promise as he did his sacred work, leaving for posterity, if not eternity, that most fascinating of all relics: the mummy.

Some, such as the mummy of Ramses II (opposite), tell us tales. His X-rays showed he had eaten rough grains that had worn down his teeth, had gum disease and blackheads—and endured cold feet because of poor circulation. Long before his time, mummification had evolved from royal rite to civil right. But you got what you paid for. And the poor often got little more than burial in the sand.

Embalmings began with removal of organs that would decay. They usually were put into canopic jars (below), so called after a city where a god was worshiped in jar-like form. They were filled by a code linking each stopper-head to an organ: jackal, stomach; baboon, lungs; falcon, intestines; human, liver. The heads invoked Horus's protective sons.

The heart, as the site of intelligence, was blessed with a scarab, which Anubis the funerary god seeks (right) in a tomb painting. A hook put up the nose yanked out the worthless brain. The body was packed in salts, dried until leathery, and wrapped in some 20 layers of linen.

"Eternity . . . for those who were righteous"

Well-buried Egyptians would not be caught dead without a helpful tract we misname Book of the Dead. They knew it as a "book" of spells for helping the dead return to the land of the living. The book, such as the papyrus one excerpted here, went into the tomb with the mummy. Those who recited the spells could, as "the justified dead," join the afterlife.

Key rituals, illustrated in detail, recalled aspects of the regeneration myth of Osiris. His avenger Horus plays roles (right) as white-skirted priests. He brings his jar-shaped sons full of water, important in resurrection rites. This will soften the lips of the mummy, which is being propped up by jackal-headed Anubis, death's master of ceremonies. Next Horus raises his adz-like wand to pry open the mummy's mouth so the deceased can eat, drink, and speak. Finally Seth in a leopard skin symbolically surrenders the Eye of Horus —in the form of food, water, and incense. Such opening-the-mouth ceremonies were also enacted on gods' statues in temples.

Now active and in the netherworld, the white-robed deceased (upper left, below) kneels before 14 gods. He will be judged by them—and 28 others—with such frightful names as Breaker of Bones and Eater of Blood. In a long, negative confession, he must deny having committed specific sins, ranging from mistreating cattle and hoarding water to blasphemy and murder. He also stresses the positive: He is "pure of mouth and pure of hands" and "without sin, without guilt, without evil."

His judgment comes on the scale of Maat (whose figurehead tops it). His heart is weighed against the plume of Maat—truth, justice, order—as he prays, "O heart of my body . . . don't weigh heavy against me . . . for you are my ka, who is in my body." Anubis supervises the weighing, while the crocodile-lion-hippo-bodied Swallower of the Dead hopes for the worst. But ibis-headed Thoth, divine scribe, records a happy verdict, dipping his brush—to write on this papyrus. Finally, the justified deceased, escorted by Horus, meets Osiris, the goddesses Isis and Nephthys, and, standing upon a flower rooted in the throne-supporting Nile, the four sons of Horus.

Egyptians did do things "which are not done." But because they denied all—in writing—the gods had to believe them.

Through the final gate to a "Happy Land"

Though the justified deceased need no longer fear the Swallower of the Dead, he had to face other perils—including the netherworld's Swallower of the Stars. A painting in the royal tomb of Seti I illustrates this terrifying realm of snakes and flames. Egyptians navigated it with the help of the Book of Gates, which described the sun god's nocturnal passage. In his boat he voyaged through the 12 divisions—or hours—of the land of night. The great swallower here is a snake identified as the "pythoness Hereret," a form of the sky goddess. Each linked figure eight of her coils stands for an "hour star" gulped at dawn. So the 12—also called her starry children—represent the variable length of night. Below, men bend before "pits of fire" stoked for foes of Osiris.

But those who had "fought against the spirit of evil" would prevail against the demons of this infernal place. They would join the ranks of the justified dead to dwell beyond the Nile "in the Happy Land of the Setting Sun."

Overleaf: The king who became immortal

Tutankhamun, who gave posterity the gift of rediscovered splendor, lies in a burial chamber that dramatizes his triumph over death. His successor Ay (at the right), wearing the blue crown of reigning pharaoh, performs the opening-the-mouth rite on the mummified Tutankhamun. Then Nut, goddess of the sky and mother of Osiris, receives him as her son; he carries club and staff, symbols of power. Finally, the mummiform Osiris greets the pharaoh, who wears a striped headdress, and his ka, or conscience, who clutches the ankh, symbol of life. Hieroglyphs proclaim that he has been "given life forever and ever." Baboons, one for each hour of day, adore their new sun, the risen, gleaming king.

He rested in a nest of three mummiform coffins, which enhanced his resemblance to Osiris, usually portrayed as a mummy. The Sacred Eye and winged goddesses adorn his sarcophagus, guarding a pharaoh who could say in death to us: "It goes well with me and with my name."

199

Change in a Changeless Land

Edna R. Russmann

You rise in perfection on the horizon of the sky,
Living Aten, who started life.
Whenever you are risen upon the eastern horizon
You fill every land with your perfection. . . .
You have made a far-off heaven in which to rise. . . .
Yet you are alone.

Thus, according to the inscriptions, Akhenaten, king of Egypt some 1,350 years before the birth of Christ, hymned his praises to the sun. This extraordinary man, perhaps physically deformed, husband to one of the most famous beauties in history, has been hailed as the inventor of monotheism—the worship of a single, all-powerful god. But, as we will see, Akhenaten's god was not entirely new, nor was it quite the only god. And Akhenaten himself would become a prophet dishonored in his own land. His memory would be reviled, his very existence expunged from the record by later rulers. Official documents would refer to him, if at all, as "that criminal." Nevertheless, one aspect of Akhenaten's ideas did survive, and would influence Egyptian culture for centuries—the arts.

Almost nothing is known about Akhenaten's childhood. He was the son of Amunhotep III and Queen Tiy. That much is certain. But where he grew up, how and when he acquired his revolutionary ideas—even the date of his birth—are questions that perhaps no amount of scholarly work will ever be able to resolve.

We do know that during the reign of Akhenaten's father Egypt basked in a golden age of power and prosperity. The court of Amunhotep III must have been as rich and cosmopolitan as any the world had yet seen. Such a court would have glittered with wealth and ideas from every quarter. Amunhotep's harem, for example, included even an Asiatic princess who, along with the customary gold and jewels, brought a retinue that included 316 ladies-in-waiting.

As for the idea of a sun god, Egyptians had worshiped Re in his human and animal forms since earliest times. From the beginning of the 18th Dynasty the

"Their arms are lifted in praise at your rising"

Words from the "Hymn to the Aten," Akhenaten's prayer to the sun, echo a scene of royal piety on a tablet (opposite) found at Amarna. Akhenaten and his queen, Nefertiti, pray before flower-laden stands, offering libations to the solar divinity that ruled over Egypt during their reign. The rays end in little hands that accept the offerings and, in turn, dangle before the royal couple symbols signifying "life." The king's breast bears the sun-god's name in cartouches. Fluid, curving lines and exaggerated physical features typify early Amarna art. Offering tables laden with meat, bread, and wine (left) represent a scene from the Great Temple at Amarna. About 3,000 such tables, placed row upon row in the compound, bore gifts to the sun.

importance of the sun itself, as the shining disk—or *Aten*—that traveled the heavens, had taken on a power of its own. People had begun to worship it, while the king, as ruler, had become identified with it. Amunhotep III himself was called "the dazzling sun disk."

From the beginning of his reign Akhenaten paid homage to the sun. A few early monuments show that at first he represented his deity in a traditional form—as a falcon-headed man. During these years he allowed other gods to coexist, and even continued to use the name he had been given as a child, Amunhotep, "Amun is pleased." By our numbering, he was Amunhotep IV. Only in the fifth or sixth year of his reign did he change his name to Akhenaten—"The Effective Spirit of the Aten." By then he had come to believe that there was no god but the sun, and that it took the form of the Aten, the radiant disk by whose light man lives.

Other gods—especially the state god, Amun—fell into eclipse. Some of their statues were smashed, their names chiseled away. Amun's great temple at Karnak was closed. So impassioned was the campaign against the state god that even the name of Akhenaten's father suffered mutilation because of its reference to Amun. Such was Akhenaten's "heresy."

To represent his deity, Akhenaten devised a hieroglyph-like symbol—a disk with rays of light ending in little hands. He created for it a new worship that took place, not in temple sanctuaries, but in the open—in large courtyards filled with altars and offering stands. No statues were carved of the Aten; it simply was present everywhere, shining down upon Akhenaten and his wife and daughters as they celebrated its rites.

Worship of the Aten was a public spectacle, with chariot processions to the temple, offerings heaped upon rows of altars, and crowds of followers lined up according to rank. But only the royal family actually took part in the services, and only the royal family received the blessings of the disk's many hands. The cult of the Aten was essentially a dialogue between Akhenaten and the disk, his divine father. Akhenaten even

had his own priests. Mortals could worship only him.

In exalting himself so far above mankind, Akhenaten elevated his family as well. His wife Nefertiti—"fair of face . . . mistress of happiness"—and their six daughters became far more prominent in public appearances than female and junior royalty had ever been. They also shared the spotlight in sculptures that portray their affectionate home life in charming detail—the girls swarming over their parents' laps.

The intimate nature of many scenes showing the royal family, and their evident fondness for one another, should not obscure from us their divine stature. Their affection also had a religious function. Akhenaten seems to have used the Egyptian love of family, and the tendency to endow nearly every god with a wife and child, to suggest a "Holy Family" of his own. It may be that Akhenaten intended the children and their mother to supply, in the new religion, the warmth and tenderness that the Aten so conspicuously lacked.

At about the time he changed his name to Akhenaten, the king journeyed to a place on the east bank of the Nile midway between Memphis and Thebes. Here he found virgin territory, a sandy plain hemmed by desert hills and cliffs. It was barren land that belonged, he tells us, to no god or goddess, nor to any prince or princess or any man. Here he founded a new city, marking its boundaries with huge stelae cut into the cliffs. On the stelae he named the temples and palaces he intended to build, and described the tombs he would carve for himself and his followers. He vowed he would be buried nowhere else.

Akhenaten called his city Akhetaten—"The Horizon of the Aten." We know the site as Amarna—or Tell el-Amarna—and it has given its name to the entire period of his reign. Those who travel to Amarna today find the same unproductive waste Akhenaten first saw, strangely empty and desolate. But the foundations of huge temples, palaces, and villas now lie under the drifting sand, all that remains of a city erected almost

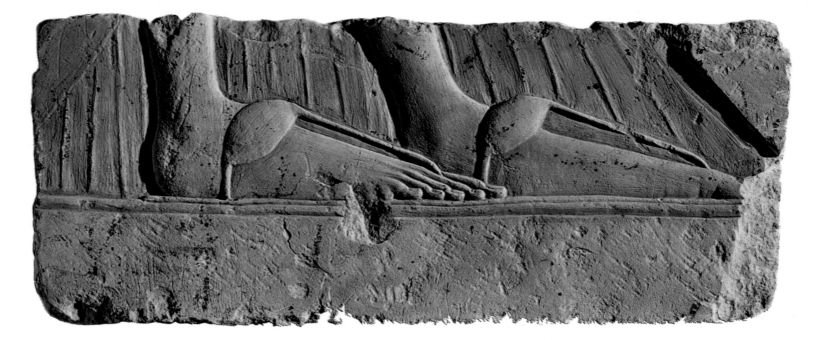

overnight—and abandoned nearly as quickly after its founder's death. The royal tomb is a shattered wreck. Akhenaten probably kept his promise to be buried there. Because his mummy has not been found, we may never know. But Amarna was Akhenaten's home for the rest of his life; from Aten's city he sought to spread his ideas throughout the Egyptian empire.

The extent to which the new Aten cult touched the lives of the people is difficult to tell. Outside of Amarna, few records of Akhenaten's reign survive. Those that do are inconclusive. But when the king moved against the temples of the old gods, he must have given the country a jolt. If so, there is no trace of open resistance or revolt as long as he lived.

Interfering with temple rites may not have had much effect on the ordinary person. Egyptian ritual had always been mostly the business of priests performing their duties privately, in sanctuaries from which the public was barred. The Aten cult probably had little popular appeal, and certainly the people of Egypt must have found it hard to accept this god with no face, no personality, and no richness of myth or superstition. The people appear to have done what they had always done: offered their prayers to the humble gods, the homely little spirits who presided over practical matters like warding off snakes and scorpions and protecting women in childbirth. These household gods had no temples to lose, but they did hold people's hearts.

Whether or not Akhenaten actually wrote the sun hymn, he must certainly have been involved in the modernization of the written language that took place during his reign. He may also have had his own ideas about music. Unlike other gods, the Aten was serenaded by string ensembles that had previously performed at banquets. Troupes of foreign musicians were among them, some playing the giant lyre, an eastern instrument known in Egypt only during this time. Even the orchestras reflected the topsy-turviness of the new order. Male musicians now played certain women's instruments, like the boat-shaped harp, while women danced to the warlike trumpet.

But the innovations most visible to us, and in which we can most clearly see his personal intervention, lay in the visual arts—statuary, relief, painting. It may seem strange that a man so fanatically involved with restructuring the religion of his time should rethink the arts as well. It would probably not have occurred to Akhenaten to do otherwise. Every aspect of Egyptian life was permeated—had been formed—by religious belief. Every expression of what we today call art was, in a real sense, a religious expression. Ancient Egyptians had no word for "art," nor would they have understood our use of the term. The individual expected to live forever in human form through statues and other representations in his tomb. These images were far more potent than mere symbols. In a magical way, they *were* the being represented. We know of many cases in which posthumous revenge was taken by smashing a person's statue—or by simply breaking off its nose, so that he could no longer "breathe." When Akhenaten ordered the images of Amun destroyed, he may have intended, quite literally, to kill the rival god.

The inherently religious nature of Egyptian art imposed a conservatism that, to us, seems one of its main characteristics. But we must remember that this conservatism would not have been perceived as a restriction by the artist. A deliberate, conscious resistance to change was as deeply ingrained in ancient Egyptians as their hope that the sun would rise every morning. By their unchanging worship of the gods, they sought to maintain the pattern of the universe. The only thing wrong with life was its impermanence. Human life should—must—be made to go on forever. Stone was imperishable; wood and bronze, in that dry climate, nearly so. By means of his image, god, king, or mortal could last forever. Eternity was perhaps the most important single determinant of Egyptian art.

The rules of this art were laid down early. During the first three dynasties, from about 3100 to 2600 B.C.,

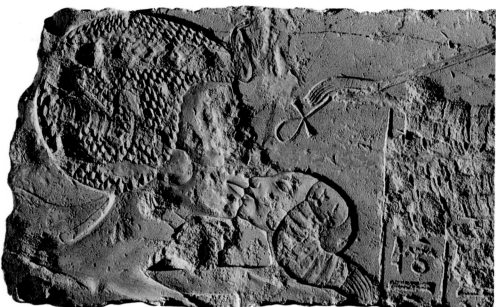

motifs and themes going back to prehistoric times were conventionalized—the human figure, the lordly animals including the lion and the falcon, and such evil ones as the hippopotamus and the crocodile. By the time of Cheops, the important artistic conventions had been decided upon. Almost all of them served to enhance solidity, clarity, harmony, balance. These criteria, not technical limitations, led Egyptian sculptors to leave a stone fill between the limbs of a statue so that it would be less vulnerable to breakage.

These rules endowed the human body with an ideal set of proportions, and determined that a standing man should be shown with the left leg forward, but with the weight comfortably and equally distributed on both feet. They dictated that the fist, whether holding an object or empty, should be clenched, so that the forearm muscles are visible, but not painfully tense.

The Egyptian sculptor could be a master at rendering an individual face. We see a few superb examples from Cheops's time. But individuality, alas, is impermanent. Far more prudent to make the face as idealized as the body, to eliminate any signs of age, illness, or care.

Carved and painted reliefs on tomb and temple walls presented special problems. Here it was necessary to show scenes of activity, often involving several figures, animals, and equipment. It was most important that there be no doubt as to what was going on. Short hieroglyphic statements explain the action, but no more describe the scenes than the scenes illustrate the writing. Egyptian writing and representation were part of each other to an extent that was possible only because the writing itself consisted of pictures. At about the time of the First Dynasty, the figures as well as the hieroglyphs had settled into orderly rows—registers, they are called, each with its base line. There is no perspective, no distance. Simply the surface along which the eye travels to "read" the design.

Ideals of clarity and comprehensibility governed the human form as well: A face in profile shows the eye frontally, its most important view; both shoulders are

The pursuit of a different vision

The dawn of a new religion brought a flowering of realism to ancient Egyptian art. Akhenaten's artists, seeking to "humanize" the abstract Aten, discarded old conventions and adopted new ones. Right and left feet—and hands—became clearly differentiated for the first time. Children began to look, and act, like children, not small-scale adults. Members of the king's family now were portrayed in informal poses—as in the reliefs of a princess dining on duck and one of the court ladies kissing a royal child.

seen, no matter what the position of the arms; both arms are visible, even when one is theoretically behind the body; hips and legs are drawn in profile, but the navel is also depicted because it is there. Only since the Greeks taught us to look at art the way we look at nature have these conventions come to seem in any way unnatural. The method is so logical and consistent, the transitions from one angle to another so gracefully worked out, that only an occasional awkwardness reminds us that we are looking, not at the imitation of a figure, but at the *idea* of one.

Every aspect of the artist's training and work helped reinforce his conservatism. He began as an apprentice, doing simple tasks. Because professions tended to run in families, he might well be introduced to his future trade while still a toddler, playing about his father's workshop. But the shop did not belong to his father. The artist was always in the service of a king, a temple, or a leading citizen. He did not choose his project; he did not own the materials he manipulated. In most cases, he probably did not even work on a single piece from start to finish.

The sculptor worked almost exclusively with stone tools, pounding and bruising away the excess, rubbing with abrasives to create the fine details and the final polish. Such a slow, laborious process could be made efficient only by using large numbers of less skilled workmen to prepare and rough out the stone. More highly skilled workers handled the advanced stages. The chief of the shop was a supervisor as much as he was a craftsman; his responsibilities included training

Baby amuses herself with mother's crown in the carving (lower), while father playfully plants a kiss on his eldest daughter—an act of parental fondness gleefully observed by a third child, perched on her mother's knee. Scenes of unabashed domestic bliss among members of the royal family add warmth and zest to art styles developed during Akhenaten's reign. Nefertiti here has usurped the ornately decorated royal stool, while her husband contents himself with a plain one next to a rack of wine jugs. Inscriptions identify the royal couple and their daughters (from left) Merytaten, Meketaten, and Ankhesenpaaten. As the wife of King Tutankhamun (bust at left), Ankhesenpaaten would one day rule as Egypt's queen. Akhenaten's mother, the dowager Queen Tiy, here appears to view the proceedings with matriarchal misgivings.

apprentices, mostly by having them copy model pieces.

From our point of view the Egyptian artist was little more than a craftsman. But to Egyptian eyes he was a special craftsman because of the special nature of what he made. In a way, he worked on the fringes of the religious profession. In the early days, the sculptor was sometimes represented and named in the tomb he carved. His being there had nothing to do with vanity or signing his work. He was present as a witness that the job had been properly executed to meet religious specifications and guarantee the owner's immortality. He ranked higher, socially, than most other craftsmen, especially if his employer were the king. The king's chief sculptor was one of the high officials of the land.

All these pressures toward imitation and conservatism did not affect the quality of Egyptian art. And they certainly did not prevent it from changing. The very intimacy of its relationship to people's thoughts and beliefs made art as vulnerable to change as life itself. For this reason we can distinguish the art of different periods, and even individual reigns, simply by the style. One rarely confuses the stocky, confident-looking figures of the Pyramid Age, say, with the large-eyed, expressive figures of the later Old Kingdom.

By Akhenaten's time, art styles reflect a luxury and opulence surpassing even that known during his father's reign. And they show a new spirit of freshness and verve. The palaces at Amarna were designed to give pleasure, from their sensuously rounded columns to furniture shaped to fit the human form—and sumptuously cushioned. In luxuriant gardens painted on palace walls and floors sprang plants seldom seen in earlier forms of Egyptian art. Glazed tiles imitated the real-life brilliance of flowers and, in some rooms, jewel-like clusters of faience grapes hung as if in an arbor. Akhenaten was no ascetic. To celebrate nature's boundless variety was to recognize the manifold greatness of the Aten who had created all. Amarna art is full of detailed and loving observation of

the beauties of life, whether bird, plant, or human foot.

But some elements of Amarna art also disturb—the portrayals of Akhenaten himself. In the few years before he founded Amarna, Akhenaten built prodigiously at Karnak, near Amun's temple. There seem to have been at least eight of his buildings in the area. We do not know much about them, for their excavation has just begun. But we do know something of their decoration and we still have the remains of several colossal statues of the king that stood within them.

Each of these huge images is full of majesty, half smiling—and grotesque. The elongated, emaciated head with its slit eyes and pendulous lips and chin; the scrawny neck, seeming to bend under the weight of head and crown; the puny, bony torso with its frankly feminine contours. Did he really look like this? And if he did, what caused his deformities?

Many attempts have been made to suggest a disease or condition that would account for Akhenaten's appearance: Akhenaten was a woman in the guise of a man; Akhenaten was a man presenting himself as a maternal deity; Akhenaten suffered a malfunction of the pituitary gland. None of the theories is satisfactory. His six daughters are the problem. Any disorder that could have so drastically affected his appearance would also have made it unlikely for him to father children. Perhaps the statues and reliefs greatly exaggerate Akhenaten's peculiarities. After all, his whole family was made to look like him—even Nefertiti. Whatever their relationship to Akhenaten's actual appearance, such images could have been made only with the king's approval, and probably at his own instigation.

Akhenaten's artistic innovations went far beyond distortions of the human form and a new symbol for a god. From the scattered remains of his buildings we can see they were planned on a grand scale. Instead of separate registers moving in linear progression, some whole walls contain single compositions of palaces and temples. Busy little figures go about their work, carrying on animated conversations, even taking catnaps.

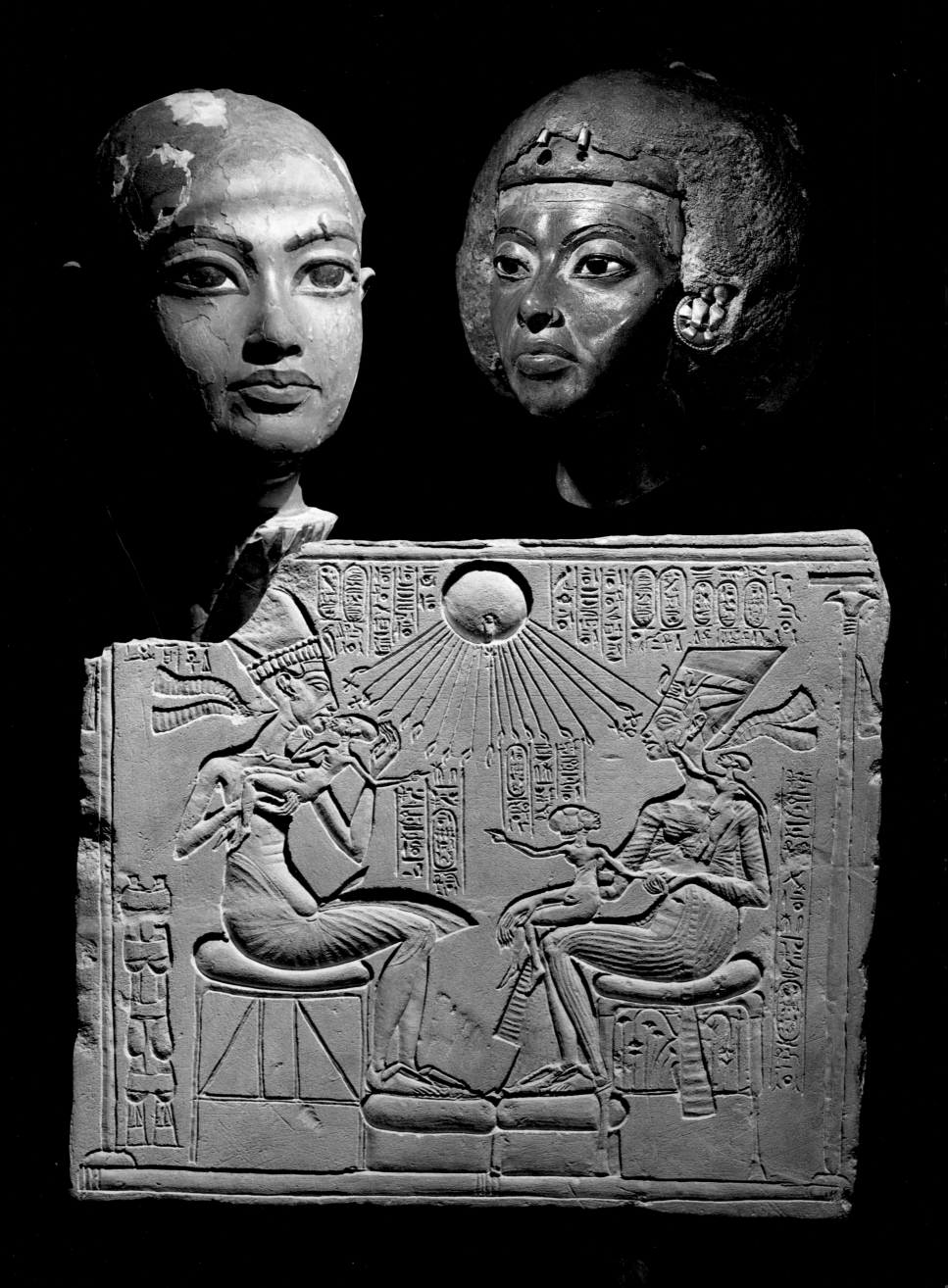

The sense of unified space is entirely new to Egyptian art, and so is the interaction between the figures.

Before Akhenaten, groups had been shown when necessary, but each individual performed his own action. There was no great sense of communication between them. Statues of married couples, their arms about each other, stared straight ahead, independently, into space. So did the ramrod-stiff children at their sides. How different are the representations of Akhenaten and his family—full of tender gestures and human love and warmth.

When Akhenaten shifted his attention to Amarna, he stopped the Karnak projects and sent his chief sculptor, Bak, to carry on the artistic revolution in the new city. But after a few years, art at Amarna began to change in subtle ways. The great compositions, the lively little figures, the wealth of detailed observation of nature continued. Representations of the royal family now became softer and more idealized. The remote gaze of the fanatic is replaced by a dreamy, somewhat melancholy expression; the jaw and neck droop less; even the gross swells of flesh have been toned down to an almost childlike pudginess.

The workshop of Bak's successor, excavated at Amarna, revealed a number of trial sketches, models, and works in progress, among them the great painted head of Nefertiti (page 247). The head was never intended to be part of a whole statue; it is complete as it was made. The superb workmanship makes it fairly certain that the head served as a model, the perfect image of the queen for lesser sculptors to use as a guide. Her prominent bone structure, full mouth, and swan neck bear a resemblance to the statues from Karnak, but they have been refined into the essence of beauty and elegance. By this head we remember the woman whose name meant "The Beautiful One Is Come."

Called the loveliest of women, most sublime of all the queens who ever reigned in Egypt, Nefertiti even today has the power to fascinate and mystify. Just who her parents were is uncertain. The likeliest candidate for her father was a powerful official named Ay, who would one day himself succeed to Egypt's throne.

Even more mysterious—and controversial—than Nefertiti's parentage was her sudden disappearance from the scene a couple of years before her husband's death. Some scholars believe she died. Others think she lived but fell from favor, or that she had broken with the king. One scholar has recently gathered evidence suggesting that Nefertiti changed her name to Smenkhkare and joined the king on the throne as his co-regent and heir apparent. Whatever became of her, the legend of Nefertiti's beauty endures. As Akhenaten probably intended, it is Nefertiti, beautiful and serene, embracing her husband and children, who seems to embody all that was graceful and lovely in Amarna.

Akhenaten died in the 17th year of his reign. We do not know what caused his death. He may have foreseen his approaching end because he established Smenkhkare as his co-regent. Akhenaten cannot have realized how quickly his elaborately constructed reforms would collapse. Smenkhkare may never have lived to reign independently. The last kings of the 18th Dynasty—Tutankhamun, Ay, Horemheb—bent their efforts to restoring Egypt to pantheism. The Aten temples ceased to function and, as the need arose for building materials, they were dismantled. Amarna itself was abandoned. As orthodoxy triumphed, most Egyptians probably breathed a sigh of relief.

And yet memory survives in unforeseeable ways. When these counter-reformers made their new statues, every feature bore the stamp of Amarna art. From the full-lidded eyes to the puny, paunchy bodies, their images of orthodoxy traced back to Akhenaten. His legacy remained long after the youngest sculptor trained at Amarna had passed from the scene.

The great battle reliefs in which the Ramesside kings of the following dynasties immortalized their real or imaginary victories owe their grandeur, their scale and complexity, to the compositions in Akhenaten's

temples and palaces. Figures tend to be squat and dumpy, or impossibly long and skinny. The sculptors turning out statues of Ramses the Great never managed to settle on a satisfactory likeness of the king's face. This uncertainty and variability, as well as the retention of telltale details like the full mouth, stem from Amarna. Akhenaten had jolted Egyptian art out of its complacency. Like it or not, the Egyptian artist now had to face the existence of choices.

On the political front, Akhenaten's death left a power vacuum, but there was at least a legitimate successor to the crown—the child Tutankhaten. He was a king's son, but we are not sure whether his father was Akhenaten or the elderly Amunhotep III. He was only about nine when he ascended the throne. In his name a mighty program of restoring and rebuilding the old temples was undertaken. A stela found at Karnak commemorates the pious work, describing how the temples had "fallen into neglect."

Tutankhaten did not repudiate the Aten religion. After all, Akhenaten had been a close relative, and the new cult was probably the only one the boy had known. But the handwriting was on the wall. In the third year of his reign, the king and his court were moved from Amarna to the capital of Memphis. Shortly thereafter, the young king's name was changed to Tutankhamun in recognition of Amun's ascendency.

We know little else of Tutankhamun's life. It was a short one: His mummy indicates that he was no more than 18 when he died. He would probably rate little more than a footnote in scholarly histories had not the miraculous preservation of his small, makeshift tomb brought him so stunningly to light in this century. The lavishness of his tomb furnishings caught the imagination of the world, and holds it still. Much of the treasure is simply what happened to be on hand. Some of it had been made early in his reign—the magnificent throne and several objects on which his name still appears as Tutankhaten. There are even objects with the cartouche of Akhenaten. The funerary trappings were

"All the cattle are content . . . birds fly up to their nests"

Ducks take wing and bull calves romp through fields of sedge and reeds on a fresco evoking the sun hymn's paean to a new day. Sweeping strokes of the new art graced the floor of the royal harem at Amarna. The artist faltered only once—with his lapse into the stiffly drawn papyrus at extreme right. The fish, from an earlier floor decoration, pops up through a plaster chink. Farmers angered by field-trampling tourists demolished the floor in 1910.

partly second-hand. In several places we can see that Tutankhamun's name has been added over the erased name of Smenkhkare.

Represented with Tutankhamun on many of the objects is his wife, Akhenaten's third daughter, Ankhesenamun (originally Ankhesenpaaten). But the couple produced no heirs, and with Tutankhamun's death, the extraordinary family that had ruled so long and so brilliantly as the 18th Dynasty reached its end.

The crown passed to the now elderly Ay, but he lived only four years as king. His successor, Horemheb, was a military man with no blood ties to the extinct family. By the time we encounter him under Tutankhamun, he was important enough to build a magnificent tomb for himself near Memphis. Horemheb never used the tomb. His burial, after a reign of some 27 years, took place in a proper royal tomb at Thebes, not far from Tutankhamun's. Apparently it was Horemheb who finally closed the Aten temples and began tearing them down. Akhenaten's blocks were incorporated in the interiors of Horemheb's massive structures, invisible, but preserved to this day.

Having no son, Horemheb chose another general, one Ramses, as his successor. The Ramesside kings were in no way beholden to Akhenaten; they did their best to cast a pall of silence over the whole period of the heresy. They venerated Horemheb, their benefactor, and credited him not only with the 27 years of his own rule, but with Ay's, Tutankhamun's, and Akhenaten's as well. Fifty-nine years reigned Horemheb, according to a Ramesside document. Akhenaten had never existed. Egypt had never changed.

The power and the glory of Amarna art

Breathtaking beauty of a queen thought to be Nefertiti shines undimmed through the ages—lending credence to inscriptions that call her "fair of face . . . lady of grace, great of love." Her serene expression here contrasts with the baleful, almost malevolent presence of her husband. His effigy, a 13-foot colossus, exudes power and majesty. But the sagging paunch, bulbous hips and thighs, and thin, cat-like face also perturb. One hand holds a flail, royal symbol of authority.

The queenly head, not yet finished and polished, bears sculptor's guide marks and represents another Amarna innovation—the composite statue. Such works were carved in separate pieces by various specialists, who then assembled them into a completed whole. A limited number of master craftsmen were thus able to build many statues at one time. Credit for devising the process generally goes to Bak, chief sculptor early in Akhenaten's reign. History has forgotten the name of the master who carved this lovely "Nefertiti."

The royal family: exuberance and tragedy

Two little princesses, caught for eternity
in a moment of sisterly affection,
enliven a fragment of an Amarna painting.
Other members of the family—including
Nefertiti, whose giant heel and sandal
strap appear at upper right—once shared
the mural portrait. Fragments not seen
here depict tantalizing glimpses
of the king, his three oldest daughters—
even little Sotepenre, baby of the family.
The girls here probably are the royal
family's fourth and fifth daughters,
Neferneferuaten and Neferneferure.
Frontal views of the eyes and the two left
hands of Neferneferuaten hark back to
pre-Amarna artistic conventions. Grace,
warmth, informality—and grossly elongated
skulls—typify the new art.

The finely modeled head of an unidentified
princess repeats in stone the superhuman
qualities Amarna artists bestowed
on their royal subjects—with royal approval.
Portrayals of the girls as adults show no
traces of such skull deformities.

In other scenes of Akhenaten's family,
the girls help their father "drive"
the royal chariot, toss out gold necklaces
at awards ceremonies, or clamber upon
their parents with boundless energy.
In one of the most poignant episodes,
the king and queen stand grief-stricken
before the body of Meketaten, their second
daughter. Did the young princess die while
giving birth to the child? Perhaps.
And perhaps no one will ever know.

A general's monument, a king's immortality

Jigsaw puzzle in stone, Akhenaten's wall rises again after some 3,300 years of concealment within a general's monument. A French-Egyptian restoration team discovered the blocks in the 1960's when they dismantled Pylon IX at Karnak to shore up its crumbling foundations. Horemheb, a military commander under Akhenaten, who eventually succeeded to the throne of Egypt, had filled his massive pylon with some 6,000 blocks taken from his predecessor's buildings and temples. Egyptologists matched thousands of photographs to rebuild a 60-foot section of the temple wall that stood at Karnak. On this segment, workers believed to be temple attendants carry wine, food, and other offerings from well-stocked larders and storerooms (shown at right). Ducks quack and cattle bellow as herdsmen coax them toward an unseen destination—presumably a nearby temple to the Aten.

Each of the blocks measures about three handspans in length, inspiring modern handlers to call them talatat, the Arabic word for "threes."

Over the years, some 45,000 talatat have turned up, many of them remarkably well preserved. But it is only recently, with the development of computerized matching and cataloguing techniques, that the task of reassembling them—at least photographically—has seemed feasible.

Tutankhamun's throne, glory of empire

"Below . . . stood another of the great artistic treasures of the tomb . . . a throne overlaid with gold from top to bottom. . . ."

So wrote Howard Carter, discoverer of Tutankhamun's tomb in the Valley of the Kings. The throne, made of gold-sheathed wood inlaid with colored glass, faience, and lapis lazuli, dazzled Carter's eye. Its glorious back panel was to him "the most beautiful thing . . . found in Egypt."

It depicts "a room decorated with flower-garlanded pillars" and topped with a frieze of royal cobras. "Through a hole in the roof the sun shoots down his life-giving protective rays. The king himself sits . . . upon a cushioned throne, his arm thrown carelessly across its back. Before him stands the girlish figure of the queen" (Nefertiti's third daughter), who anoints her husband with perfumed oil. A jeweled collar rests on a stand next to her. "A simple, homely little composition," wrote the discoverer, "but how instinct with life and feeling it is, and with what a sense of movement."

Heavenly scents for the afterlife

Skillfully wrought alabaster containers held perfumes and unguents fit for a king's life in the hereafter. These vessels, and dozens of others found in Tutankhamun's tomb, held more than 100 gallons of scented oils and emollients—before tomb robbers emptied them. The vase at left, over two feet high, symbolizes the union of Upper and Lower Egypt. Twin figures of the Nile god Hapi support looping papyrus and lily-like plants and scepters twined by royal cobras. A vulture goddess, signifying maternal care, embraces the vessel's lip with sheltering wings. A stylized "ibex" and gold-fanged lion, both with painted ivory tongues, also held scented ointments. The lion's paw rests on the symbol sa, meaning "protection."

To shade the kingly brow

Coursing along at breakneck speed, reins looped about his middle to free his hands, Tutankhamun brings down his quarry—a pair of ostriches of a species that lived in Egypt until early this century. Such is the drama of the chase, as recorded on the head of a gold-sheathed fan found in Tutankhamun's tomb. The king's hound springs to finish off the birds, while an animated ankh symbol lopes behind the royal hunting chariot. It holds aloft a fan similar to the one seen here (the plumes of which have long since disintegrated).

The king, in short wig, wearing a kilt and leopard-skin corselet, rides behind a team richly caparisoned with feathered headpieces. Symbols within the arc of his bow proclaim him the "possessor of a strong arm." Other hieroglyphs record one of Tutankhamun's names and a royal motto: "The good god Nebkheperure [Tutankhamun's throne name], given life for ever like Re." Inscriptions on the handle of the fan (not shown here) state that it was made of "ostrich

The Crest of Empire

Anthony J. Spalinger

Lo, the god knows me well . . .
He made me rule Black Land and Red Land as reward,
All foreign lands are my subjects,
He placed my border at the limits of heaven.

Intrigue in royal palaces was hardly new by the time of the New Kingdom. The Thutmosids, empire-building rulers of Dynasty 18, were strong-willed people, and even the gods sometimes upstaged one another. Still, the coup that took place about 1490 B.C. must have disturbed many tradition-bound Egyptians. Overnight, the tip of the power pyramid had shifted. Now when the supreme god Amun made mystic contact with the pharaoh, a woman's voice answered.

Hatshepsut had been the chief royal wife of the previous pharaoh. The eldest son of a king's main wife was his heir apparent. But when Thutmose II died without a male heir in the direct line, Hatshepsut became regent. At first it was with the understanding that she would give up her powers to Thutmose III, the son of her husband by a lesser wife, when he came of age. But her plans changed. With the aid of her able minister and temple designer, Senmut, Hatshepsut sidestepped her young stepson and assumed the Double Crown of Egypt. And she called herself king.

Even the language was caught unawares. The hieroglyphs for "queen" translate as "king's wife." Although a woman had sat on the throne of Egypt before Dynasty 18, the monarchy was masculine by definition. Scribes, at a loss for appropriate words, vacillated between "he" and "she" in writing the records of Hatshepsut. Of possible throne names, one phrase was omitted: Mighty Bull. In an attempt to harmonize the myth of the pharaoh's divine origin, Hatshepsut had herself born again. In a series of reliefs at Deir el Bahri, the god Amun visits Hatshepsut's mother, Queen Ahmose; the queen conceives; Khnum, the gods' potter, molds the royal infant and its ka; the child is born, presented to Amun, and launched on its royal career. In spite of her anomalous position, Hatshepsut reigned ably. Some have called her history's first great woman. Says the biography of Ineni, a court official who had served and outlived three earlier pharaohs: "Egypt was made to labor with bowed head for her, the excellent seed of the god ... bow-rope of the South ... stern-rope of the Northland is she; the mistress of command, whose plans are excellent. ..."

Execution of one of those excellent plans took place in her ninth regnal year. Hatshepsut sent a fleet far south on a trading expedition to the marvelous land of Punt, close to present-day Somalia. The myrrh terraces of "God's Land" produced the incense and fragrant ointments Egyptians used for religious purposes and cosmetics. Scenes on the temple walls at Deir el Bahri preserve some of the vivid detail.

Five ships carrying goods for exchange sailed the length of the Red Sea. Traversing the sea both ways in safety, the pharaoh's vessels in time returned to Thebes amid a flurry of excitement, for the Egyptians had a lively interest in foreign lands and peoples. Some of the people of Punt came back on the ships, along with native flora and fauna. Down the gangplanks and through the streets to the palace came baboons, monkeys, dogs, a leopard—and enough live myrrh trees for Hatshepsut to make for Amun "a Punt in his garden, just as he commanded me." Among an array of other valuables the cargo contained large amounts of myrrh resins, eye cosmetics, leopard skins, throw sticks for hunting birds, ebony, ivory, and electrum, a natural blend of silver and gold.

She did not rely solely on peaceful expeditions, however. The army was sent into Asia and Nubia, and Hatshepsut herself may have taken part in one campaign. These were prosperous times in Egypt. Under the New Kingdom, the state owned most of the land. From persons who controlled and worked parcels of property the state collected taxes in the form of cattle, grain, wine, and other goods the land yielded. Adding to Egypt's vast internal revenues was tribute paid from outside. Hatshepsut channeled the funds to explora-

tion, building projects, and good works such as repairing neglected temples. Her own magnificent mortuary temple, constructed by Senmut, ranks as her foremost architectural achievement.

Toward the end of her reign Hatshepsut came to depend more on her stepson and co-regent, Thutmose III. She had no male heir and her daughter had recently died. The personal advisers who had supported her usurpation were nearly all gone. Her co-regent had ripened into vigorous manhood. When Hatshepsut died, Thutmose III automatically became the new king, with no opposition. Later in his life he vilified the memory of Hatshepsut. He hacked away her images and titles from the walls of temples, often crediting her accomplishments to Thutmose I, Thutmose II, or himself. And he omitted her name from the official list of Egypt's kings, erasing her from history. The woman who had herself "reborn" fit to be king thus, in effect, died a second death.

Pharaoh, a term commonly used for all kings of ancient Egypt, originally had meant "Great House." It first came to mean the person of the king sometime in Dynasty 18. Surely no monarch merited it more than Thutmose III, the great warrior king. We know he led at least 14 military campaigns into the Levant. He also put a cap on Egypt's conquests up the Nile. South to the Fourth Cataract and north to the Euphrates he marched. With him we can truly see Egypt rise to be a major military power in the Near East.

Within months after Thutmose III acceded to power, the army of Egypt marched into Asia, the king at its head. Since the campaigns of Thutmose I, Egypt had held loose dominion over numerous city-states of Syria and Palestine as far north as the Euphrates. But without an army on the scene to reinforce her claims, total supremacy was impossible. Now a coalition of these restless rulers, stirred to revolt by the king of Kadesh, had massed their forces at the strategic city of Megiddo. Sited above the plain of Esdraelon, Megiddo—the

Puntites bearing gifts fit for a female pharaoh

Exception to the rule that queens do not rule, Hatshepsut donned the *nemes* headdress and kilt of a king (opposite). At times a monarch's false beard hid the pretty chin of the odd-gendered "Son of Re." Blood and marriage entangled Hatshepsut with a series of kings named Thutmose. Daughter of I, half-sister and wife of II, she ousted III, her nephew and stepson. Though not a pacifist, Hatshepsut made her mark in trade, not war. She renewed Egypt's commerce with Punt, an exotic realm on the African coast. Its king and his ungainly queen (left) bartered such valuables as aromatic myrrh and 31 live myrrh trees to be transplanted. Sharing the treasure with Amun-Re, Hatshepsut thanked the god for a successful mission, "her limbs fragrant as the dew of the gods with ointment and myrrh."

"I set the war-cry of your majesty throughout the Nine Bows"

Biblical Armageddon—commanded the pass through the Carmel ridge on the main road between Egypt and the upper Euphrates. Spurning the advice of his officers to take a less dangerous detour, Thutmose in his gilded war chariot charged directly through the narrow pass. Not anticipating such a daring move, the enemy had not even a token guard on the pass. Thutmose led his army through, emerging safely in open terrain south of Megiddo. In the battle next day they overwhelmed the enemy who "fled headlong to Megiddo . . . abandoning their horses, their chariots of gold and silver, so as to be hoisted up into the town by pulling at their garments."

Flushed with their immediate success, the sight of all that free transportation proved too much for the Egyptians to resist. They took the spoil first and let Megiddo wait. Eventually, by long siege they took the city too—and even more booty. Duly recorded by battle scribes, the spoil of Megiddo included 340 prisoners, 2,041 mares, 191 foals, 6 stallions, 924 chariots, 200 suits of armor, 502 bows, 7 tent poles wrought with silver, some 24,000 head of cattle and other livestock, and more than 100,000 bushels of grain standing ripe in the fields and ready for harvest.

Then hard on the heels of Megiddo, Thutmose III marched his army on into southern Lebanon, taking more cities and building a fort before returning to Thebes. The entire first campaign took about 175 days. Thutmose was in his mid-twenties.

Year after year, at the end of the spring rainy season in Syria and Palestine—as promptly as May flowers—the Egyptian army would appear there. The reputation gained at Megiddo spared Thutmose the need for aggressive action for a few years. He went about receiving tribute and homage, securing Egypt's hold over the subdued city-states.

By the fifth campaign he ranged northward into new territory, again on the attack, again victorious. He listed among the plunder some Phoenician ships. Thereafter he began to transport the army to and from Egypt by water, capturing port cities and using them as supply points for his forays inland.

On his eighth campaign, which marked a pinnacle of achievement in his long series of Asiatic wars, he advanced beyond the Euphrates to challenge the powerful King of Mitanni. To ferry across that misguided river—it flowed north—he provided the army with boats on the coast of Lebanon, hauling them on ox-drawn wagons over rugged and barren land to the Euphrates. That invading horde must have made an incredible spectacle: plodding oxen towing the landborne fleet, followed by horses and chariotry—the shock troops of New Kingdom warfare—then the ranks of long-suffering infantrymen with their spears, bows, and quivers, and finally perhaps a donkey train bearing food and supplies. All this from a traditionally peaceful, rather insular country that had not long known the horse.

Triumphant over Mitanni, Thutmose III set up a stela of victory at the scene. The event had a special significance: He had exceeded the deepest penetration into Asia by any previous pharaoh, that of his grandfather Thutmose I. He had stretched the boundaries of the Egyptian empire to its northern limit, one that would hold more or less intact for a hundred years.

Before returning home from the Euphrates country, the hard-driving pharaoh allowed himself some relaxation, an elephant hunt in the nearby marshes. A trusted officer named Amunemheb who would follow his king and commander on bivouac and battlefield for many years was one of those who accompanied him on the hunt. The Lord of the Two Lands, says Amunemheb's biography, "hunted 120 elephants, for the sake of their tusks." "Then an elephant attacked and the king would have lost his life but for his faithful officer." "I engaged the largest . . . which fought against his Majesty; I cut off his hand [trunk] while he was alive."

This same biography tells of a ruse employed in battle by the King of Kadesh, a strong and persistent foe of

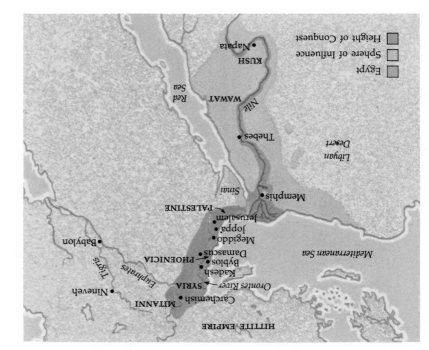

Words of Amun hallow Egypt's dominion over its known world—the Nine Bows—and hail the conqueror. Thutmose III (right), quintessence of the young warrior pharaoh, vitalized the martial spirit of the New Kingdom: Dynasties 18, 19, 20. In his first campaign at Megiddo he crushed a massive coalition of small city-states of Palestine and Syria. With an effective war machine—supported by the aristocracy, manned by levies—he solidified and stretched Egypt's wavering empire. At its zenith (left) in the mid-1400's B.C., it spanned 1,000 miles, from the Euphrates to the Nile's Fourth Cataract. Trade ships poured the world's wealth into the Delta and stirred a lively cultural exchange. Ably juggling government and war on the semester plan, Thutmose set "forth at the head of his army himself, showing the way."

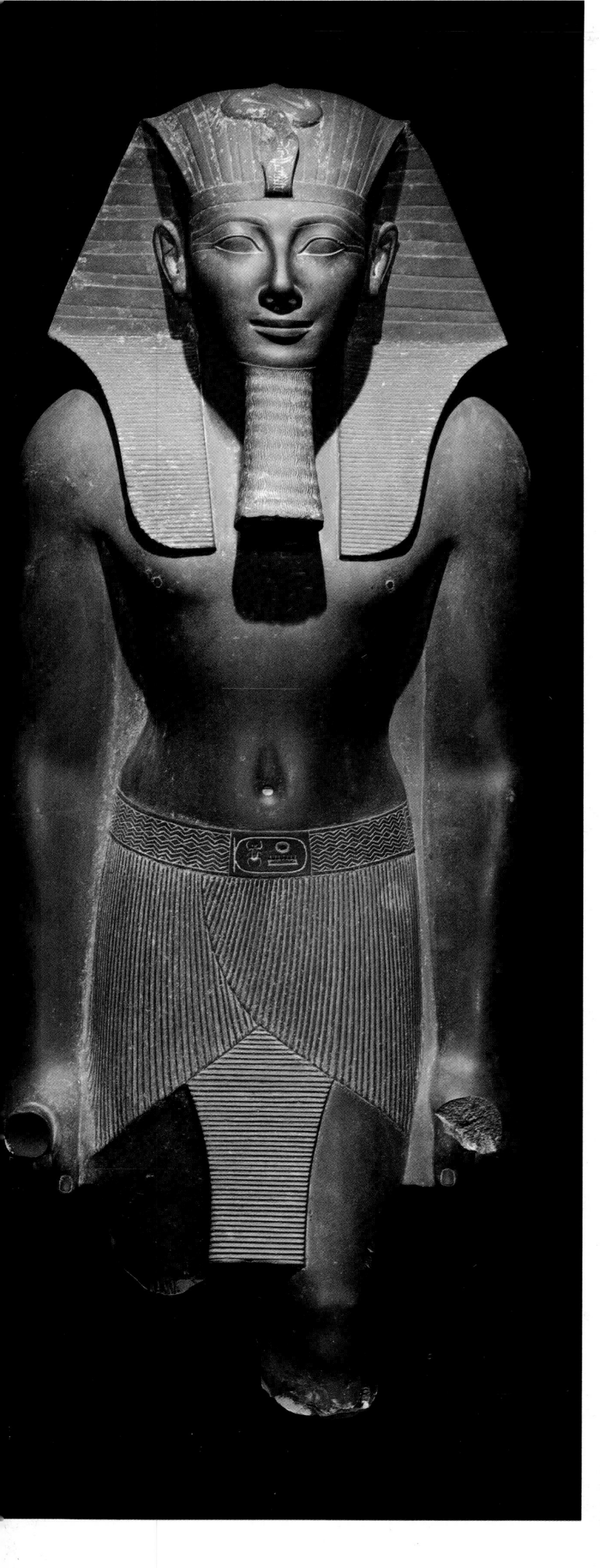

Egypt. Noticing that Egypt's chariots were drawn by stallions, he loosed a mare in their midst to break their pattern and thwart the impending charge. Amunemheb "pursued her . . . on foot, with my sword, and I ripped open her belly; I cut off her tail, I set it before the king. . . ." Amunemheb's deeds did not go unrewarded. His services on the battlefield and off earned him the Gold of Valor several times through the years, along with other rich gifts and the personal gratitude and affection of his sovereign.

A war story about Thutiy, one of Thutmose's generals, has a familiar ring. To capture the city of Joppa in Palestine, Thutiy made a fake surrender. Then, offering to present booty, he smuggled 200 hand-picked soldiers inside the city gates concealed in the panniers used to haul burdens on the backs of donkeys. The trick has an echo in the plot of "Ali Baba and the Forty Thieves," one of the most popular tales of the *Arabian Nights*. There the hidden men are robbers, and the scheme is foiled by Morgiana's boiling oil.

Under the reign of Thutmose III the Egyptian empire was firmly established. A campaigner all his life, he continued to spend part of nearly every year abroad with his army, sometimes in battle, sometimes by the military presence renewing some old, frayed allegiance. Tribute and booty regularly flowed back to Egypt from his wars. Every year an impost was expected from the small tributary countries of the north and from Nubia to the south. Much of this wealth above the actual cost of the wars went to enrich the temples and priesthood of the state god Amun, with full credit to the king and his deeds of glory. Thutmose III built extensively at Thebes, especially at the Karnak temple, where he erected the Sixth and Seventh Pylons. He also reformed the government. Two viziers were appointed instead of one. Memphis in the north and Thebes in the south became the administrative centers.

The empire that Thutmose forged had been in the making for a long time. Ahmose, founding pharaoh of Dynasty 18 and of the New Kingdom, had expelled the occupying Hyksos from the Nile Valley and chased them into Asia. His successor Amunhotep I had fought in Asia and led troops up the Nile to capture a Nubian rebel leader. Thutmose I, after his invasion of Syria, advanced north to the Euphrates, as we have seen. In the south this resolute warrior extended the conquest of Nubia beyond the Third Cataract of the Nile, returning with the body of the slain African chief hanging head down from the royal barge.

At the First Cataract, Thutmose I had encountered an obstacle: The old Middle Kingdom canal of Sesostris III was stopped up with stones and he was obliged to clear it. Thutmose III, sailing up the Nile to pacify some recalcitrant Nubians, met the same obstacle his grandfather had. Twice was enough. Naming the canal "Opening-of-This-Way-in-the-Beauty-of-Thutmose-Living-Forever," he left orders for the fishermen of Elephantine to clear the canal of debris each year.

Nubia with its valuable gold mines formed a major financial pillar of the empire. Egyptian officials took personal command of the lands they called Kush and Wawat, milking them for all they were worth. From the south, in addition to gold, came such exotic goods as leopard skins, ivory, live monkeys, Sudanese ebony, ostrich plumes and eggs, carnelian, amethyst, and some copper. Some of the land's attractions had to be enjoyed on the scene—there is a record of the pharaoh hunting rhinoceros on the upper reaches of the Nile.

In the Asian part of the empire, however, a different situation prevailed. These countries, though valuable to Egypt commercially, did not possess the wealth of gold and precious natural materials that the south held. Thus, the New Kingdom pharaohs exercised less control over those governments than over Nubia's. More interested in extracting wealth from the northern lands through trade than in annexing them, Egypt allowed the local kings of Syria and Palestine to remain on their thrones, so long as they swore allegiance to the pharaoh. Egypt did sometimes send governors, but they acted more as inspectors than overseers.

As a form of insurance of future loyalty, the pharaohs would bring the sons of those local kings back to Thebes to be educated, and presumably Egyptianized. Then when a ruler died, his son would be sent home to replace him. Egypt, of course, expected its annual tribute from the vassal kings—gold, silver, semiprecious stones, copper, horses, chariots, fine furniture. In a wood-scarce land, a yearly impost of cedar from the forests of Lebanon held special importance. Costly coffins, temple doors, flagpoles that stood before temples, and seagoing ships that plied the lanes to the trading center of Byblos—all used the straight, fine-grained wood of the cedars of Lebanon.

Under Thutmose III a military flavor came to pervade the country. The long wars against the Hyksos had established the need for a large standing army of professional soldiers, a New Kingdom innovation. The pharaoh, active as well as titular commander-in-chief, led major campaigns. War annals of Thutmose III evoke a vivid picture of the young pharaoh in his chariot galloping first into the thick of battle, inspiring—and sometimes shaming—the troops with his own courage and skill at arms. He was no towering figure—his mummy indicates he measured a hair over five feet. But he possessed brilliance as tactician and administrator, as well as unflagging energy. And charisma. James Breasted calls him the "first world-hero."

A worthy heir loomed in his son. Amunhotep II served as a general in his father's army. The kings' sons, in fact, often fought beside their fathers at the head of the army. Among his martial skills, Amunhotep II claimed prowess in handling horses and boats. And, says a stela, no man could draw his bow.

Soon put to the test—Asian princes revolted—Amunhotep II passed with honors. He returned triumphant to Thebes with the bodies of seven rebel princes hanging head down from his flagship. In spoil the campaign yielded some 1,650 pounds troy of gold, 50 tons of copper, and 550 captured Syrian nobles—plus their wives, horses, and chariots.

Captives brought back from military forays provided a permanent pool of labor for Egypt's building projects. Some of the Semitic tribesmen were allowed to settle lands in the Delta as taxpaying serfs. Many of these northern foreigners joined the army of their recent foe. More and more in the New Kingdom we hear of mercenary contingents lending their skills in battle on the side of Egypt.

Late in Dynasty 18 the laissez-faire attitude Egypt had adopted toward the northern sector of her empire would lead to trouble. The Hittites, a rising empire, flexed military muscle, expanding southward. While a Thutmose III would have charged "forth at the head of the army himself," the aging Amunhotep III preferred to continue his relaxed policy in foreign affairs. After he died, Hittite chariots rumbled in northern Syria, and Akhenaten was left to face the problem. This young king had his own dazzling dream—and the sun of the Aten rose.

The aftermath of the Amarna Revolution has often been described as a conservative counter-revolution in politics, art, literature—in society itself. Actually, the immediate response to the Amarna Period was not particularly violent at all. Instead, we see an energetic return to tradition and normalcy from Egypt's floundering as the Amarna Period ended.

With the death of all of Akhenaten's relatives—Smenkhkare, Tutankhamun, and Ay—a new dynasty came to the fore. Its predecessor, the general Horemheb, occupies a unique place within the New Kingdom. He is related neither to the dynasty of Akhenaten (18) nor to that of the Ramessides who follow (19).

Upon his accession, Horemheb issued an Edict of Restoration to put an end to the anarchy of the late Amarna Period. From one end of the land to the other, corrupt tax collectors, soldiers, and petty civil servants had greedily lined their own pockets under the pretext of collecting for the state. The lax central government—which had been losing revenues—had not interfered. But the new pharaoh made it his business to find out what was going on and then cracked down.

Among its provisions, Horemheb's edict specifically prohibited: robbing the poor of dues for the royal breweries and kitchens, robbing the poor of food of the king, use of the labor of slaves by unauthorized persons, stealing vegetables under the pretense of collecting taxes, and connivance of crooked tax inspectors with thievish tax collectors for a share of the take.

For each specific kind of offense, the edict prescribed an equally specific penalty. For misappropriating the share of a poor man's crop due as taxes, for instance, the guilty collector would have his nose cut off and then be banished to the boondocks, a remote place called Tharu on Egypt's northeastern frontier.

The edict also cites crimes committed by soldiers stationed on Egyptian soil. The huge cattle herds owned by the state and placed in the care of peasants were expected to return revenue, partly in the form of hides. Soldiers also had many uses for leather, but one caught rustling cattle hides from the king's herds would be punished "by beating him a hundred blows, opening five wounds," and forfeit of the stolen goods.

While very specific in some of its provisions, the new king's declaration clarified for his subjects general principles he expected them to follow, ideals rather than laws. For Horemheb's edict basically was a renewal of Egypt's ancient code of maat.

Horemheb ruled about 27 years, efficiently but not gloriously. Although originally a military man, he concerned himself primarily with bettering the country's internal condition. With the capital moved from the south at Thebes to the age-old center at Memphis in the north, the bureaucracy concentrated there. From this time on, Memphis and the Delta increasingly came to dominate the country. Of course Thebes, with its shrines of Karnak and Luxor and sacred burial grounds of the Valley of the Kings and of the Queens, remained the focus of priestly power. The priests of Amun had supported Horemheb. Now he honored the

Chariot makes the rounds in peace and war

Keeping up with the Hyksos and other Asian foes pushed Egypt into the chariot age, putting war on wheels, bringing mobility to New Kingdom nobility. This luxury, two-horsepower model of bentwood—gilded, embossed, and inlaid with faience—was one of four in the tomb of Tutankhamun. Though this king led no battles, a conventional scene of bound enemies showing submission decorates the dashboard (left). A charioteer, royal or not, rode standing—there was no seat. Meshed leather straps made a resilient floor. An open back let riders jump to the ground. Used mainly for war and sport, the new vehicles also carried high-echelon mail in a relay postal service.

debt, building pylons to Amun with blocks taken from Akhenaten's temple at east Karnak. Yet, though the old order resumed in Thebes, the distinct social and political tenor of the new age comes from the north.

As the head of Egypt's army, Horemheb appointed his vizier Paramesses—the future Ramses I and founder of Dynasty 19. His origins lay in the eastern Delta. Paramesses came from a military family, and the appointment exemplifies Horemheb's policy of alignment with the most powerful houses of Egypt. Paramesses filled a void in the pharaoh's life: Horemheb had no son to succeed him so he made the vizier his heir. Thus the death of the old general who as king "spent the whole time seeking the welfare of Egypt" did not cause—as it might have—a civil war.

Less vigorous in tone and not quite so glorious in deed as the golden years of Dynasty 18, the Ramesside Period nevertheless deserves to be called Egypt's Silver Age. Ramses I, an old man upon accession, reigned but briefly, bequeathing the kingdom to his son Seti I, also a man wise in the military.

Too long had Egypt accepted the Hittite expansion in Syria. The rise of the kingdom of Hatti had forced economic realignments, slashing into Egypt's former zone of influence. Immediately upon becoming king, Seti I marched his army into Palestine and up to the coastline of Phoenicia. This "first campaign of might" launched an all-out effort to dislodge the Hittites from southern Syria and regain lost tributaries.

In an 11-year reign Seti I fought brilliantly in the north, conquering port cities such as Ugarit and Tyre and Palestinian city-states. In one long campaign Seti moved inland against Amurru, a Syrian ally of the Hittites. When Kadesh, an important Amorite city, fell to Seti's legions, the Hittites counterattacked. They lost the battle and shied away from a full-scale war against Egypt at this time. Seti had opened a new age of warfare that his famous son and successor Ramses II would vigorously continue.

The military flavor of Dynasty 18 also pervaded 19. The scribes penned attacks deriding the military, who were the nouveaux riches of the New Kingdom. Strong builders as well as strong warriors, Seti I and Ramses II built extensively at the religious centers of Thebes and Abydos.

The Ramessides had a penchant for drama, preferring hyperbole to history. Both the plastic arts and literature switch from older models to a bombastic, flamboyant style. Ramses II's Kadesh inscriptions, telling of his great battle against the Hittites in his fifth year, show the new direction. Upon a meager core of narration the account weaves a highly personal and exciting piece of military literature.

Ramses had assembled his army in four divisions, named for the gods Amun, Pre, Ptah, and Seth. They had marched north along the Orontes in Syria. Enemy spies tricked the pharaoh into believing the Hittite coalition was still far distant; actually it awaited him at Kadesh. Ramses plunged ahead with the Amun division, the bulk of his army trailing far behind. At Kadesh the Hittites sprang their surprise. As Ramses tells us himself, had it not been for his own personal valor Egypt would have completely lost the day:

"His Majesty was alone. . . . But the wretched Chief of Hatti stood in the midst of the army . . . multitudinous like the sand, and they were three men on a chariot . . . and they were equipped with all weapons of warfare. . . . His Majesty girt himself with his corselet. . . . Then his Majesty started forth at a gallop, and entered into the host . . . being alone by himself and none other with him."

The king's heroic fight saved his army from utter rout. Since it almost cost Ramses his life, he wished to broadcast the account of his personal victory throughout Egypt—and severely berate his army for leaving him in such a fix. And broadcast he did, inscribing vainglorious and inflated statements of victory over the Hittites on nearly every temple in Egypt.

In truth, the morning after the battle Ramses and his Hittite opponent, Muwatallis, declared a truce. The Egyptians left for home, defaulting the battle. The Hittites had not been dislodged from Kadesh.

Warfare in the Levant did not end with this encounter. The tough and tenacious Ramses returned year after year, regaining much of Egypt's former territory. He fought repeatedly, in Transjordan and against the Hittites in Syria. It took a decade or more of inconclusive shuttlecock warfare to make him realize that he could not retake Syria. The new Hittite king, Hattusilis III, had troubles at home: Assyrians and others stabbing at his empire. These factors, and simple weariness of war on both sides, led them to sign a peace treaty in Ramses' twenty-first year of rule. The Egyptian version in hieroglyphs reads as if the Hittite king had sued for peace; the cuneiform version (in Akkadian, the lingua franca of the day) omits that section.

Once at peace, Ramses and Hattusilis kept up a correspondence, as did their queens. The kings' letters stress a brotherly relationship—no mere diplomatic sham, it seems; 13 years after the treaty Ramses married a daughter of Hattusilis, and later a second. Ramses had numerous wives and concubines. But this international union nevertheless helped to cement friendship between the two powers. Indeed, Ramses II's son and successor, Merneptah, in later years sent grain to the Hittites to relieve famine.

The end of foreign entanglements gave Ramses II the time and resources to indulge in the building activity that—far more than his wars—made his name a household word. The work at Karnak, Luxor, the Ramesseum on the west bank at Thebes, the temple of Ptah at Memphis, the gigantic grotto-temple of Abu Simbel—all testify to his power. Ramses forced his

memory upon us; he had his image and his name carved on almost every monument in Egypt. The Greeks knew of him in a garbled form as Ozymandias, and the English poet Percy Bysshe Shelley composed a sonnet about this great king:

Half sunk a shattered visage lies, whose frown,
And wrinkled lip, and sneer of cold command,
Tell that its sculptor well those passions read
Which yet survive, stamped on these lifeless things,
The hand that mocked them, and the heart that fed;
And on the pedestal these words appear:
"My name is Ozymandias, king of kings,
Look on my works, ye Mighty, and despair!"

Ramses ruled for 67 years, outliving 12 of his sons as well as his most famous queen Nefertari. His thirteenth son Merneptah, already an old man at his coronation, probably had little heart for conquest. He soon had to go to war in Egypt's defense. Libyan tribes, the Meshwesh and Libu, united for the purpose of settling in the Delta. In hordes—with wives and children, personal goods, cattle and other livestock—they moved on Egypt's borders. Before the campaign, Merneptah relates in an inscription at Karnak, the god Ptah of Memphis came to him in a dream and gave him a sickle sword for victory. The famous Israel Stela, in a more poetic way, sings of the pharaoh's triumphs:

The princes are prostrate saying: "Mercy!"
No one raises his head among the Nine Bows.
Desolation for Tehnu; Hatti is pacified . . .
Israel is laid waste, its seed does not exist.

The mention of Israel in the stela, unique in Egyptian literature, has led scholars in the past to equate Merneptah with the Biblical pharaoh of the Exodus. After his death, court intrigues plagued the country. Dynasty 19 exhausted itself. A later account of this time claims that a Syrian ruled Egypt for a while.

Horemheb, a pharaoh who came up from the ranks

General Horemheb, "King's messenger as far as the sun disk shines," sits in the typical cross-legged pose of a scribe (right). He added spine to the splendor of the weak Amarna regime. Tutankhamun heaped gold collars and duties on the shoulders of this military man. As King's Deputy (left) he receives homage of Egyptians and Asiatics—two of whom throw themselves in the dust "seven times and seven times" on belly and back. Not of royal blood, Horemheb was both king and kingmaker. He gained the throne as Dynasty 18 ran out, then launched the Ramessides of Dynasty 19. Before his accession, Horemheb built a tomb at Saqqara. Buried under drifted sands, it was found again in 1975. As archeologists under Geoffrey T. Martin excavate and analyze, fragments that long ago found their way into museums gain context, and light is shed on a career that bridged two dynasties.

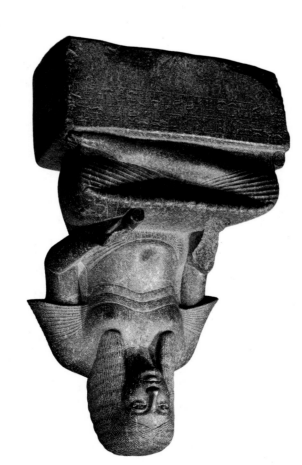

Ramses III, Egypt's last truly great pharaoh, belongs to Dynasty 20, a second line of Ramesside kings related only distantly, if at all, to Dynasty 19. In his fifth regnal year, Libyans, chiefly the Meshwesh, again invaded. An inscription on the walls of Medinet Habu temple—in the bombast typical of the Ramesside age—tells us: "His Majesty went forth against them like a flame . . . They were threshed as sheaves, made ashes and cast down prostrate in their own blood . . . made into pyramids on their own soil."

Ramses had to thresh another invading Libyan army six years later. New crops of Meshwesh continued to sprout like seeds blown east onto Delta soil.

Between the two Libyan conflicts, Ramses III faced an onslaught of Sea Peoples: "Peleset, Tjeker, Shekelesh, Denyen, and Weshesh, lands united." The Peleset were the Philistines, the Tjeker their cousins, the Shekelesh possibly Sicilians. This coalition posed a great threat on land as well; they had already smashed the Hittite empire before the Egyptian army met and stopped the Sea Peoples in Palestine. Simultaneously, the invaders sent a navy to the Delta. There Egypt's fleet destroyed them.

These wars bought peace, but at a price. Egypt's empire was crumbling. Palestine was a shambles. Philistines settled in former Egyptian territories. Egypt lost control of her sea trade to Phoenicia. She faced collapse, as Ramses grew old and fat in his palace. Inflation was rampant. The bureaucracy grew more and more degenerate. Near the end of Ramses' reign history's first recorded sit-down strike took place. Necropolis workmen had not been paid and a gang protested, "saying 'We are hungry!' . . . And they sat down . . .'" So the symptoms of Egypt's ills piled up.

Eventually an attempt was made on the king's life by a son and a wife. Dozens of high-ranking persons had a hand in the harem conspiracy—royal butlers, army officers. Many were foreigners. And judges on the bench who convicted them included Syrians.

Ramses III died peacefully, having ruled for 32 trou-ble-filled years. His sons constantly quarreled. One Ramses after another ruled Egypt in a century of decline. While other nations advanced into the Iron Age, Egypt even lost her copper mines in the Sinai. Commerce halted. Starvation stalked the land. Idle workmen and marauders plagued the countryside.

As the prestige of the pharaohs ebbed, the priests of Amun gained power. Under Ramses XI, Hrihor, commander of the army and viceroy of Kush, was also the high priest of Amun. At about the same time an ambitious local magnate of the Delta, Smendes, assumed control over Lower Egypt. These two powers bided their time. But when this last of the Ramesside kings went to his grave, the New Kingdom with its concept of divine kingship died with him. Egypt split in two.

In the "Report of Wenamun" we have a picturesque account from Egypt's dying days as an international power. Wenamun, the "elder of the portal of the temple of Amun," was sent by Hrihor to Byblos, to get cedars for the holy bark of Amun. The mission—once routine—had become hazardous. Troubles beset Wenamun from first to last. In Palestine a sailor stole his money, then jumped ship. The local authorities made little effort to get his money back and Wenamun sailed on. When he got to Byblos, its prince, Tjekerbaal, refused to see him, and he cooled his heels for a month. When Wenamun finally got to state his request for cedars, Tjekerbaal arrogantly told him off:

"'I am not your servant and neither am I a servant of the one who sent you. I have but to let out a cry unto the Lebanon so that the heavens open up, and the logs are already lying here on the seashore.'"

Wenamun complained. He invoked the god Amun and the omnipotence of Egypt. Tjekerbaal smiled—and refused to provide the wood without payment.

Compare Wenamun's tale with that of Sinuhe (page 144), set in a time when Egyptians were considered among the strongest people in the world. Sinuhe prospered. But a Levantine prince now scoffs at Wenamun, the emissary of a "broken reed."

"Bringing the tribute . . . from the country of Kush"

Ramses II enthroned receives emissaries from the conquered land of Kush, in Nubia. Its viceroy, an official answerable only to the king, carries a table draped with leopard skins. Common dress for Nubians, the skins in Egypt were kept for robes worn by priests or the king while offering incense to the gods. Among the Nubians' other tribute: rings of gold, jars of incense, bows, spears, shields, fans, ostrich eggs, elephant tusks, ebony and ivory furniture. And live cattle, a giraffe, gazelle, monkey, lion, and leopards. Taken as cubs, leopards and lions sometimes were trained as pets or hunting companions. Ramses II had a tame lion that sat by his throne and paced beside his war chariot, "doubtless hastening the enemy into retreat." Among other epithets, Ramses called himself in battle "strong-hearted lion."

Ramses II as a thumb-sucking infant

Nestled under the wing of the falcon god, Horus, Ramses II—famed for mighty war deeds and mightier boasts about them—appears helpless and shy in typical child's pose. Yet the statue implies he commands the powers of Horus. Symbols form a rebus of the name Ramses: *Re:* the sun disk resting on his head; *mes,* the child; *su,* the plant held in his left hand.

Overleaf: Ramses, "firm in the chariot like the lord of Thebes, lord of victory, fighting millions, mighty Bull . . . crushing the rebellious upon the mountains."

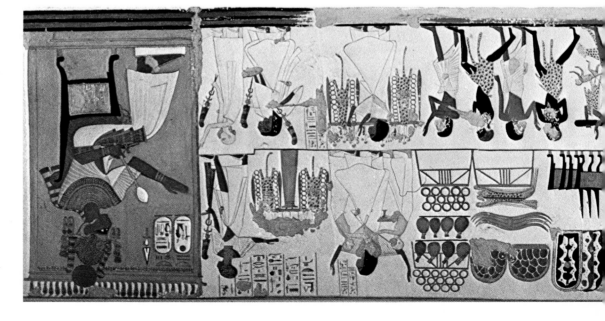

Egypt, a defensive country, preferred to follow its age-old practices in religion and daily life, avoiding alien influences. Its pharaohs did not set out to conquer the world. In a Thutmose III you will scarcely find an Alexander. In a Ramses II, the merest trace of a Caesar. Nor did they have in mind economic domination in any modern sense. To the warrior kings there were a few major enemies that had to be defeated—foes of the eternal status quo established by the creator god. They inherited wars and fought them, never fully understanding the effect of the Hittites, Nubians, Libyans, Sea Peoples. They would have laughed at the notion that strife could mean the end of their empire or lead to foreign domination of their own land.

This idea contains, in a nutshell, the strengths and weaknesses of Egypt. By separating themselves from other men and by considering their land to be independent of the rest of the world, the pharaohs of Egypt developed a unique civilization with its own merits and faults. However, this very feeling of separateness ill-equipped them to evaluate their enemies.

At a glance the history of Egypt during the first millennium B.C. shows a rapid change of foreign dynasties—first Libyans, then Kushites—in a lengthy period of disunity. Then followed one brief bright era, the Saite Period (664-525 B.C.) when Egyptians ruled once more, in turn succeeded by on-and-off Persian domination. The close of Egypt's independence witnessed a new star rising. Alexander the Great in 332 B.C. took the land easily and ushered in a vibrant new era under Greek domination. Enter the Ptolemies. Their rule would end with Cleopatra and the rise of Rome.

Egypt's decline before new peoples and new empires did not occur suddenly at the end of the reign of Ramses III. It was long and protracted. Nor does the fadeout of its empire prove exhaustion of the Egyptians' political or intellectual spirit. The Saite kings managed to rally the people for a final show of glory. Yet, when the tally was drawn up, the aegis of civilization had passed from the land of the pharaohs.

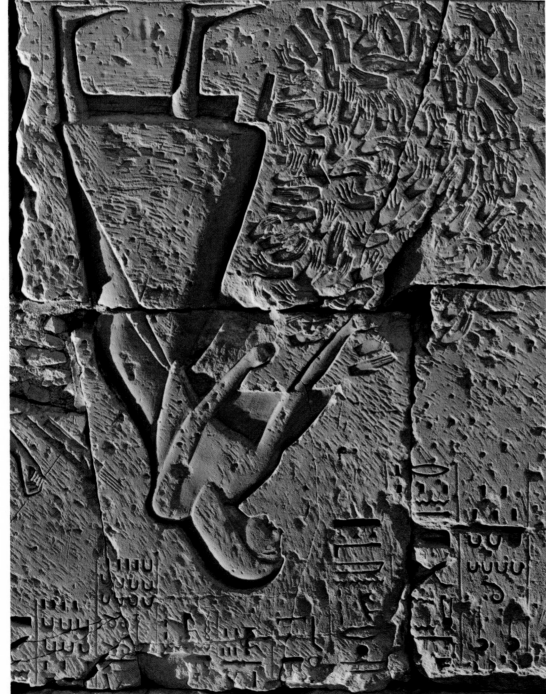

After the battle, the post mortem

Gory tokens of triumph—severed hands of slain enemies—pile up to be tallied and presented to the glory of the pharaoh. Inscriptions surrounding this detail from murals of Ramses III's second Libyan war put the trophy count at 2,175; living captives numbered another 2,052 (including 558 females). The traditional review might take place on the battlefield, with the pharaoh watching from his chariot, or, as here, from a rostrum.

In motifs and language of their battle monuments Egypt's warrior kings copied freely from their predecessors, altering only details and—of course—the star. Prisoners paraded before the pharaoh come "bound like fowl," bent in obeisance. Those below: Nubians in a frieze at Abu Simbel. Slavery awaited most captives. Relief (opposite) enacts a bloody ceremony of ancient origin requiring the king to sacrifice foes to Amun. Ramses II grasps the selected victims and ritually smites them with a mace.

Booty, the beauty of battle, included chariots, horses, asses, herds of cattle, weapons, gold, and other valuables of the vanquished that could be taken back home. Plunder enriched the estate of Amun, the king's coffers, and soldiers who showed special valor in the campaign. At the review of the spoils, a victor claimed a share based on the number of hands he put in the pile, proof of enemies killed. Fruits of incidental pillage of a downed village—food, wine, facilities for fun—strewed fringe benefits on the soldiers. What they seized was what they got.

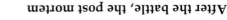

"Let me tell you the woes of the soldier!"

"He is called up for Syria. He may not
rest. There are no clothes, no sandals.
The weapons of war are assembled. . . ."
For the infantryman new wars, old woes.
His life had changed little since these
40 model spearmen marched into the
tomb of a nomarch, ruler of a nome,
in the strife-torn Middle Kingdom.
Frequent wars of the empire needed
personnel trained and ready. Chariots,
each manned by driver and a fighter,
paced a more sophisticated warfare.
But most soldiers—bowmen, axmen,
spearmen—still traveled and fought on foot.
Spears, shorter than those shown above,
measured about three feet. Uniforms still
suited the climate: a short linen skirt,
a shield of raw cowhide with the spotted
hair outside, a helmet also of leather.
"His march is uphill through mountains.
He drinks water every third day. . . . His body
is ravaged by illness. The enemy comes,
surrounds him with missiles. . . . He is told:
'Quick, forward, valiant soldier!'"

"He has made his monuments like the stars of heaven"

Colossal quartet—all images of Ramses II—surveyed their first Nile sunrise 3,200 years ago. From Abu Simbel's rock bluff artisans hewed away what was not Ramses, leaving the four seated figures, 67 feet high and weighing 1,200 tons each. Their lips measure some three feet wide.

One of the heads broke off from its torso centuries ago. In a niche above the portal of the temple stands a hawk-headed human figure crowned with a sun disk, depicting the pharaoh merged with Re-Harakhty. Not only absolute monarch, Ramses II was worshiped as a deity in his own time. Celebrating himself, he built grandiose monuments up and down the land.

"The All-Lord himself. . . gave to me the land while I was in the egg; the great kissed the earth before me," boasts a Ramses inscription at the Abydos temple of his father, Seti I. Seti made Ramses co-regent while yet a child "that I may see his beauty while I live." He also gave him official duties and a harem. After warring at Seti's side in boyhood, Ramses as king and commander fought to maintain Egypt's Asian empire. "His might is in all lands, bringing for him multitudes of workmen from the captivity of his sword," says a notation on one of Ramses' Abu Simbel reliefs.

With the relentless building activities of the Rameside kings, particularly Ramses' namesake city, scholars have linked the Biblical oppression of Israel. Multitudes of Ramses' workmen not only labored making sun-dried bricks but quarried the building blocks of previous pharaohs. Determined to eradicate relics of the hated Akhenaten, Ramses II left no Amarna stone unturned.

Abu Simbel, 180 miles above Aswan, had its own building material. The facade (above) fronts Ramses' Great Temple hewn 200 feet back into a sandstone monolith. Little damaged after a vigil of three millenniums, this and a smaller temple nearby were threatened in the 1960's by rising waters of the Aswan High Dam. In a massive international effort to save the priceless monuments, rescue crews cut the statues and their temples into huge blocks for transport to higher ground. Aware that vibration might break the crumbly sandstone—and leave scars on Ramses' faces—craftsmen hand-sawed the surfaces, then power-sawed from the back to finish cuts. Painstakingly reassembled, Ramses, "house of myriads of years" resumed its watch on the Nile.

"One long level beam . . . falls like fire"

Twice each year, rays of the rising sun penetrate to the sanctuary deep inside the great temple at Abu Simbel, flushing figures of the gods (left). A deified Ramses II shares the light with Amun of Thebes, at Ramses' right hand. Ptah of Memphis and Re-Harakhty of Heliopolis sit in shadow. The stone pedestal in the foreground served as a resting place for the sacred bark of the god.

Four 30-foot pillars having features of Osiris, god of the underworld, flank each side of the hall (right).

Reliefs on the walls show Ramses the king offering cloth and incense before the bark of Ramses the god. One reads "incense to Ramses-meramen, may the incense come twice, may the perfume of Seth come, may the eye of Horus come . . . and the perfume of Nekhbet. . . ."

In the temple's new site the original orientation has been preserved. Maximum illumination by the dawning sun still occurs around October 20 and February 20. Egyptologist Louis Christophe believed the temple may have been planned so that sunshine would glorify Ramses' 30-year jubilee, about October 20, 1260 B.C.

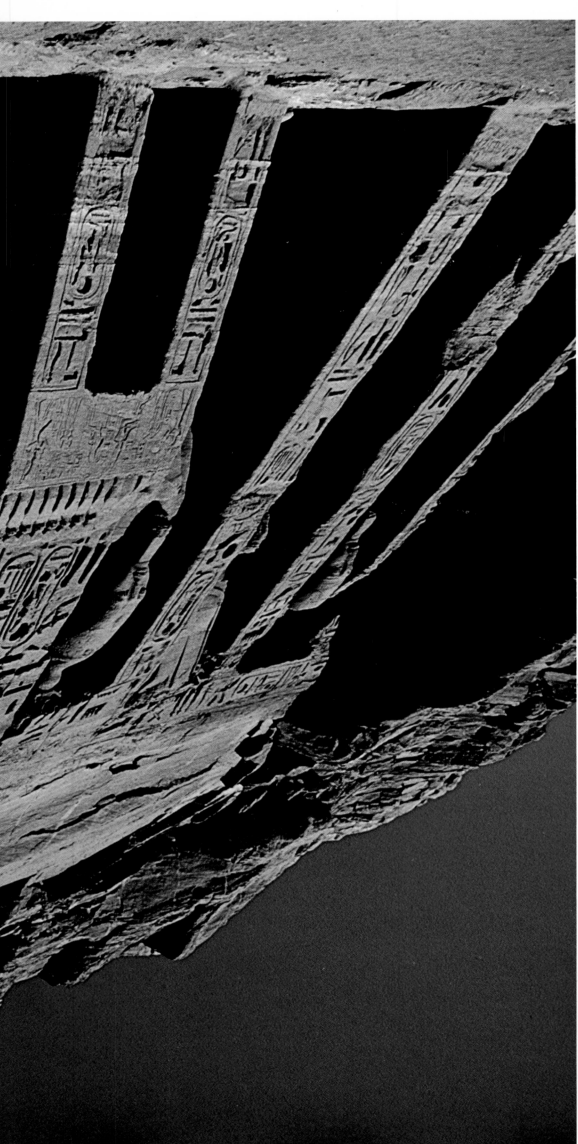

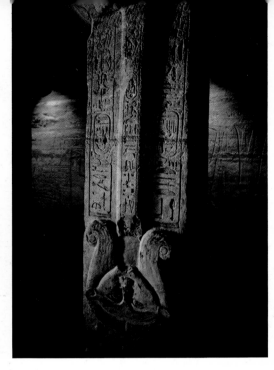

For the Great Royal Wife, a mansion

Before Nefertari's temple at Abu Simbel Ramses II put the ultimate status symbol: statues of his "Beautiful Companion." Married to Nefertari before he became king, he gave her first place in a vast harem. Twice cherished, each image of the queen is flanked by two of Ramses (right). As part of her high, feathered crown, Nefertari wears the cow horns and solar disk of the sky goddess Hathor.

The relief (above) pictures the queen's divine coronation by Hathor and Isis. A huge head of Hathor dominates a pillar (below), one of six in the temple. Nefertari's smaller temple complements the Great Temple of Ramses at Abu Simbel.

"On every pillar . . . names of Ramses and Nefertari" coupled and inseparable,'" wrote traveler Amelia Edwards. "We see that the Queen was fair . . . the King was in his prime. We divine the rest; and the poetry of the place . . . is ours . . . a breath from the shores of old romance."

To speak of the dead, in the religion of the ancient Egyptians, is to make them live again. While such monumental stones endure, inspiring awe and wonder in all who see, speech is automatic. And the people who raised them long ago seem to move again to the rhythms of the Nile, "given life, like Re, forever."

Time chart

Across a span of 5,200 years, this overview of ancient history sketches events in Egypt against a backdrop of happenings in the rest of the world.

Dates in the chronology here—and throughout the book—are approximations. New archeological findings or fresh interpretations of old ones, along with new developments in dating methods, make for recurring revisions. And for all the ancient world, dates are so interdependent that a change in one can affect a number of others, domino-fashion. We have used those currently accepted by major authorities.

Problems arise too with the spelling of Egyptian names. The lack of vowels in hieroglyphic writing has already been touched on (page 143). But there can be bewildering turns. Some scholars argue, for example, that "Amun" should be spelled with a "u" when the stress falls on that vowel—as in the god *Amun*—but with an "e" when the stress is elsewhere—as in "Amenhotep." Others disagree. In addition, scholars around the world have spelling conventions based on their own languages, and sometimes these show up in English translations of their works.

Further complications crop up in spellings based on Egyptian words from Babylonian tablets written in cuneiform, which does not set down vowels. From this we get such forms as "Amanhatpi" instead of "Amunhotep." But experts argue that this derivation, from a foreign tongue, is no certain guide to ancient Egyptian usage.

Then there is the fact that Greek domination of Egypt for centuries brought indelible change. Greeks put a veneer of their words on people and gods and places. As a result, we are more familiar with Cheops than Khufu, Osiris and Isis than Usir and Aset, Memphis and Thebes than names long lost or obscure.

Modern Arabic pronunciation adds to the complexities. Archeological sites and place names are known by Arabic words that are difficult to transliterate in our Western alphabet. So no one meets Idfu as well as Edfu, Saqqara and Sakkara, Qurna or Qurneh or Gurna.

Even among experts, no general agreement resolves such problems as those reviewed briefly above. We have tried, in this book, to conform to the simplest and the most common spelling.

5200 B.C.

Egypt's Predynastic Period begins around 5200 B.C. Small bands of hunter-gatherers roam the Nile Valley. Herding and agriculture are known, but little practiced. Excavations of camps, cemeteries, and settlements have unearthed pottery, baskets, beads, stone tools, slate palettes for cosmetics. Pottery found near El Badari has given the name "Badarian" to one early culture.

VASE/COOK POT, CA 4750 B.C.

4600 B.C.

Farms and farming villages expand in **Mesopotamia.** Mud bricks used in building. Wheat and barley established as staple crops; farmers have domesticated goats, sheep, cattle, and swine. Earliest evidence of the taming of pigs found in Turkey, where the pottery figure above was unearthed near Hacilar. First use of hammered copper for tools and ornaments occurs in Iraq, spreads throughout Mesopotamia, presumably by trade.

Agriculture develops in **China** and the valley of the **Indus River.** Hunting-fishing cultures in **Europe** leave rock carvings and animal sculptures of stone and amber. In **Middle America,** after big game dies out, hunter-gatherers experiment with food plants—corn, beans, squash.

POTTERY PIG, CA 5600 B.C.

BIRD DEITY, CA 4000 B.C.

3500 B.C.

Sumerian city-states come into existence along the Tigris and Euphrates rivers, centering around temples of mud brick. Work in copper becomes highly sophisticated. Impressions from stamp seals used as identification tags. They lead to cylinder seals, and eventually to the development of writing.

People of the **Danube River** basin produce skillful copperwork, and, by the end of this period, goldwork. Metalworking may have developed independently at several places in Europe not long after its beginnings in the Near East.

Megalithic—huge rough stone—tombs are erected in western **Europe.** They date from 4000 B.C., the oldest known stone structures.

SUMERIAN STAMP SEAL, CA 3500 B.C.

GOLD ORNAMENT, DANUBE, CA 3500 B.C.

Farming takes over from a hunting-fishing way of life along the Nile. Towns, sometimes fortified, become established. Sailboats ply the Nile and explore Mediterranean shores. Fine flintwork and pottery with crosslined designs in white are made. People of late predynastic times develop a single culture archeologists call the Amratian, or Nagada I.

3200 B.C.

Sumerian civilization climbs to new heights with invention of the cart wheel and the potter's wheel (and first mass-produced pottery). At the same time the first writing—pictographs—develops; earliest known use dates from about 3200 B.C. Pictographs and the wheel spread quickly to neighboring areas. Sumerians also devise the numbering system that would give us our 360-degree circle and our 60-minute hour.

Farmers in **China** cultivate rice, millet—and the silk moth. In **Middle** and **South America,** nomadic hunter-gatherers settle into permanent villages, develop agriculture. People of the Peruvian Andes domesticate the llama. In **North America,** signs of a settlement appear in a sheltered site in the Illinois River Valley.

SUMERIAN PICTOGRAPH TABLET, CA 3000 B.C.

Influences from outside the Nile Valley spark development of the Gerzean, or Nagada II, culture. Larger towns, rudimentary irrigation mark the change. Wattle-and-daub houses give way to rectangular structures of mud brick. Pottery shows new painting techniques, incised decoration, lug handles. Tombs become more elaborate; chambers, wall paintings are added.

GERZEAN VASE, CA 3400 B.C.

NARMER PALETTE, CA 3000 B.C.

FUNERARY STELA, CA 3000 B.C.

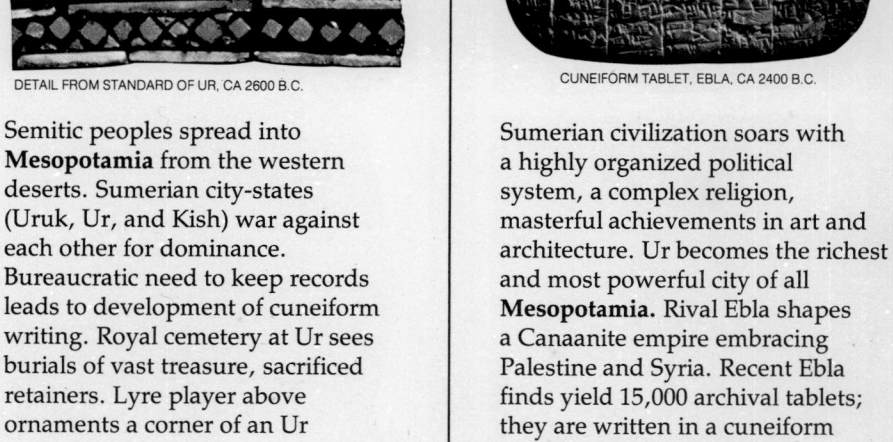

STEP PYRAMID, SAQQARA, CA 2650 B.C.

GREAT SPHINX, GIZA, CA 2550 B.C.

Separate political units—districts or provinces called "nomes"—begin to join forces. In time a single leader wins control of all nomes in Upper Egypt and achieves status as god-king. Unification with nomes of Lower Egypt is accomplished about 3050 B.C., and the pharaohs of Dynasty 1 rule all Egypt. The name of conquering King Narmer shows on a slate palette in an early form of hieroglyphs.

A new capital for the unified Egypt rises at Memphis. Royal and religious pomp and power grow as Dynasty 2 gains the throne. Pharaohs and noblemen build even more elaborate tombs. Egyptians devise an accurate stellar calendar, become expert at working copper and gold. Hieroglyphic writing, with many pictographic elements, decorates temples and tombs. A cursive form develops for writing on newly invented papyrus.

The Pyramid Age emerges in Egypt. Architect Imhotep builds a step pyramid for King Djoser of Dynasty 3. It stands as the world's first massive monument of hewn stone. Cult of the sun god Re flourishes at Heliopolis, stimulating the sciences of astronomy and mathematics.

Building of Bent Pyramid for King Snefru of Dynasty 4 ushers in construction of true pyramids. Cheops's great monument rises at Giza and shortly afterwards Chephren's with its guardian Sphinx. Egyptians war against Nubia and Libya, undertake trade expeditions in the Mediterranean. Old Kingdom reaches its zenith.

Sumerians usher in the Bronze Age, alloying copper first with arsenic, later with tin. Artistic skills and technology in bronze spread throughout the **Near East.** Sumerians also develop techniques for layering mud brick into solid, towering ziggurats—"mountains." Ceremonial stairways rise past intricate stepped terraces to temples at the top.

Large and complex semicircular structures of limestone blocks, perhaps the world's first stone temples, take shape on the Mediterranean island of Malta. "Fat lady" figurines found there may represent a mother goddess or fertility cult symbol—a central

Flourishing Sumerian city-states establish royal dynasties, reach populations as large as 50,000. Their cultural influence spreads across the **Near East.** Stone figurines and a bull-shaped vase found in Iran reflect a close relationship to the classic art of Sumer. Trade routes develop. Trading posts and towns are established in Palestine, Syria, and Anatolia—including the first settlement of Troy.

The horse is domesticated in southwestern **Asia** and the soybean in **China.** Earliest cultivation of cotton appears in the **Indus Valley**—and in **Peru.**

Pictographs come into use in

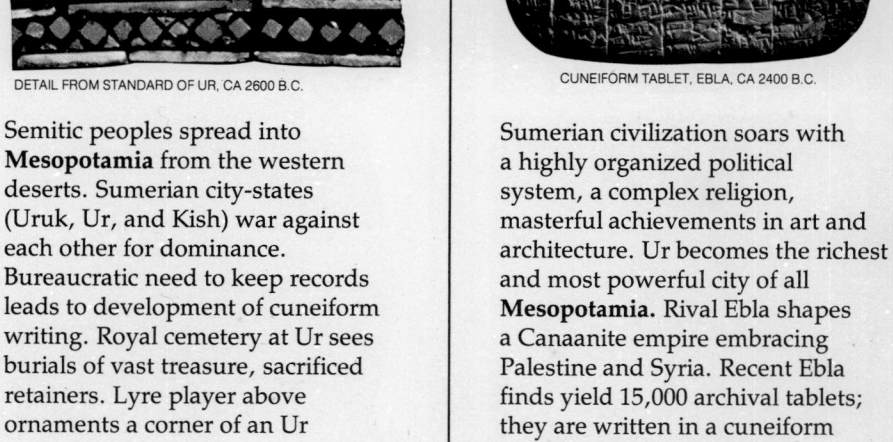

DETAIL FROM STANDARD OF UR, CA 2600 B.C.

Semitic peoples spread into **Mesopotamia** from the western deserts. Sumerian city-states (Uruk, Ur, and Kish) war against each other for dominance. Bureaucratic need to keep records leads to development of cuneiform writing. Royal cemetery at Ur sees burials of vast treasure, sacrificed retainers. Lyre player above ornaments a corner of an Ur

CUNEIFORM TABLET, EBLA, CA 2400 B.C.

Sumerian civilization soars with a highly organized political system, a complex religion, masterful achievements in art and architecture. Ur becomes the richest and most powerful city of all **Mesopotamia.** Rival Ebla shapes a Canaanite empire embracing Palestine and Syria. Recent Ebla finds yield 15,000 archival tablets; they are written in a cuneiform text that reflects a previously unknown Semitic language.

Indus Valley civilization flourishes. Sophisticated planned cities such as Mohenjo-Daro and Harappa have straight streets, buildings of fired brick, a sewer system. Water buffalo and yak are domesticated in **India** and **Tibet.**

Pottery making spreads from centers in **Ecuador** and **Mexico.**

MALTESE FIGURINE, CA 3100 B.C.

BULL VASE FROM IRAN, CA 3000 B.C.

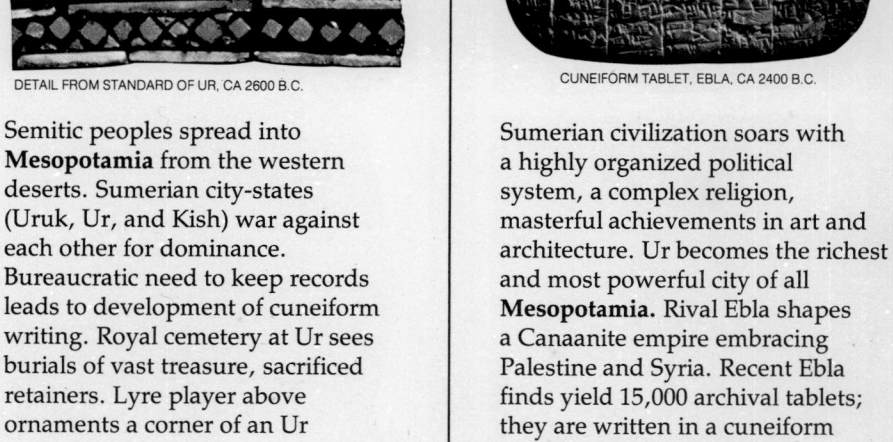

STONEHENGE, CA 2600 B.C.

feature of early religions across **Europe** and **Asia.** The example above is 19 inches tall.

Potters in **China** and **Japan** produce elaborately modeled and painted jars. Earliest pottery in the **Americas** appears in Ecuador and Colombia, with techniques and designs that some archeologists believe may have been brought by visitors from Japan.

northern **India** as the remarkable Harappan culture takes root along the Indus River.

mosaic depicting a victory celebration.

Early Minoan civilization flowers on **Crete.** Wheel comes into use in the **Indus Valley.**

Peoples of **Europe** construct megalithic chamber tombs, passage graves, and shrines such as England's Stonehenge. First stages of the latter, apparently laid out with astronomical observation, date to first half of third millennium B.C.

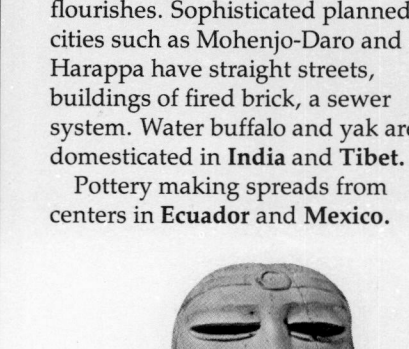

PRIEST-KING STATUE, MOHENJO-DARO, CA 2500 B.C.

2400 B.C.

TOMB OF MERERUKA, CA 2350 B.C.

Pharaohs begin calling themselves "Son of Re" and build elaborate sun temples. Pyramid Texts appear in royal tombs. High officials extol their own achievements in tombs nearby. Cedar from Lebanon and gold, ebony, incense, and ivory flow from Africa into Egypt. Internal decay sets in during long reign of Pepy II, last major king of Dynasty 6. Power shifts to the nomarchs—rulers of the provinces. Egypt splinters.

BRONZE HEAD OF SARGON (?), CA 2300 B.C.

Sargon of Akkad, Semitic warrior-king, unifies **Mesopotamia**, founds an empire stretching from the Mediterranean to the Persian Gulf. But his empire falls around 2200 B.C., to the Guti, nomads of the Zagros Mountains. Mesopotamian city-states again become autonomous. Farming spreads in northern and eastern **China**; hunter-gatherer culture still marks the south. Hittite tribes filter into central **Turkey**. Skilled metalsmiths there fashion treasures of gold, silver, copper, and bronze and experiment with smelting iron. In northern, central, and western **Europe** villagers cultivate wheat and barley, raise cattle and sheep. Farming people erect huge stone monuments in the Orkney Islands.

2200 B.C.

LADY KAWIT, CA 2040 B.C.

Social and political chaos marks First Intermediate Period; tombs are ransacked, cultural traditions disrupted. Provinces engage in petty warfare against each other. Herakleopolitans restore order in the north, then Theban princes of Dynasty 11 reunite the country and initiate the Middle Kingdom. Thebes becomes the capital. Monumental building projects are revived, trade routes renewed. Egyptians begin to smelt bronze.

GUDEA OF LAGASH, CA 2140 B.C.

From ashes of the Akkadian empire, Gudea of Lagash revives southern **Mesopotamia**, sets stage for final resurgence of Sumer. Ur-Nammu becomes king of Sumer and Akkad, issues the first known law code, erects magnificent buildings—including the storied ziggurat at Ur. In northern **China**, Hsia Dynasty is founded, based on slavery. Minoan civilization on **Crete** builds planned cities with royal palaces, develops a writing system. Migrant "beaker people," named for their pottery, introduce copper and bronze to western and northern **Europe**. The wheel reaches the North Sea. Scandinavians first use skis. **Peruvians** work designs in cotton textiles. Maize agriculture spreads through **Middle America**. Native peoples of the **Great Lakes** and the Mississippi Valley hammer out copper tools. Ancestors of Eskimos reach Greenland.

2000 B.C.

CYCLADIC IDOL, CA 2000 B.C.

Minoan civilization undergoes a meteoric rise on **Crete**. People of the Cyclades Islands in the Aegean make stylized statues and carvings of ivory. Their culture spans from 2600 to 1800 B.C. Mycenaeans advance into Greece from the north. At Avebury in England, builders raise one of the largest megalithic centers in **Europe**. Pottery making and cultivation of maize take root in **Peru**. **North America**'s earliest pottery appears on south Atlantic coast. Eskimo culture develops in Alaska.

1800 B.C.

SHRINE OF SESOSTRIS I, KARNAK, CA 1950 B.C.

Powerful monarchs undertake large irrigation projects, intensify trade, build fortresses in the south. Egypt controls Nubia by the time of Sesostris III. He curbs nobles, helps rise of middle class based on trade, bureaucracy. Court and royal burials shift north to a site near Memphis, but Thebes remains a center of worship. Cultural splendor grows—pyramids at Dahshur, a shrine at Karnak, sculpture in the round.

Sumerian *Epic of Gilgamesh*, one of the world's oldest literary compositions, is compiled. Amorites of Arabia's desert and Elamites of Iran shatter Sumerian renaissance. Amorites rule from Babylon. Pictographic writing develops in **China**.

1600 B.C.

NOBLEMAN, 1790-1750 B.C.

Parade of pharaohs—some 50 in 150 years—marks Dynasty 13. At the same time western Delta secedes and 76 kings rule there as Dynasty 14. Nubia becomes independent. Decline of central government leads to the Second Intermediate Period. Hyksos—"chiefs of foreign lands"—arise in eastern Delta and set up Dynasties 15 and 16. They introduce the chariot and horse, and their influence spreads over all Egypt.

Hammurabi, great ruler of the first **Babylonian** empire, sets down his law code. Babylonians make strides in mathematics and astronomy. Indo-Europeans settle in Iran, eventually to form Persian empire. Scholars date Abraham's Biblical trek to Canaan and Egypt in this period. Natural disasters—floods, mud

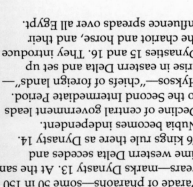

MINOAN "SNAKE GODDESS," 1600-1550 B.C.

volcanoes—spur collapse of **Indus** civilization; less advanced cultures of Aryan invaders are established in Bombay and Ganges regions. Shang Dynasty rises in Hwang Ho Valley of **China**. Its warrior-landlord society is to last five centuries. Advances in architecture and plumbing stand among achievements of **Minoan** civilization, now at its height. Multistoried palace at Knossos dominates a city of 80,000. People of **Europe** become identifiable as Slavs, Teutons, Finns, and ancestors of Celts.

HATSHEPSUT, CA 1485 B.C.

BUST OF NEFERTITI, CA 1355 B.C.

ARTIST'S TOMB, CA 1150 B.C.

God Triad: Horus, Osiris, Isis, 874-850 B.C.

Theban princes expel the Hyksos, reunite Egypt. Dynasty 18 begins the New Kingdom and Egypt's golden imperial age. Warrior pharaohs extend Egypt's boundaries, embrace Palestine, Syria, Nubia. Tomb of Thutmose I becomes the first to be cut in the cliffs of the Valley of the Kings. Book of the Dead recorded on papyri, placed in tombs.

The Mitanni form a new empire in northern **Mesopotamia**. Hittites maintain a flourishing iron industry. Alphabetic use of pictographs by Semitic people in the Sinai is possible forerunner of the Phoenician alphabet.
    Warlike Mycenaeans, established

MYCENAEAN MASK, CA 1550 B.C.

in citadels in mainland **Greece,** move into Crete, overthrow Minoans. Mycenaean rulers are interred with gold treasures in shaft graves.
    Bronze Age expands in **Europe.** New technology prompts improved designs in jewelry, tools, weapons.
    Aryans spread Sanskrit language and many elements of Hindu religion in **India**. Shang Dynasty spurs **Chinese** civilization; cities emerge as trade centers, agrarian fiefdoms shape the countryside. High art develops in bronze.
    Farm-village cultures in **Middle America** grow more complex; large communities develop in **Peru.**

Amunhotep III reaps splendor of Egypt's empire; court life at Thebes is luxurious, cosmopolitan. His son Amunhotep IV defies powerful priests of Amun and proclaims a worship of the sun's disk, the Aten. He changes his name to Akhenaten, builds a new capital at Amarna, ushers in realistic art. His successors, including Tutankhamun, restore old ways. First Ramesside dynasty renews military activity abroad.

LION GATE, MYCENAE, CA 1250 B.C.

Moses leads Hebrews from Egypt in the Biblical Exodus. Hittite empire collapses, conquered by invaders from Thrace. Use of iron becomes common in the **Near East.**
    Mycenaean civilization peaks;

OWL-SHAPED BRONZE WINE VESSEL, CHINA, 11TH CENTURY B.C.

it dominates all **Greece**; its trade covers the eastern Mediterranean.
    Aryan caste system evolves in **India.** Shang Dynasty founds its capital near An-yang in **China.**

Ramses III, the last strong pharaoh, drives back invading Libyans and Sea Peoples. But Egypt sinks into a decline. Tomb robbery grows flagrant, workers strike for lack of rations, conspirators plot the king's assassination. By the end of Dynasty 20, the pharaoh, the high priest at Thebes, and the viceroy of Nubia share power. A procession of Ramesside rulers marks the close of the New Kingdom. Unrest of the Third Intermediate Period follows.

Iron Age brings advances to the Aegean, Syria, and Palestine. Hebrews establish monotheism in Canaan, make Saul their first king. Phoenicians become a force in Syria and Lebanon.
    In **India,** rice farming develops, Hindu Rig Veda hymns are set down.
    Mycenaeans conquer Troy, then

WARRIOR VASE, MYCENAE, 12TH CENTURY B.C.

are overthrown by Indo-European northerners swarming down the Peloponnesian Peninsula.
    Olmec civilization appears in **Middle America.** Tlatilco villagers in the area of present-day Mexico City model elaborate figurines for use in burials.

TLATILCO FIGURINE, MEXICO, CA 1000 B.C.

Pharaonic capital moves to the Delta; Amun's high priest rules a theocratic state from Thebes. Dynasties 22 and 23 see a joint reign by Libyan families that had become Egyptianized in the western Delta. The first Libyan pharaoh, Sheshonq I (the Shishak of the Bible), pillages Jerusalem. By end of Dynasty 23 the Delta is dividing into city-states. Sculptors in this period produce exquisite statuettes in metal.

PHOENICIAN NORA STONE, 9TH CENTURY B.C.

Phoenicians build trading colonies, such as Carthage and Cadiz, around the **Mediterranean.** Their script is adopted by the Greeks, in turn to find its way into our alphabet. David makes Jerusalem his capital; his successor, Solomon, builds the Temple.
    Ancestor worship, with elaborate ritual, reaches a peak in **China.**
    Etruscans settle in **Italy.** Crete and Greece endure a period of darkness, accompanied by major migrations.
    Platforms of earth or stone for use as ceremonial centers are built in **Mexico** and **Peru.** Adena culture, with elaborate burials, centers in **Ohio Valley.**

OLMEC HEAD, 1000-850 B.C.

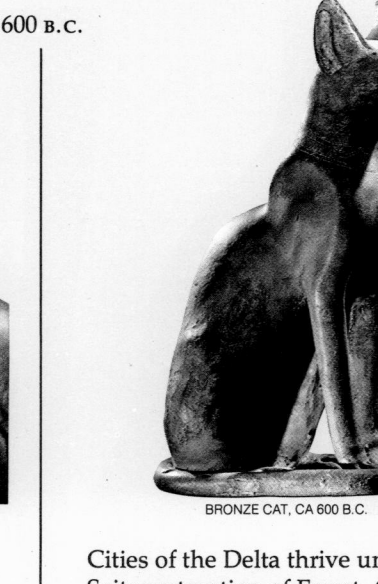

MENTUEMHAT, CA 660 B.C.

Nubians from Kush, under King Piankhy, conquer Egypt. Kushite rule ends with Assyrian conquest and sack of Memphis and Thebes. Saite Dynasty reunites Egypt and rebuilds its power and prestige, but Pharaoh Neko II's attempt to regain its empire is defeated by Nebuchadnezzar II. The Iron Age and camel reach Egypt in this period. Mentuemhat has a long tenure as a powerful governor of Upper Egypt.

BRONZE CAT, CA 600 B.C.

Cities of the Delta thrive under Saite restoration of Egypt. One of them, Bubastis, is the cult city of the goddess Bastet whose sacred animal is a cat. Neko II sanctions an attempt to build a canal from the Nile to the Red Sea, sends an expedition to sail around Africa. Streams of immigrants—Greeks, Syrians, Hebrews—flow into Egypt. In 525 B.C. King Cambyses II of Persia adds Egypt to his empire.

LION VESSEL, 525-404 B.C.

Persian rulers adopt the trappings of the pharaohs and maintain Egyptian culture. Egypt's legal system is codified. But revolts break out, spurred by Greek victories against Persians such as that at Marathon. Finally in 404 B.C. the Egyptians throw off the Persian yoke.

HEAD OF WESIRWER, CA 360 B.C.

Political turmoil and uncertainty mark rule of Egypt's last native kings. Persians again briefly gain control in 341 B.C. Their defeat in Asia by Alexander the Great leads to his whirlwind conquest of Egypt and establishment of dynasties under Macedonians and the Greek Ptolemies. Scholarship and trade flourish in Alexandria, their capital. It would boast a luxurious court, a university, and a library housing 400,000 scrolls.

"MONA LISA OF NIMRUD," 8TH CENTURY B.C.

Assyria reaches its pinnacle; Nimrud, one of its capitals, is rebuilt. But fall of the capital at Nineveh in 612 B.C. topples the nation. Mounted Scythians raid from their Black Sea home, join with Medes to bring down Assyria. **Babylon** climbs again into importance as an empire.

Etruscan civilization flourishes. Rome is founded (753 B.C.). Greece rises. First Olympic games take place, Homer's *Iliad* and *Odyssey* are written down. Celts emerge as a distinct people, spread ironworking through northern and central **Europe**, move into England.

Iron replaces bronze in **China**. Chou Dynasty struggles with rising challenge of rival warring states.

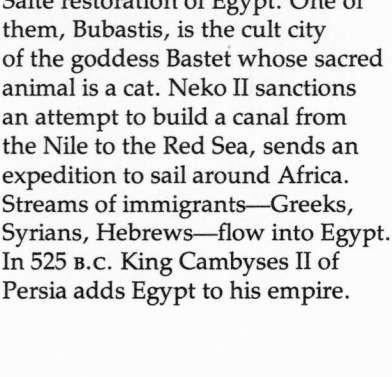

WARRIOR FRIEZE, PERSEPOLIS, 6TH-5TH CENTURIES B.C.

Nebuchadnezzar II takes over the fertile crescent of the **Near East.** He rebuilds Babylon, razes Jerusalem, carries Jews into captivity. Persians led by Cyrus the Great conquer **Babylonia.** Jews gain freedom. Darius I founds the Persian capital of Persepolis, extends Persian empire to the Indus.

Mahavira Jina rebels against **India**'s ritualistic religion, sets out the ascetic philosophy of Jainism. Teachings of Gautama Buddha begin Buddhism.

Etruscans expand in **Italy,** but in 509 B.C. rebelling Romans found the Roman republic. The Greek city-state of Athens expels a tyrant, Hipparchus, and creates a democracy.

China undergoes upheaval in a change from a slave to a feudal system. Lao Tzu forges Taoism; Confucius preaches his concepts.

ETRUSCAN SARCOPHAGUS SCULPTURE, CA 500 B.C.

Greeks, under leadership of Sparta, defeat Persian armies. Persians also gradually lose dominions in the **Near East, India.** Their liberal and brilliant civilization wanes.

Athens rises as a power. Golden Age of Pericles, named for the Athenian statesman, sees great works of literature, philosophy, and art and such immortals as Socrates, Hippocrates, Herodotus, Sophocles. Envy and hostility of other Greek states leads to Peloponnesian Wars.

PARTHENON, FINISHED 432 B.C.

Etruscan power ebbs. **Rome** firms independence, sets laws guaranteeing liberty, property, due process.

China slips into anarchy, a time of constantly warring states.

Olmec civilization in **Middle America** begins decline.

POT WITH SPOUT, PERU, 500-250 B.C.

Greek city-states jockey for supremacy. In 338 B.C. Philip II of Macedon subdues the quarreling Hellenes and adds **Greece** to the Macedonian empire. After his assassination, his son Alexander consolidates the inherited realm, sweeps on to defeat Persia, Syria, and Egypt, and marches as far as the Indus Valley. Hellenistic culture washes over **Asia Minor.**

Rome, now mistress of the Italian peninsula, builds on

ALEXANDER, THRACIAN COIN, 3RD CENTURY B.C.

traditions of the Etruscans—a sophisticated, exuberant, and civilized folk. Rampaging Celts, whom the Romans call Gauls, sack Rome in 387 B.C. but are driven back; the city is soon rebuilt.

Scythian culture reaches a peak in the **Ukraine.**

Chandragupta founds the first Indian empire. It spreads over **India** and parts of central Asia. The epic poems *Mahabharata* and *Ramayana* are set down.

Internal strife and attacks by nomads plague **China,** but rival rulers foster trade. "Golden Age" of Chinese philosophy blossoms.

Farm settlements begin in **North America**. Pottery appears in the southwest; coastal tribes of the northwest build plank houses.

Egypt's periods and dynasties

The list includes the number of kings and some notable rulers. Dates are B.C. and—before 664—approximate.

Predynastic Period, 5200-3050

Early Dynastic Period
DYNASTY 1, 3050-2890
Eight kings, including Namer (Menes), Aha, Djer, Djet
DYNASTY 2, 2890-2686
Six kings

Old Kingdom
DYNASTY 3, 2686-2613
Five kings, including Djoser
DYNASTY 4, 2613-2494
Six kings . . . Snefru, Cheops, Chephren, Mycerinus
DYNASTY 5, 2494-2345
Nine kings . . . Userkaf, Unas
DYNASTY 6, 2345-2181
About seven kings . . . Pepy I
DYNASTY 7, 2181-2173
About nine kings
DYNASTY 8, 2173-2160
About eight kings

First Intermediate Period
DYNASTIES 9 & 10, 2160-2040
Five kings . . . Menthotep I

Middle Kingdom
DYNASTY 11, 2040-1991
Three kings . . . Menthotep II
DYNASTY 12, 1991-1780
Eight kings . . . Sesostris I
DYNASTY 13, 1780-1633
About 50 kings

Second Intermediate Period
DYNASTY 14, 1786-1603
Seventy-six kings
DYNASTIES 15 & 16, 1674-1558
The Hyksos kings
DYNASTY 17, 1650-1558
About 15 kings

New Kingdom
DYNASTY 18, 1558-1303
Fourteen kings . . . Ahmose, Amunhotep I, Thutmose I, Thutmose II, Queen Hatshepsut, Thutmose III, Amunhotep III, Akhenaten, Smenkhkare, Tutankhamun, Horemheb
DYNASTY 19, 1303-1200
Eight kings . . . Ramses I, Seti I, Ramses II, Merneptah, Seti II
DYNASTY 20, 1200-1069
Ten kings . . . Ramses III

Third Intermediate Period
DYNASTY 21, 1069-945
Six kings
DYNASTY 22, 945-715
Eight Libyan kings . . . Sheshong I
DYNASTY 23, 818-715
Six Libyan kings
DYNASTY 24, 727-715
Two kings
DYNASTY 25, 760-656
Six Kushite kings . . . Piankhy

Saite Renaissance
DYNASTY 26, 664-525
Six kings . . . Psamtik I

Late Dynastic
DYNASTY 27, 525-404
Five Persian kings
DYNASTY 28, 404-398
One king
DYNASTY 29, 398-378
Five kings
DYNASTY 30, 378-341
Three kings
DYNASTY 31, 341-330
Three Persian kings
Alexander's Conquest, 332
Macedonian Domination, 332-304
Ptolemaic Dynasty, 304-30
Fourteen Ptolemaic kings . . . Ptolemy I, Cleopatra VII.
Roman Conquest, 30

A.D. 1

Tax revolts, animosities between ethnic stocks and classes continue. Under Rome's protection, Egypt's independent status slips. Ptolemies' hold weakens. Cleopatra VII, last of the dynasty, works her wiles on Julius Caesar and Mark Antony, but Egypt still falls to Rome in 30 B.C. Emperor Augustus assumes attributes of the pharaohs. Rome builds temples in Egyptian style. Exquisite temple at Dendera, begun by Ptolemies, is finished by Romans.

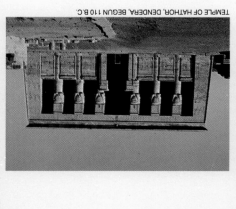
TEMPLE OF HATHOR, DENDERA, BEGUN 110 B.C.

Political unrest and violence rack the Roman republic. Caesar, with Pompey and Crassus, forms the First Triumvirate. Caesar assassinated in 44 B.C. Rivalry among successors ends with Octavian (Augustus) becoming the first Roman emperor. Augustan Age witnesses the peak of Roman art, the literature of Cicero, Ovid, Virgil, Horace.

JULIUS CAESAR, 1ST CENTURY B.C.

Waterwheel comes into use in Greece and the Near East. Parthians rule from Euphrates to Indus. Birth of Jesus ushers in Christian era. Architects in Mexico engineer the massive Pyramid of the Sun. Peruvian Indians weave some of the finest textiles of the New World.

PERUVIAN EMBROIDERY, CA. A.D. 1

---

100 B.C.

Ptolemaic Dynasty begins to fade. Egyptians riot over living costs, heavy taxes—there is even a tax on tax receipts! Trouble breaks out in Alexandria among Egyptians, Greeks, and Jews. Threatened by Syrian and Macedonian invaders, Ptolemies place Egypt under the protection of Rome. Rosetta Stone is inscribed to honor Ptolemy V.

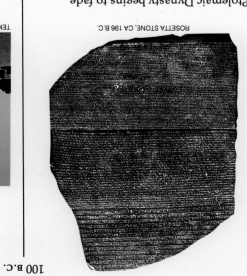
ROSETTA STONE, CA 196 B.C.

Maccabean revolt frees the Jews from Syrian rule; independent Jewish state is formed, 142 B.C. Roman legions engulf eastern Mediterranean, Greece, Asia Minor. Carthage falls. Romans adopt Greek forms in art, building, literature.

VENUS DE MILO, 2ND CENTURY B.C.

Chinese invent paper. Emperor Wu Ti of Han Dynasty develops the Silk Route to the West, revives art and literature. In North America, people of the Hopewell culture raise huge burial mounds, tap a vast trade network.

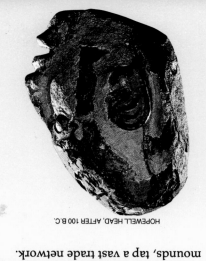
HOPEWELL HEAD, AFTER 100 B.C.

---

200 B.C.

Under Ptolemies, Greek influence pervades Egyptian art and culture. Ptolemy III introduces leap year into Egypt's calendar. Manetho, an Egyptian priest, groups the pharaohs into dynastic divisions. In Alexandria, Eratosthenes calculates earth's circumference, Euclid formulates fundamentals of plane geometry, Archimedes makes basic discoveries in science.

TEMPLE OF HORUS, BEGUN 3RD CENTURY B.C.

Parthians weld a kingdom in Iran. In the Punic Wars, Carthage loses Sicily and Spain to Rome despite Hannibal's thrust across the Alps. Roman fleets sail the Mediterranean.

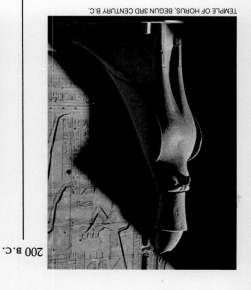
WINGED VICTORY, SAMOTHRACE, 200-190 B.C.

Warrior-horsemen from the steppes drive Scythians into the Crimea. Huns, nomadic warriors, grow powerful in Mongolia. Ch'in Shih Huang Ti unifies China, builds the Great Wall, standardizes weights and writing—and is buried with a life-size pottery army of 6,000. Forebears set stage for rise of Maya civilization in Middle America.

CH'IN DYNASTY WARRIOR, 210 B.C.

Notes on the Authors

WILLIAM KELLY SIMPSON, editorial consultant for this book and author of the chapter on writing, is professor of Egyptology at Yale University and curator of Egyptian and ancient Near Eastern art at the Boston Museum of Fine Arts. He serves as a trustee of the American Research Center in Egypt and the American School of Classical Studies in Athens.

J. CARTER BROWN, who wrote the Foreword, is the director of the National Gallery of Art and a trustee of the National Geographic Society.

KARL W. BUTZER is professor of anthropology and geography at the University of Chicago and a professor in The Oriental Institute there. He is co-author of *Desert and River in Nubia* and author of many other books and articles.

VIRGINIA LEE DAVIS has taught courses in Egyptian art, history, mythology, and hieroglyphics at Harvard and Yale universities, and served as guest curator of Egyptian art at the New Orleans Museum of Art.

I. E. S. EDWARDS retired recently as Keeper of Egyptian Antiquities at the British Museum. He is joint editor of *The Cambridge Ancient History*. His many publications include authoritative studies on the pyramids and on Tutankhamun.

BARBARA MERTZ is the author of *Temples, Tombs and Hieroglyphs* and of *Red Land, Black Land*. She also draws on her background in archeology and history to write popular novels.

WILLIAM H. PECK is curator of ancient art at the Detroit Institute of Arts and adjunct professor of Egyptian art and archeology at Wayne State University.

EDNA R. RUSSMANN is assistant curator of the department of Egyptian art at the Metropolitan Museum of Art.

ANTHONY J. SPALINGER is lecturer of Egyptology in the department of Near Eastern languages and literatures at Yale University.

Acknowledgments

In the preparation of this volume we had the unstinting assistance of many individuals and organizations, and we gratefully acknowledge our indebtedness to them. Staff members of the Library of Congress and the National Geographic Society Library were generous with advice and cooperation. We would like also to thank particularly the following individuals:

Dr. Morsi Saad el-Din, director of information, Egyptian Ministry of Information and Culture; Dr. Dia Abou-Ghazi, Egyptian Museum, Cairo; Dr. and Mrs. Labib Habachi, Cairo; Dr. Ahmed Mousa, director of antiquities, Saqqara; and Ahmed Majahlawi, Cairo.

Dr. Lanny Bell, director of Chicago House at Luxor, and Mrs. Bell provided invaluable aid, as did May Trad, librarian of Chicago House; Abd El Hamid El Daly, Luxor; Said Higazi, director of antiquities, Luxor; Abdalla El Sayed M., director of the Luxor Museum; Sheikh M. Negdi, Qurna; and Jean Lauffray, of the Franco-Egyptian Center, Karnak.

Jennifer Moseley, London, gave liberal assistance, as did Carol Andrews of the British Museum; Dr. Jurgen Settgast and Jurgen Liepe of the Ägyptisches Museum, West Berlin; Frau Dr. Kischkewitz, Ägyptisches Museum, East Berlin; Bernard Bothmer and Richard Fazzini of the Brooklyn Museum; David W. Nasgowitz of The Oriental Institute; Dr. James B. Pritchard, University of Pennsylvania Museum; and Dr. Timothy Kendall, Boston Museum of Fine Arts.

We are grateful also for permission to reprint excerpts from *The Literature of Ancient Egypt*, edited by William Kelly Simpson © Yale University Press, New Haven, 1973.

Bibliography

In the extensive literature dealing with the civilization of ancient Egypt, we found many books helpful in preparing this volume. Those of a general nature with information applicable to most of the chapters included *Art in Ancient Egypt* by Cyril Aldred, London, 1968-72; *The Egyptians*, Cyril Aldred, New York, 1961; *A History of Egyptian Architecture*, Alexander Badawy, Berkeley, 1954-68; *Egypt and the Sudan*, Karl Baedeker, Leipzig, 1929; *Ancient Records of Egypt*, James H. Breasted, New York, 1906; *A History of Egypt*, James H. Breasted, New York, 1912; *The Cambridge Ancient History*, London, 1923-1977; *Living Architecture: Egyptian*, Jean-Louis de Cenival, New York, 1964; *Food: The Gift of Osiris*, William J. Darby and others, London, 1977; *The Egyptian Kingdoms*, A. Rosalie David, London, 1975; *Ancient Egyptian Paintings*, Nina M. Davies and Alan H. Gardiner, Chicago, 1936; *Description de l'Égypte*, France, Commission des Monuments d'Égypte, Paris, 1809-28; *Tutankhamen*, Christiane Desroches-Noblecourt, New York, 1963; *Tutankhamun: His Tomb and Its Treasures*, I. E. S. Edwards, New York, 1976; *Studies in Ancient Technology*, R. J. Forbes, Leiden, 1955-64; *Egypt of the Pharaohs*, Alan H. Gardiner, Oxford, 1961; *Magic and Medical Science in Ancient Egypt*, Paul Ghalioungui, London, 1963; *The Ancient Near East: A History*, William W. Hallo and William Kelly Simpson, New York, 1971; *The Legacy of Egypt*, J. R. Harris, Oxford, 1971; *The Scepter of Egypt*, William C. Hayes, Cambridge, Mass., 1953, 1959; *Technology in the Ancient World*, Henry Hodges, New York, 1970; *Ships of the Pharaohs*, Björn Landström, Garden City, N.Y., 1970; *Egypt*, Kurt Lange and Max Hirmer, London/New York, 1968; *Saqqara*, Jean-Philippe Lauer, New York, 1976.

Ancient Egyptian Materials and Industries, A. Lucas and J. R. Harris, London, 1962; *Egyptian Painting*, Arpag Mekhitarian, Geneva, 1954; *Temples, Tombs and Hieroglyphs*, Barbara Mertz, New York, 1964; *Art of Ancient Egypt*, Kazimierz Michalowski, New York, 1977; *Eternal Egypt*, Pierre Montet, New York, 1964; *The Splendor that was Egypt*, Margaret A. Murray, New York, 1963; *Egyptian Museum, Cairo*, Newsweek, New York, 1969; *Ancient Egyptian Art*, Eberhard Otto, New York, 1967; *Topographical Bibliography of Ancient Egyptian Hieroglyphic Texts, Reliefs, and Paintings*, Bertha Porter and Rosalind L. B. Moss, Oxford, 1927-64; *Dictionary of Egyptian Civilization*, Georges Posener, New York, 1962; *Ancient Near Eastern Texts Relating to the Old Testament*, James B. Pritchard, Princeton, 1969; *The Ancient Near East in Pictures*, James B. Pritchard, Princeton, 1969; *The Egyptians*, John Ruffle, Ithaca, N.Y., 1977; *Egyptian Architecture*, E. Baldwin Smith, New York/London, 1938; *The Art and Architecture of Ancient Egypt*, W. Stevenson Smith, Harmondsworth, Eng., 1958; *Treasures of Egyptian Art from the Cairo Museum*, E. L. B. Terrace and H. G. Fischer, Boston, 1970; *Painting, Sculpture, and Architecture of Ancient Egypt*, Wolfhart Westendorf, New York, 1968; *The Burden of Egypt*, John A. Wilson, Chicago, 1951; *The Art of Egypt*, Irmgard Woldering, New York, 1963; *Treasures of the Pharaohs*, Jean Yoyotte, Geneva, 1968.

For specialized study on particular chapters, we found these references helpful:

The Constant Lure *Narratives . . . in Egypt and Nubia*, G. B. Belzoni, London, 1820; *The Tomb of Tut-Ankh-Amen*, Howard Carter, New York, 1923; *Who Was Who in Egyptology*, Warren R. Dawson, London 1972; *Travels in Upper and Lower Egypt*, Vivant Denon, London, 1803; *The Rape of the Nile*, Brian Fagan, New York, 1975; *Egyptian Obelisks*, Henry H. Gorringe, New York, 1882; *The Discovery of Egypt*, Leslie Greener, London, 1966; *The Obelisks of Egypt*, Labib Habachi, New York, 1977; *Bonaparte in Egypt*, J. Christopher Herold, New York, 1962; *The History of Herodotus*, trans. by George Rawlinson, London/Toronto/New York, 1910; *The Great Belzoni*, Stanley Mayes, London, 1959; *Ten Years' Digging in Egypt*, W. M. Flinders Petrie, London, 1891; *A History of Egyptian Mummies*, Thomas J. Pettigrew, London, 1834; *A Description of the East and Some Other Countries*, Richard Pococke, London, 1743; *Egyptian Mummies*, G. Elliot Smith and Warren R. Dawson, London, 1924; *Signs and Wonders Upon Pharaoh*, John A. Wilson, Chicago, 1964; *Excavations at Deir el Bahri*, H. E. Winlock, New York, 1942.

The People of the River *Egypt to the End of the Old Kingdom*, Cyril Aldred, New York, 1976; *Early Hydraulic Civilization in Egypt*, Karl W. Butzer, Chicago, 1976; *The Prehistory of Africa*, J. Desmond Clark, New York, 1970; *Archaic Egypt*, Walter Emery, Baltimore, 1961; *Ancient Kingdoms of the Nile*, Walter A. Fairservis, Jr., New York, 1962; *Barrow, Pyramid, and Tomb*, Leslie V. Grinsell, London, 1975; *Most Ancient Egypt*, William C. Hayes, Chicago, 1965; "Stone-age Man on the Nile," Philip E. L. Smith in *Scientific American*, August, 1976; *Beyond History: The Methods of Prehistory*, Bruce G. Trigger, New York, 1968; "Egyptian Prehistory: Some New Concepts," Fred Wendorf and others in *Science*, Sept. 18, 1970.

Pyramids: Building for Eternity *The Pyramids of Egypt*, I. E. S. Edwards, New York, 1972; *The Pyramids*, Ahmed Fakhry, Chicago, 1961; *Egyptian Pyramids*, Leslie Grinsell, Gloucester, Eng., 1947; *The Pyramids and Sphinx*, Desmond Stewart, New York, 1971.

The Pleasures of Life *Jewels of the Pharaohs*, Cyril Aldred, London 1971; *Furniture in the Ancient World*, Hollis S. Baker, London, 1966; *Daily Life in Ancient Egypt*, Lionel Casson, New York, 1975; *Life in Ancient Egypt*, Adolf Erman, London, 1894; *The Ancient Egyptians*, Jill Kamil, Chester Springs, Pa., 1977; *Red Land, Black Land*, Barbara Mertz, New York, 1966; *The History of Musical Instruments*, Curt Sachs, New York, 1940; *The Daily Life of the Ancient Egyptians*, Nora Scott, Metropolitan Museum Bulletin, New York, Spring 1973; *Egyptian Jewellery*, Milada Vilímková, London, 1969; *Everyday Life in Ancient Egypt*, Jon Manchip White, London/New York, 1963; *Ancient Egyptian Jewellery*, Alix Wilkinson, London, 1971; *The Manners and Customs of the Ancient Egyptians*, J. Gardner Wilkinson, Boston, 1883; *Models of Daily Life in Ancient Egypt*, H. E. Winlock, Cambridge, Mass., 1955.

The Gift of Writing *Paper and Books in Ancient Egypt*, Jaroslav Černý, University College, London, 1947; *The Alphabet*, David Diringer, New York, 1968; *The Literature of the Ancient Egyptians*, Adolf Erman, trans. by A. H. Blackman, London 1927; *Egyptian Grammar*, Alan H. Gardiner, Oxford, 1957; *The Hekanakhte Papers*, T. G. H. James, New York, 1962; *Papyrus in Classical Antiquity*, Naphtali Lewis, Oxford, 1974; *Ancient Egyptian Literature*, Miriam Lichtheim, Berkeley, 1973, 1976; *The Literature of Ancient Egypt*, ed. by William Kelly Simpson, New Haven, 1973.

Pathways to the Gods *The Egyptian Book of the Dead*, E. A. Wallis Budge, London, 1895; *Thebes*, Jean Capart, New York, 1926; *Ancient Egyptian Religion*, Jaroslav Černý, London, 1952; *Myth and Symbol in Ancient Egypt*, R. T. Rundle Clark, New York, 1959; *The Ancient Egyptian Coffin Texts*, R. O. Faulkner, Warminster, Eng., 1973, 1977; *The Ancient Egyptian Pyramid Texts*, R. O. Faulkner, Oxford, 1969; *Images for Eternity*, Richard Fazzini, San Francisco/New York, 1975; *Ancient Egyptian Religion*, Henri Frankfort, New York, 1948; *Kingship and the Gods*, Henri Frankfort, Chicago, 1948; *X-raying the Pharaohs*, James E. Harris and Kent R. Weeks, New York, 1973; *Egyptian Mythology*, Veronica Ions, London, 1968; *Luxor: A Guide to Ancient Thebes*, Jill Kamil, London/New York, 1973; *Egyptian Religion*, Siegfried Morenz, Ithaca, N.Y., 1973; *Thebes of the Pharaohs*, Charles F. Nims, New York, 1965; *The Priests of Ancient Egypt*, Serge Sauneron, New York, 1960.

Change in a Changeless Land *Akhenaten and Nefertiti*, Cyril Aldred, London/New York, 1973; *Akhenaten, Pharaoh of Egypt*, Cyril Aldred, London/New York, 1968; *Treasures of Tutankhamun*, Metropolitan Museum, New York, 1976; *The Akhenaten Temple Project*, Ray Winfield Smith and Donald B. Redford, Warminster, Eng., 1976; *The Life and Times of Akhnaton*, Arthur Weigall, New York, 1923.

The Crest of Empire *The Warrior Pharaohs*, Leonard Cottrell, New York, 1969; *The World Saves Abu Simbel*, Christiane Desroches-Noblecourt and Georg Gerster, Vienna, 1968; "Egyptian Military Organization," R. O. Faulkner in the *Journal of Egyptian Archaeology*, Dec., 1953; *Everyday Life in Egypt in the Days of Ramses the Great*, Pierre Montet, London, 1962; *Lives of the Pharaohs*, Pierre Montet, Cleveland/New York, 1968; *History and Chronology of the 18th Dynasty of Egypt*, Donald B. Redford, Toronto, 1967; *Thebes in the Time of Amunhotep III*, Elizabeth Riefstahl, Norman, Okla., 1964; *When Egypt Ruled the East*, George Steindorff and Keith C. Seele, Chicago, 1957.

A number of periodicals carry articles that provide valuable reference material. Two devote their pages exclusively to Egyptology. They are the *Journal of Egyptian Archaeology*, published in London, and the *Journal of the American Research Center in Egypt*, Princeton. Other periodicals include: *Archaeology*, New York; *Antiquity*, Cambridge, Eng.; *Expedition*, Philadelphia; and the *American Journal of Archaeology*, New York. In addition, occasional pertinent articles appear in such publications as *Scientific American*, *Natural History*, *Science*, *National Geographic*, *Smithsonian*, *Illustrated London News*, and bulletins of major museums.

Illustration credits

In this listing picture sources are separated from left to right by a semicolon (;) and top to bottom by a dash (—). The following abbreviations are used:
EMC—Egyptian Museum, Cairo
MMA—Metropolitan Museum of Art, New York
BM—British Museum, London
BMFA—Boston Museum of Fine Arts
ht—height; dia—diameter; m—meter
cm—centimeter; ca—circa; col—column
NGP—National Geographic Photographer
NGS—National Geographic Staff
All dates given for Egyptian objects are B.C.

Cover Hieroglyphic reliefs from the shrine of Sesostris I at Karnak, ca 1971-1928: Farrell Grehan. Pages 2,3,7 Farrell Grehan.

The Constant Lure 8 Farrell Grehan. 10 through 15 From *Description de l'Égypte*, France, Commission des Monuments d'Égypte, Paris, 1809-1828. 16 From *Egyptian Obelisks* by Henry H. Gorringe, 1882. 17 From *Six New Plates. . .*, by G. B. Belzoni, 1822, New York Public Library. 18 From *Century Illustrated Magazine*, May 1887—Radio Times Hulton Picture Library—From *Voyage dans la Haute Égypte*, by Auguste Mariette, 1893. 20,21 MMA: Harry Burton. 22 Griffith Institute, Ashmolean Museum, Oxford. 23 MMA: Harry Burton—Ledger Photo Service—MMA: Harry Burton. 24,25 MMA: Harry Burton. 26 Shrine doors, wood overlaid with gold, ht 50 cm, ca 1340, EMC: Fred J. Maroon. 27 Gilded wooden figure, ht 90 cm, ca 1340, EMC: Fred J. Maroon. 28,29 Gold funerary mask, ht 54 cm, ca 1340, EMC: John G. Ross. 30 Gold decorated dagger hilt, 12 cm long—Gilded leopard's head, ht 17 cm—Gold dagger and sheath, 32 cm long, all ca 1340, EMC: Lee Boltin. 31 Gold statuette, ht 5 cm; Gilded wooden serpent, ht 56 cm, both ca 1340, EMC: Lee Boltin

The People of the River 33 Painted clay figure, ht 29 cm, ca 4000, Brooklyn Museum—Terra-cotta vase, ht 22 cm, ca 3400, EMC—Flint and ivory knife, 23 cm long, ca 3100, Brooklyn Museum: all by Victor R. Boswell, Jr., NGP. 34,35 Front and back of slate palette, ht 64 cm, ca 3000, EMC: Victor R. Boswell, Jr., NGP. 36,37 Relief from the temple causeway of Unas, Saqqara, ca 2350: Victor R. Boswell, Jr., NGP—Farrell Grehan. 38 Lloyd K. Townsend, Jr. 39 Limestone relief, ht 45 cm, ca 1335, BMFA: Victor R. Boswell, Jr., NGP. 40,41 Wall painting from the tomb of Itat, 24x172 cm, ca 2570, EMC: Victor R. Boswell, Jr., NGP. 42,43 Farrell Grehan. 44,45 Farrell Grehan—Limestone relief in the tomb of Ti, Saqqara, ca 2400: Victor R. Boswell, Jr., NGP. 46,47 Farrell Grehan. 48,49 Thomas J. Abercrombie, NGS—Farrell Grehan. 50 through 55 Farrell Grehan. 56 Wooden statue of Kaaper, ht 109 cm, ca 2500; Painted limestone statue of the dwarf Seneb and family, ht 33 cm, ca 2350, both EMC: Victor R. Boswell, Jr., NGP. 57 Wooden statue of a Memphite couple, ht 69 cm, ca 2450, Louvre, Paris: Adam Woolfitt—Painted limestone statues of Rehotep and Nofret, ht 1.2 m, ca 2600, EMC, Joseph J. Scherschel, NGS. 58 Wooden model from the tomb of Meketre, base 1.7 m long, ca 2000, EMC: Victor R. Boswell, Jr., NGP. 59 Limestone relief in the tomb of Mereruka, Saqqara, ca 2300—Painted limestone relief, ca 2450, EMC: both Victor R. Boswell, Jr., NGP. 61 Limestone relief in the tomb of Ptahhotep, Saqqara, ca 2450—Limestone relief, ca 2450, Ägyptisches Museum, East Berlin: both Victor R. Boswell, Jr., NGP. 62,63 From *Ancient Egyptian Paintings* by Nina M. Davies and Alan H. Gardiner, courtesy The Oriental Institute, University of Chicago—Wall painting in the tomb of Menna, Thebes, ca 1400: Victor R. Boswell, Jr., NGP. 64 Wooden model from the tomb of Meketre, ht 29 cm, ca 2000, MMA—Limestone figure, woman making beer, ht 27 cm, ca 2450, EMC: Joseph J. Scherschel, NGS—Limestone figure, woman grinding grain, ht 28 cm, ca 2350, EMC: Victor R. Boswell, Jr., NGP. 64,65 Nathan Benn. 66,67 Wall relief in the tomb of Ptahhotep, Saqqara, ca 2450—wall painting in the tomb of Nakht, Thebes, ca 1410: both Victor R. Boswell, Jr., NGP. 68 Painted wall relief in the tomb of Ti, Saqqara, ca 2400: Victor R. Boswell, Jr., NGP. 69 Wall relief in the tomb of Nefer, Saqqara, ca 2400: Victor R. Boswell, Jr., NGP. 70,71 Farrell Grehan.

Pyramids: Building for Eternity 72 Farrell Grehan. 74 Limestone statue of Djoser, ht 1.4 m, ca 2650, EMC: Victor R. Boswell, Jr., NGP—Bronze statuette of Imhotep, ht 14 cm, BM: Gordon Roberton. 75,76 Farrell Grehan. 77 Lloyd K. Townsend, Jr. 78 Granite capstone, ht 1.4 m, ca 1800, EMC: Victor R. Boswell, Jr., NGP. 80,81 Farrell Grehan. 82 Schist triad of Mycerinus and goddesses, ht 95 cm, ca 2500, EMC: Victor R. Boswell, Jr., NGP. 83 Ivory statuette of Cheops, ht 8 cm, ca 2550—Diorite statue of Chephren, ht 1.7 m, ca 2525, both EMC: Victor R. Boswell, Jr., NGP. 84 Lloyd K. Townsend, Jr. 85 John G. Ross. 86,87 Farrell Grehan. 88 Rhind Papyrus, ca 1575, BM. 89 Fragment of a limestone relief, ca 1475, Brooklyn Museum; Wall relief in the tomb of Princess Idut, Saqqara, ca 2400: both by Victor R. Boswell, Jr., NGP. 90,91 Farrell Grehan; Copper and bronze tools (longest chisel 26 cm), EMC: Victor R. Boswell, Jr., NGP. 92 through 101 Michael A. Hampshire.

The Pleasures of Life 103 From *Ancient Egyptian Paintings* by Nina M. Davies and Alan H. Gardiner, courtesy The Oriental Institute, University of Chicago; Gold djed pillar ht 9 cm, ca 1340, EMC: Lee Boltin. 104 Wooden unguent spoon, 30 cm long, ca 1370, EMC: Victor R. Boswell, Jr., NGP. 105 Boxwood statuette, ht 13 cm, ca 1370, Gulbenkian Museum of Oriental Art, University of Durham, England. 106 Wooden toy animal, 13 cm long, ca 1300, BM: Gordon Roberton—Wooden "paddle doll," ht 22 cm, ca 2000, EMC: Victor R. Boswell, Jr., NGP. 106,107 From *Archaeological Survey of Egypt, Beni Hasan*, by Percy E. Newberry, 1894; Limestone statuette from the tomb of Nikauinpu, Giza, ht 21 cm, ca 2300, The Oriental Institute, University of Chicago: Robert M. Lightfoot III. 108,109 Comic papyrus, 54 cm long, ca 1000, BM. 111 Lloyd K. Townsend, Jr., based on a model in The Oriental Institute, University of Chicago. 112,113 Copy of a wall painting from the tomb of Ipuy, Thebes, ca 1250, MMA. 113 Wooden model from the tomb of Meketre, Thebes, 84 cm long, ca 2000, MMA, Rogers Fund—Fragment of a wall painting ca 1400, BM. 114,115 Reproduction of furniture from the tomb of Queen Hetepheres, Giza, chair ht 80 cm, bed 1.8 m long, ca 2600, BMFA: Victor R. Boswell, Jr., NGP. 116 Detail of a carved cedarwood chair, ht of chair 96 cm, ca 1340, EMC: Fred J. Maroon. 117 Ceremonial chair ht 1 m, ca 1340, EMC: Victor R. Boswell, Jr., NGP. 118 Painted wooden statue from the tomb of Methethy, ht 80 cm, ca 2450, Nelson Gallery-Atkins Museum, Kansas City, Mo.; Wooden sandals overlaid with bark, leather, and gold foil, ca 1340, EMC: Victor R. Boswell, Jr., NGP. 119 Painted wooden model from the tomb of Meketre, Thebes, ht 1.1 m, ca 2000; Crystalline limestone statue, ht 85 cm, ca 1330, both EMC: Victor R. Boswell, Jr., NGP. 120,121 Inlaid ebony chest, ht 37 cm, and cosmetic equipment (mirror is a reproduction), from the tomb of Sithathoryunet, ca 1880, hardwood comb, ca 1400, MMA; Limestone relief, from the sarcophagus of Kawit, ca 2040, EMC: Victor R. Boswell, Jr., NGP. 122 Gold and rock-crystal pendant, medallion dia 2 cm, ca 1900—Diadem of gold and semiprecious stones, ht 3 cm, ca 1900, both from the tomb of Princess Khnumet, EMC: Victor R. Boswell, Jr., NGP. 123 Inlaid gold headdress, ht 36 cm, ca 1450, MMA. 124,125 Collar of gold, carnelian, and feldspar from the tomb of Neferuptah, Hawara, 37 cm wide, ca 1800, EMC: Victor R. Boswell, Jr., NGP; Wall painting in the tomb of Nefertari, Thebes, ca 1250: Thomas J. Abercrombie, NGS—Rings of gold and semiprecious stones, ca 1340, EMC: Lee Boltin. 126 Bracelets of gold and lapis lazuli, 6 cm wide, ca 1250—Crown of gold and semiprecious stones, dia 19 cm, ca 1880, both EMC: Victor R. Boswell, Jr., NGP. 127 Pectoral of gold and silver with glass and semiprecious stones, ht 15 cm, ca 1340, EMC: Lee Boltin. 128,129 Wall painting in the tomb of Nakht, Thebes, ca 1410: Victor R. Boswell, Jr., NGP. 130 Painted relief in the tomb of Nefertari, Thebes, ca 1250—Wooden game, 28 cm long, ca 1295, EMC—Bone die, 2 cm wide, Coptic Period: all by Victor R. Boswell, Jr., NGP. 131 Ivory and ebony veneer game, 10x15 cm, with ivory playing pieces, from the tomb of Renseneb, ca 1795—Three knucklebones, both MMA. 132,133 Fragment of a wall painting, ca 1400, BM.—Ebony, copper, and gilt figure, ht 15 cm, ca 1425, Royal Scottish Museum, Edinburgh; Tableware, ca 1550-1300, MMA. 134,135 Fragment of a limestone relief, ht 50 cm, ca 1250, EMC: Victor R. Boswell, Jr., NGP. 136 Musical instruments, wood oboe (longest) 33 cm, ca 2000-300, Ägyptisches Museum, West Berlin: Victor R. Boswell, Jr., NGP. 137 Limestone relief from the tomb of Paatenemheb, Saqqara, ca 1340, Rijksmuseum van Oudheden, Leiden. 138,139 Painted relief in the tomb of Mehu, Saqqara, ca 2300: Victor R. Boswell, Jr., NGP.

The Gift of Writing 141 Painted limestone statue, ht 53 cm, ca 2500, Louvre, Paris: Pierre Boulat. 142,143 Painted relief in the tomb of Ti, Saqqara, ca 2400: Victor R. Boswell, Jr., NGP—Reconstructed scribe's writing kit, palette 7 cm long, The Oriental Institute, University of Chicago: Robert M. Lightfoot III. 144 Painting of Champollion by Madame Rumilly, 1823, courtesy the Champollion family. 145 Rosetta Stone, ht 1.1 m, ca 196, BM. 146 Detail from coffin lid of wood and glass, ca 350, EMC: Victor R. Boswell, Jr., NGP. 147 Details from sarcophagus in the tomb of Amunhotep II, Thebes, ca 1410: Victor R. Boswell, Jr., NGP. 148 Painted wall relief in the tomb of Nefer, Saqqara, ca 2400, Victor R. Boswell, Jr., NGP—Robert Hynes—Papyrus Institute, Cairo. 149 Farrell Grehan. 150 From the Edwin Smith Surgical Papyrus, ca 1700, New York Academy of Medicine Library. 151 Papyrus letter with mud seal, 8 cm long, ca 2000, MMA—Tutankhamun's ivory palette with brushes and wood case overlaid with gold, both 30 cm long, ca 1340, EMC: F. L Kenett from Robert Harding Associates—Tutankhamun's ivory and gold burnisher, 16 cm long, ca 1340, EMC: Lee Boltin. 152 Steatite scarab, 9 cm long, ca 1390, MMA, Rogers Fund. 153 Victor R. Boswell, Jr., NGP.

Pathways to the Gods 155 Detail, wall painting in the tomb of Pashedu, Thebes, ca 1150: Victor R. Boswell, Jr., NGP. 156 Tomb of Mereruka, Saqqara, ca 2350: Victor R. Boswell, Jr., NGP. 157 Wall painting in the tomb of Irinufer, Thebes, ca 1200: Victor R. Boswell, Jr., NGP. 158,159 Cedarwood boat, 43 cm long, ca 2550: John G. Ross. 160,161 Ceiling painting in the tomb of Seti I, Thebes, ca 1290: Victor R. Boswell, Jr., NGP. 162,163 Ceiling painting in the tomb of Ramses VI, Thebes, ca 1150: Victor R. Boswell, Jr., NGP. 164,165 Robert Hynes. 166,167 Lloyd K. Townsend, Jr. 168 through 179 Farrell Grehan. 180 Bronze cat, ht 37 cm, ca 600; Gold falcon head, ht 35 cm, ca 1900, both EMC: Victor R. Boswell, Jr., NGP. 181 Gold figurine, ht 6 cm, ca 700, BMFA; Blue faience hippopotamus, ht 10 cm, ca 1900—Bronze mongoose, ht 20 cm, ca 500, both EMC: all Victor R. Boswell, Jr., NGP—Bronze crocodile, ht 12 cm, ca 200, BM: 182,183 Painted reliefs in the Temple of Seti I, Abydos, ca 1290: Victor R. Boswell, Jr., NGP. 184,185 Painted relief in the Temple of Amun-Re, Karnak, ca 320: Farrell Grehan. 186,187 Farrell Grehan. 188,189 Detail, wall painting in the tomb of Ramose, Thebes, ca 1360: Thomas J. Abercrombie, NGS; Detail, wall painting in the tomb of Ramose, Thebes, ca 1360: Victor R. Boswell, Jr., NGP. 190,191 Farrell Grehan. 192,193 Wall painting in the tomb of Sennedjem, Thebes, ca 1200—Ushabtis, ht of tallest 24 cm, ca 1560 to 300, Ägyptisches Museum, West Berlin: both Victor R. Boswell, Jr., NGP. 194 Mummy of Ramses II, ca 1220, EMC: Nathan Benn. 195 Wall painting in the tomb of Sennedjem, Thebes, ca 1200—Alabaster canopic jars, average ht 38 cm, EMC: both Victor R. Boswell, Jr., NGP. 196,197 from the Hunefer papyrus scroll, ca 1290, BM. 198,199 Painted relief in the tomb of Seti I, Thebes, ca 1290: Victor R. Boswell, Jr., NGP. 200,201 Victor R. Boswell, Jr., NGP.

Change in a Changeless Land 202 Crystalline limestone relief, ht 1 m, ca 1350, EMC: Victor R. Boswell, Jr., NGP. 203 Fragment of a limestone relief, ht 23 cm, ca 1350, BMFA: Victor R. Boswell, Jr., NGP. 204 Limestone relief, ca 1350, Brooklyn Museum: Victor R. Boswell, Jr., NGP. 205 Drawing on limestone, ca 1350, EMC; Limestone relief, ca 1350, Brooklyn Museum, Charles Edwin Wilbour Fund: both Victor R. Boswell, Jr., NGP. 207 Painted wooden head of Tutankhamun, ht 30 cm, ca 1340, EMC: Fred J. Maroon; Painted yew wood head, ht 10 cm, ca 1370—Limestone stela, ht 33 cm, ca 1350, both Ägyptisches Museum, West Berlin: Victor R. Boswell, Jr., NGP. 208,209 From *Tell el Amarna*, by W. M. Flinders Petrie, 1894. 210 Quartzite head, ht 33 cm, ca 1350, EMC: Victor R. Boswell, Jr., NGP. 211 Sandstone statue of Akhenaten, ht 4 m, ca 1350, EMC: Victor R. Boswell, Jr., NGP. 212,213 From *Ancient Egyptian Paintings* by Nina M. Davies and Alan H. Gardiner, courtesy The Oriental Institute, University of Chicago; Quartzite head, ht 21 cm, ca 1350, EMC: Lee Boltin. 214,215 Reliefs from a temple wall, ca 1350, Luxor Museum: Victor R. Boswell, Jr., NGP. 216,217 Back panel of the throne of Tutankhamun, wood overlaid with gold and inlays, ht 53 cm, ca 1340, EMC: Lee Boltin. 218 Alabaster perfume vase, ht 70 cm, ca 1340, EMC: Victor R. Boswell, Jr., NGP. 219 Alabaster vase, 38 cm long; Alabaster lion jar, ht 60 cm, both ca 1340, EMC: Fred J. Maroon. 220,221 Ostrich fan, ht 10 cm, ca 1340, EMC: Fred J. Maroon.

The Crest of Empire 222 Indurated limestone statue of Hatshepsut, ht 2 m, ca 1485, MMA, Rogers Fund. 223 Painted wall relief from the temple of Hatshepsut, Deir el Bahri, ca 1485, EMC: Victor R. Boswell, Jr., NGP. 224 Lloyd K. Townsend, Jr. 225 Basalt statue of Thutmose III, ht 89 cm, ca 1450, Luxor Museum: Victor R. Boswell, Jr., NGP. 226,227

Bentwood chariot overlaid with gold, 2.1 m wide, ca 1340, EMC: Victor R. Boswell, Jr., NGP. 228 Wall relief from the tomb of Horemheb, Saqqara, ca 1340, Rijksmuseum van Oudheden, Leiden. 229 Granite statue of Horemheb, ht 1.1 m, ca 1340, MMA, Gift of Mr. and Mrs. Everett Macy, 1923. 230,231 Copy of a painted wall relief from the temple of Ramses II at Beit el Wali, BM—Granite statue of Ramses II as a child, ht 2.3 m, ca 1280, EMC: Victor R. Boswell, Jr., NGP. 232,233 Wall relief in the temple of Ramses II at Abu Simbel, ca 1260: Farrell Grehan. 234 Wall relief in the temple of Ramses III, Medinet Habu, ca 1170: Victor R. Boswell, Jr., NGP—Relief on the base of a colossus at Abu Simbel, ca 1260: Farrell Grehan. 235 Wall relief in the temple of Ramses II at Abu Simbel, ca 1260: Farrell Grehan. 236,237 Painted wooden models from the tomb of Mesehti, Thebes, ht 40 cm, base 2 m long, ca 2000, EMC: Victor R. Boswell, Jr., NGP. 238 through 243 Farrell Grehan.

Time Chart 244 Col 2 Pottery vase, ht 25 cm, Ägyptisches Museum, West Berlin—Pottery pig, ht 26 cm, Ankara Archeological Museum, Turkey: Ara Guler. Col 3 Bird deity, ht 29 cm, Brooklyn Museum: Victor R. Boswell, Jr., NGP—Stamp seal, ht 4 cm, Los Angeles County Museum, Heeremaneck Collection: Edith Porada—Gold ornament, ht 6 cm, Archaeological Museum, Varna, Bulgaria: Erich Lessing, Magnum. Col 4 Gerzean vase, ht 22 cm, EMC: Victor R. Boswell, Jr., NGP—Sumerian clay pictograph tablet, Louvre, Paris. 245 Col 1 Narmer palette, ht 64 cm, EMC: Victor R. Boswell, Jr., NGP—Maltese figurine, ht 48 cm, National Museum of Malta: Adam Woolfitt.

Col 2 Limestone funerary stela, Louvre, Paris: John G. Ross—Silver bull vase from Iran, ht 16 cm, MMA, Joseph Pulitzer Bequest, 1966. Col 3 Step Pyramid: Farrell Grehan—Detail from the Standard of Ur, BM—Stonehenge: W. E. Roscher. Col 4 The Great Sphinx: Farrell Grehan—Ebla tablet, ht 10 cm: Gianni Tortolli—Steatite figure, National Museum of Pakistan, Karachi: Josephine Powell. 246 Col 1 Tomb of Mereruka: Victor R. Boswell, Jr., NGP—Bronze head, ht 30 cm, Iraq Museum, Baghdad: Joseph J. Scherschel, NGS. Col 2 Relief from sarcophagus of Kawit, EMC: Victor R. Boswell, Jr., NGP—Green calcite statue of Gudea, ht 63 cm, Louvre, Paris: Adam Woolfitt. Col 3 Shrine of Sesostris I: Farrell Grehan—Cycladic marble statuette, National Museum, Athens. Col 4 Quartzite statue of a nobleman, ht 70 cm, Brooklyn Museum, Charles Edwin Wilbour Fund: Victor R. Boswell, Jr., NGP—Minoan faience "snake goddess," ht 29 cm, Archeological Museum of Herakleion, Crete: Gilbert M. Grosvenor, NGS. 247 Col 1 Head of limestone statue, MMA, Rogers Fund and contribution of Edward S. Harkness, 1929—Gold Mycenaean mask, ht 26 cm, National Archaeological Museum, Athens: Gordon Gahan, NGP. Col 2 Limestone bust of Nefertiti, ht 58 cm, Ägyptisches Museum, West Berlin: Victor R. Boswell, Jr., NGP—Lion Gate, Mycenae: Gordon Gahan, NGP—Bronze wine vessel, ht 20 cm: Robert Harding Associates, Times Newspapers, Ltd. Col 3 Wall painting in the tomb of Pashedu, Thebes: Thomas J. Abercrombie, NGS—Clay warrior vase, ht 36 cm, National Museum, Athens, Prothmann Associates—Tlatilco figurine, ht 8 cm, National Museum of Anthropology,

Mexico City: B. Anthony Stewart. Col 4 Gold triad of gods, ht 9 cm, Louvre, Paris: Adam Woolfitt—Nora stone, Museum of Archeology, Cagliari, Sardinia: Winfield Parks—Olmec head, ht 2.7 m, National Museum of Anthropology, Mexico City: B. Anthony Stewart. 248 Col 1 Black granite bust of Mentuemhat, ht 48 cm, EMC: Mario Carrieri—Ivory "Mona Lisa of Nimrud," ht 16 cm, Iraq Museum, Baghdad: Hirmer Fotoarchiv. Col 2 Bronze cat, EMC: Victor R. Boswell, Jr., NGP—Warrior frieze from Persepolis, Iran: Helen and Frank Schreider—Detail of an Etruscan terra-cotta sculpture on a sarcophagus, Museo Nationale di Villa Giulia, Rome: Dan McCoy, Black Star. Col 3 Alabaster lion vessel, ht 11 cm, Brooklyn Museum, Charles Edwin Wilbour Fund—Parthenon, Athens: Franc Shor—Ceramic pot, ht 18 cm, Museum of the American Indian, New York. Col 4 Green schist head, ht 15 cm, Brooklyn Museum, Charles Edwin Wilbour Fund—Thracian coin, dia 3 cm: Helen and Frank Schreider. 249 Col 1 Granite statue of falcon god Horus at Edfu, ht 3 m: Farrell Grehan—Marble "Winged Victory of Samothrace," ht 2.5 m, Louvre, Paris, Marc Garanger—Head of life-size terra-cotta statue, China Pictorial. Col 2 Rosetta Stone, ht 1.1 m, BM—Marble "Venus de Milo," Louvre, Paris: Bruce Dale, NGP—Clay head, ht 8 cm, Ohio Historical Society, Columbus: Robert S. Oakes, NGP. Col 4 Temple of Hathor at Dendera: Anne Dirkes Kobor, NGS—Detail of a life-size marble statue of Julius Caesar, City Council Chamber, Rome: Adam Woolfitt—Embroidered figure, National Museum of Anthropology and Archeology, Lima: Loren McIntyre.

Index

Type composition by National Geographic's Photographic Services. Color separations by Colorgraphics, Inc., Forestville, Md.; Chanticleer Company, Inc., New York, N. Y.; Progressive Color Corporation, Rockville, Md.; J. Wm. Reed Company, Alexandria, Va. Printing by Fawcett Printing Corporation, Rockville, Md.; Judd & Detweiler, Inc., Washington, D. C.; Kingsport Press, Kingsport, Tenn. Binding by R. R. Donnelley & Sons Company, Chicago, Ill.; Rand McNally & Company, Skokie, Ill. Paper by Mead Corp., Publishing Paper Division, New York, N. Y. Papyrus from the Papyrus Institute, Cairo, Egypt.

Library of Congress CIP Data

Main entry under title:

Ancient Egypt, Discovering its Splendors

Bibliography: p.
Includes index.
1. Egypt—Civilization—To 332 B.C.
I. National Geographic Society, Washington, D. C.
DT61.A6 932 78-10524
ISBN 0-87044-220-1